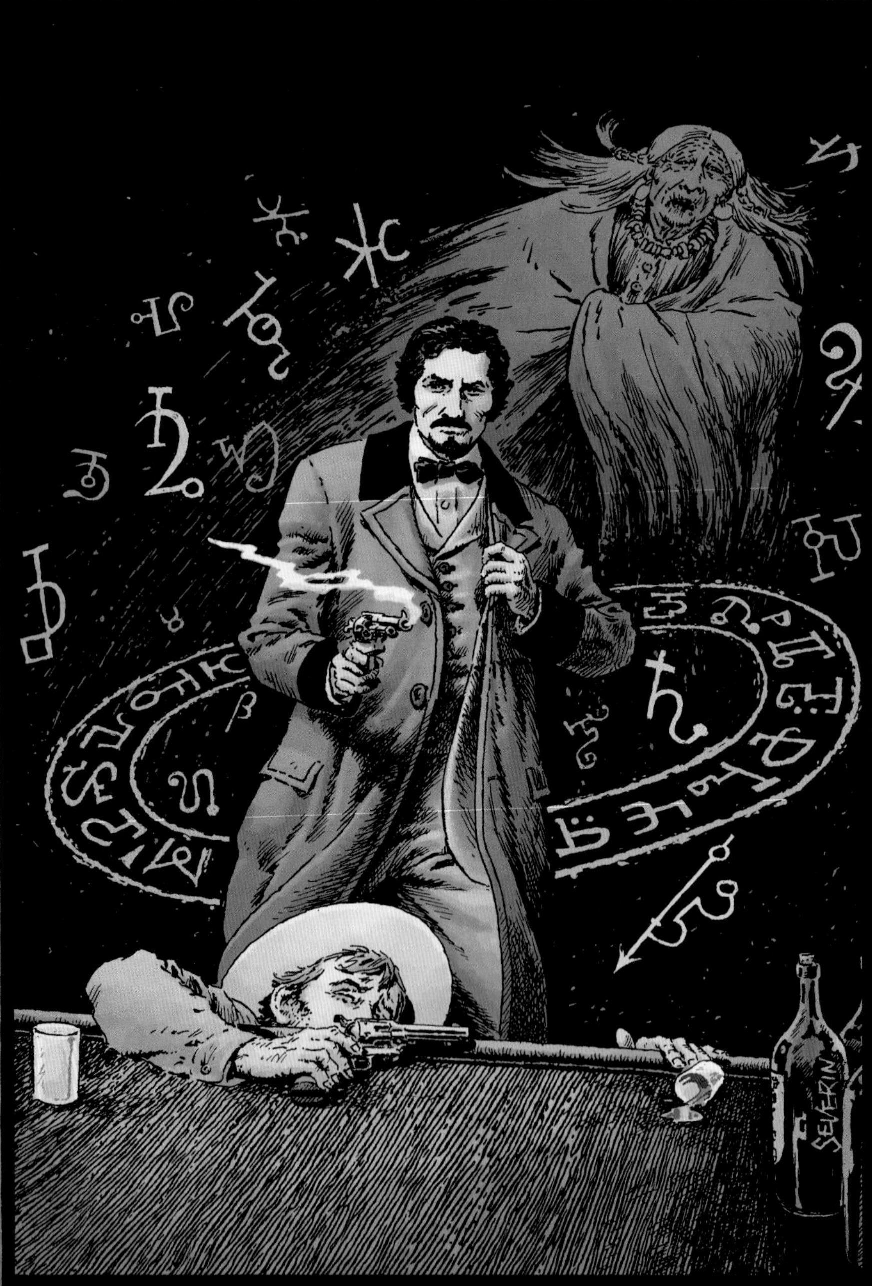
SEVERIN

SIR EDWARD GREY

WITCHFINDER™

Lost and Gone Forever

story
MIKE MIGNOLA and JOHN ARCUDI

art
JOHN SEVERIN

colors
DAVE STEWART

letters
CLEM ROBINS

cover
MIKE MIGNOLA with DAVE STEWART

editor SCOTT ALLIE

associate editor SAMANTHA ROBERTSON

assistant editor DANIEL CHABON

book designer AMY ARENDTS

publisher MIKE RICHARDSON

DARK HORSE BOOKS®

Published by
Dark Horse Books
A division of Dark Horse Comics, Inc.
10956 SE Main St.
Milwaukie, OR 97222

DarkHorse.com

First edition: January 2012
ISBN 978-1-59582-794-4

This volume collects *Sir Edward Grey, Witchfinder: Lost and Gone Forever* #1–#5, published by Dark Horse Comics.

1 3 5 7 9 10 8 6 4 2

Printed by Midas Printing International, Ltd., Huizhou, China.

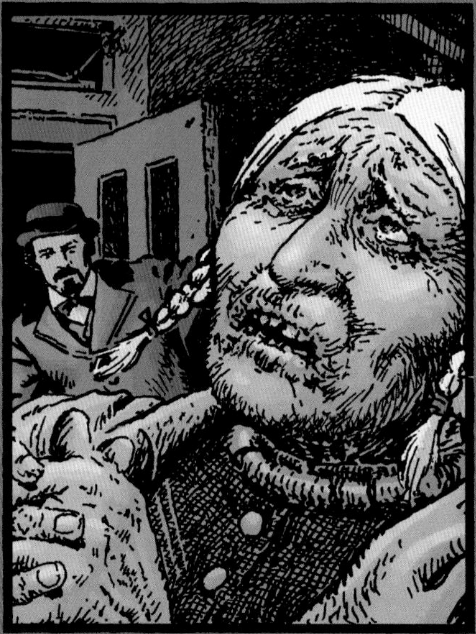

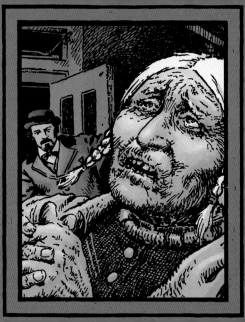

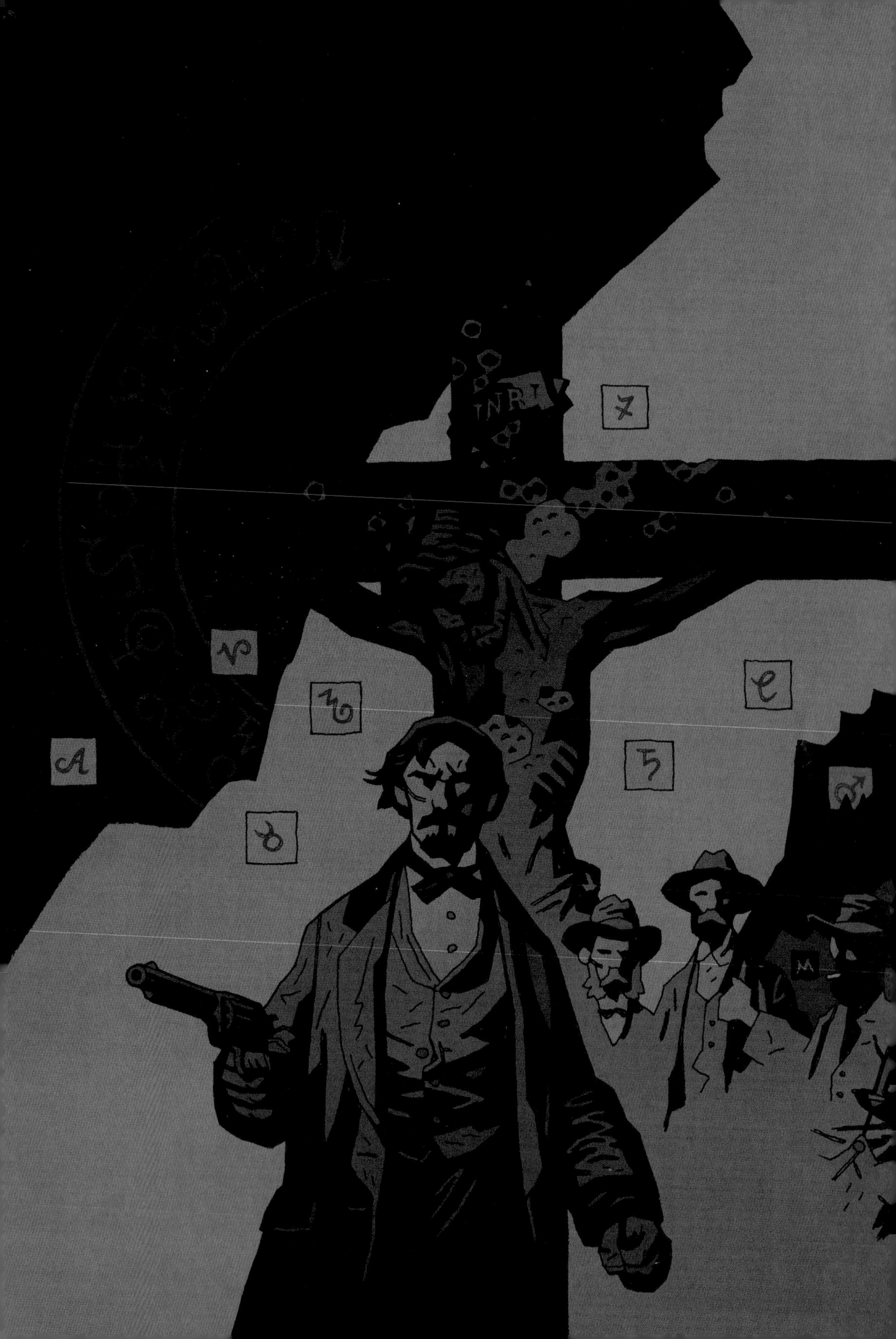
INRI

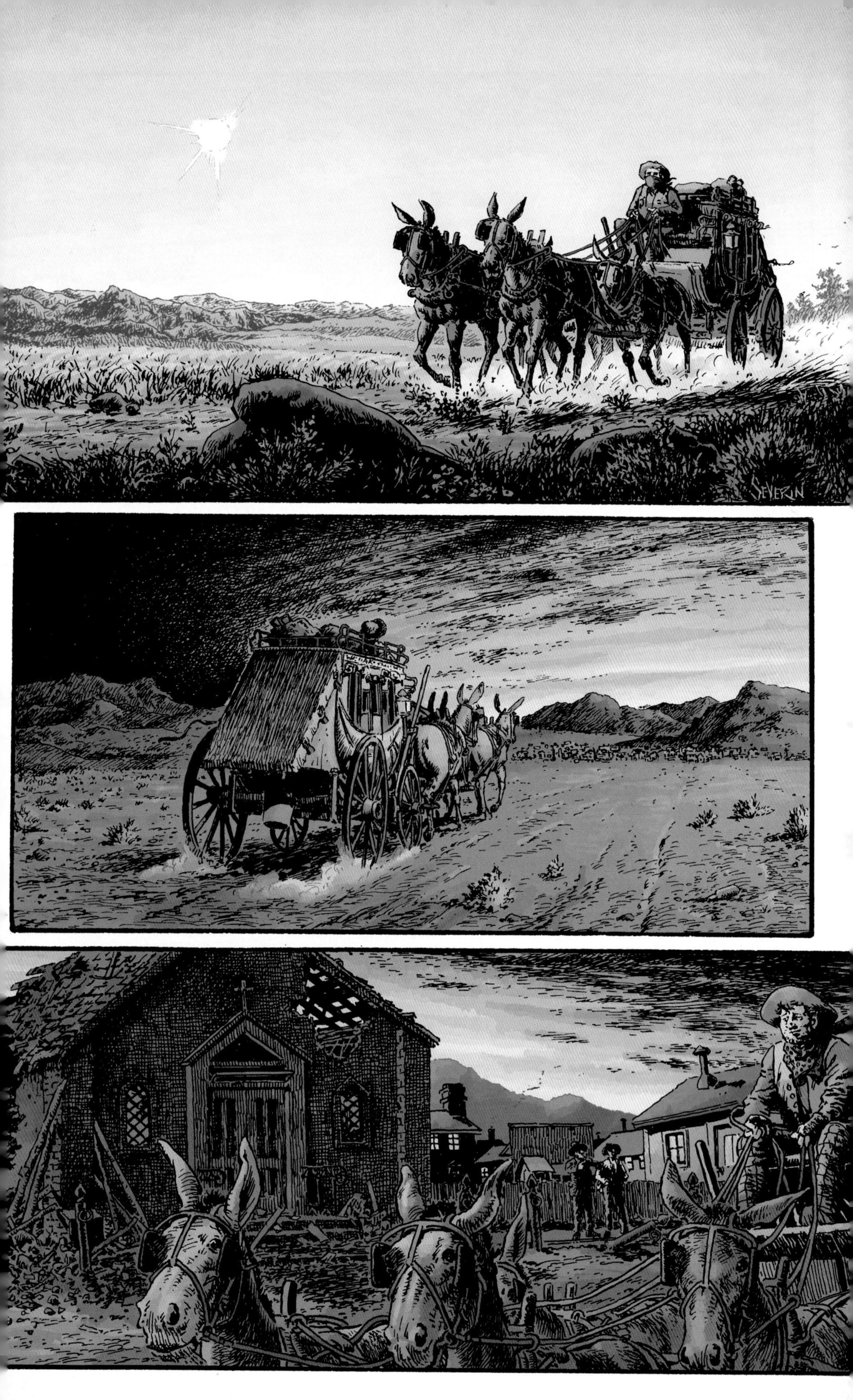
SEVERIN

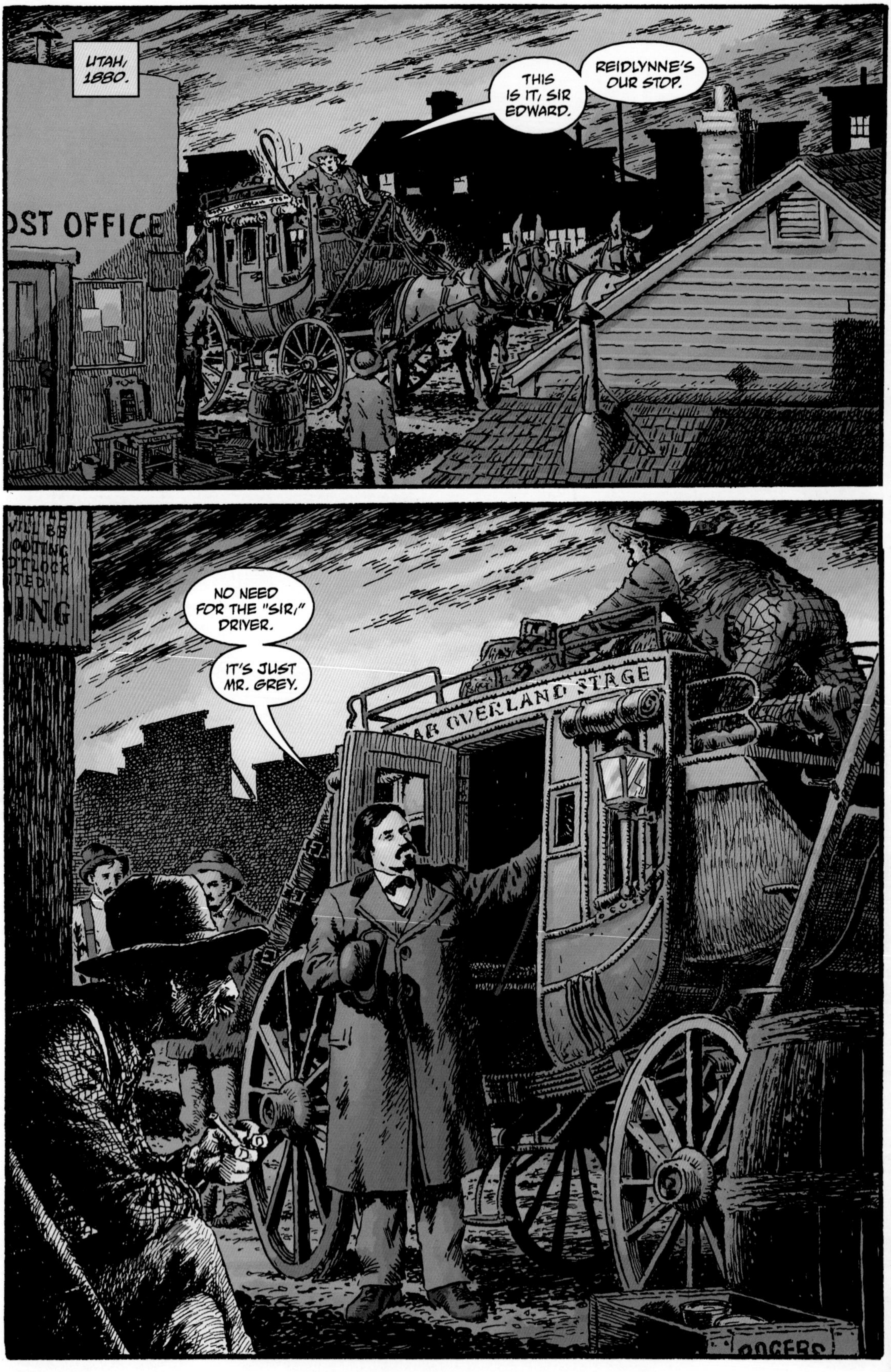
UTAH, 1880.
THIS IS IT, SIR EDWARD.
REIDLYNNE'S OUR STOP.
OST OFFICE
NO NEED FOR THE "SIR," DRIVER.
IT'S JUST MR. GREY.
OVERLAND STAGE

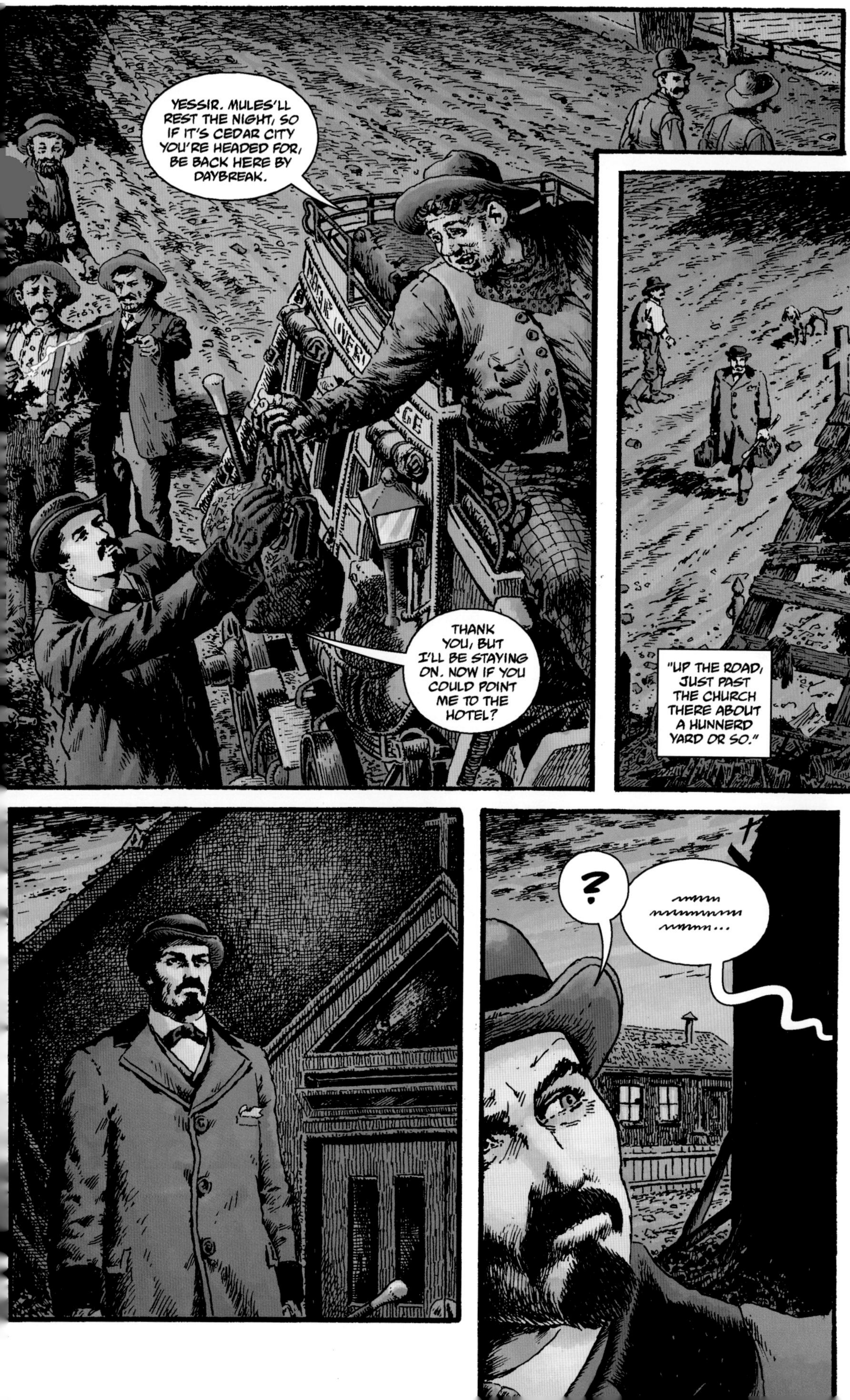
YESSIR. MULES'LL REST THE NIGHT, SO IF IT'S CEDAR CITY YOU'RE HEADED FOR, BE BACK HERE BY DAYBREAK.
THANK YOU, BUT I'LL BE STAYING ON. NOW IF YOU COULD POINT ME TO THE HOTEL?
"UP THE ROAD, JUST PAST THE CHURCH THERE ABOUT A HUNNERD YARD OR SO."
?

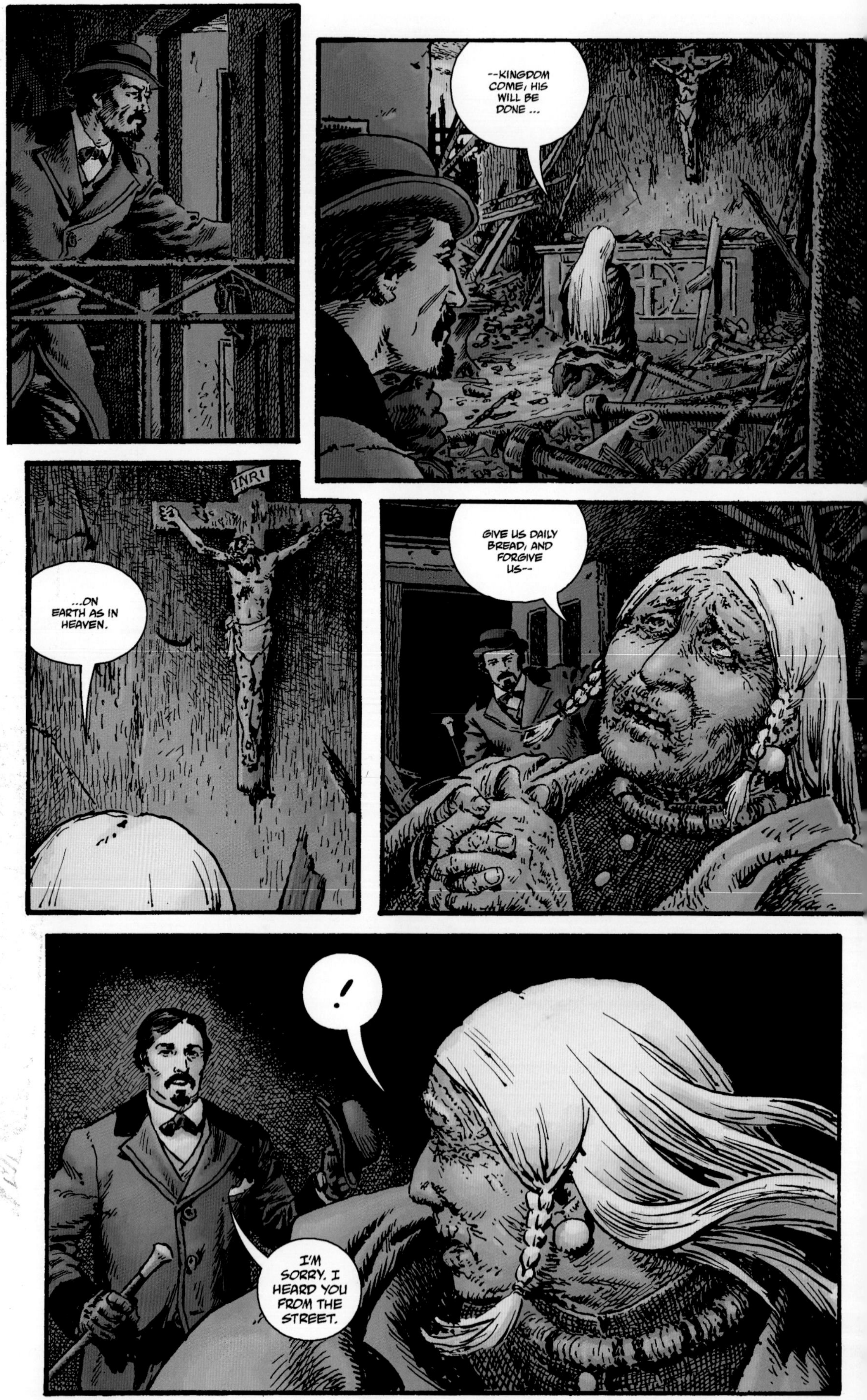
--KINGDOM COME, HIS WILL BE DONE ...
...ON EARTH AS IN HEAVEN.
GIVE US DAILY BREAD, AND FORGIVE US--
!
I'M SORRY. I HEARD YOU FROM THE STREET.

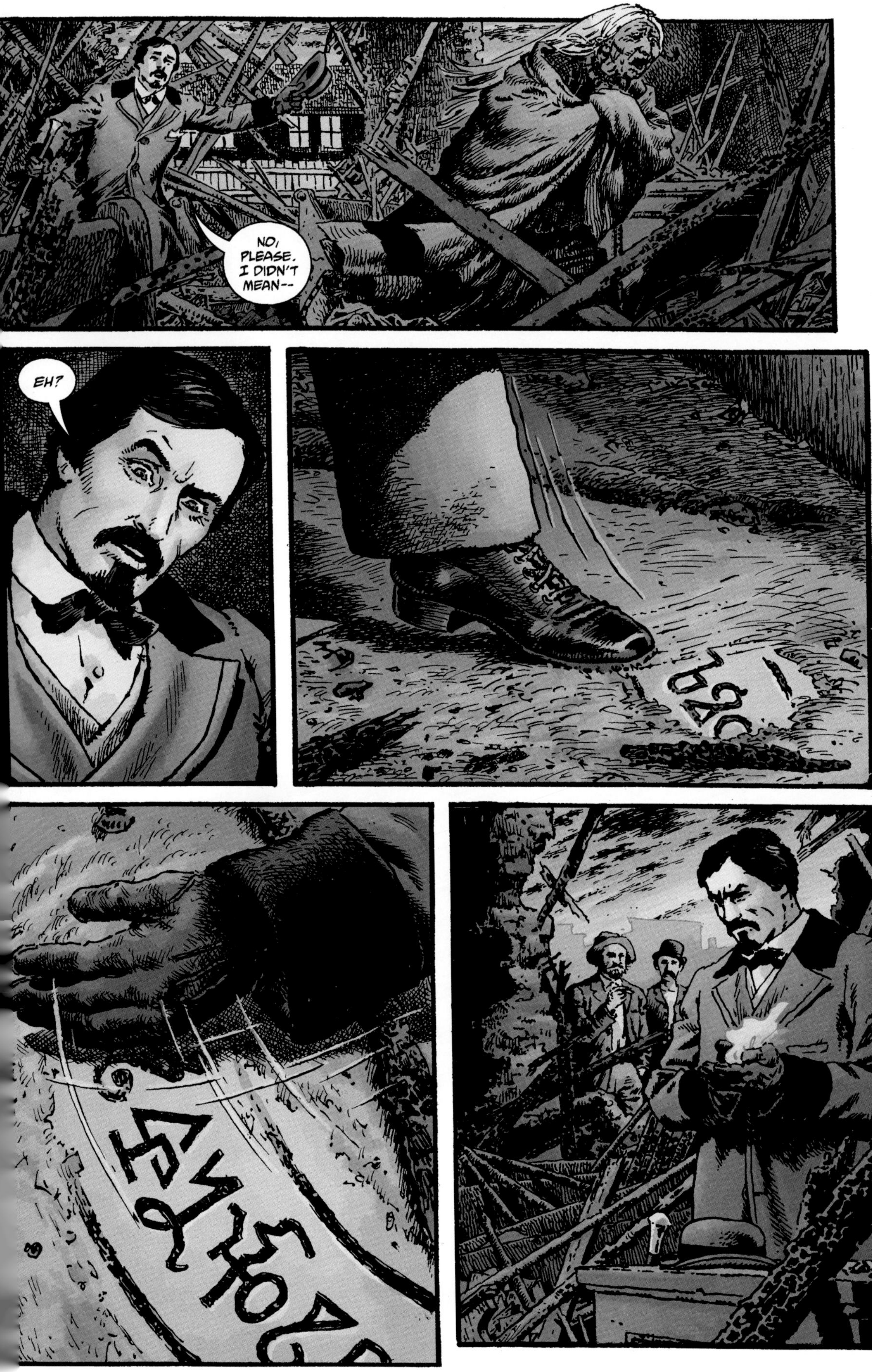
NO, PLEASE. I DIDN'T MEAN--
EH?

BE Z HOTEL
WHAT SUITS YOU, FRIEND?
I'VE JUST CHECKED IN AFTER A LONG TRIP. I IMAGINE TEA WOULD BE OUT OF THE QUESTION, BUT SOME WATER WOULD BE FINE.
ANY-THING ELSE?
MAYBE YOU COULD TELL ME THE WHEREABOUTS OF THE SHERIFF.

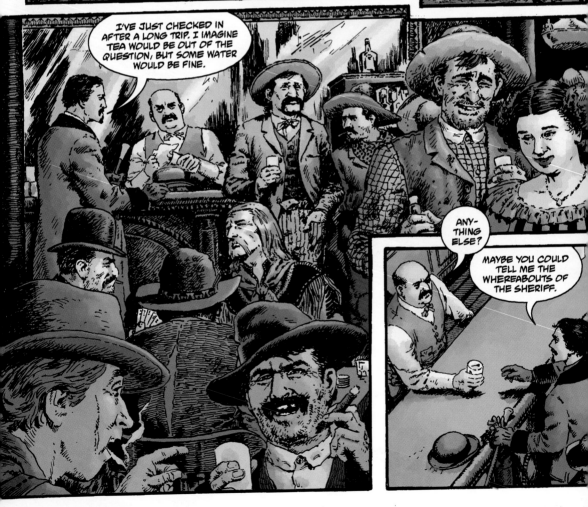

YOU SEE, THERE'S A MAN I'M LOOKING FOR.

YOU HEAR HIM? YOU HEAR WHAT HE SAY?

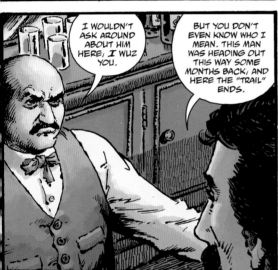

I WOULDN'T ASK AROUND ABOUT HIM HERE, *I* WUZ YOU.

BUT YOU DON'T EVEN KNOW WHO I MEAN. THIS MAN WAS HEADING OUT THIS WAY SOME MONTHS BACK, AND HERE THE "TRAIL" ENDS.

MAYBE *YOU* CAN HELP ME. IT WOULD HAVE BEEN BACK IN JUNE--

OH NO. NOT *ME*. AND DON'T BOTHER WITH THE SHERIFF, NEITHER. TAKE MY *WORD* AS TO THAT.

BEST YOU JUST FORGET ABOUT THIS GENT YOU'RE LOOKIN' FOR.

I THINK NOT. BUT THANK YOU FOR THE WATER.

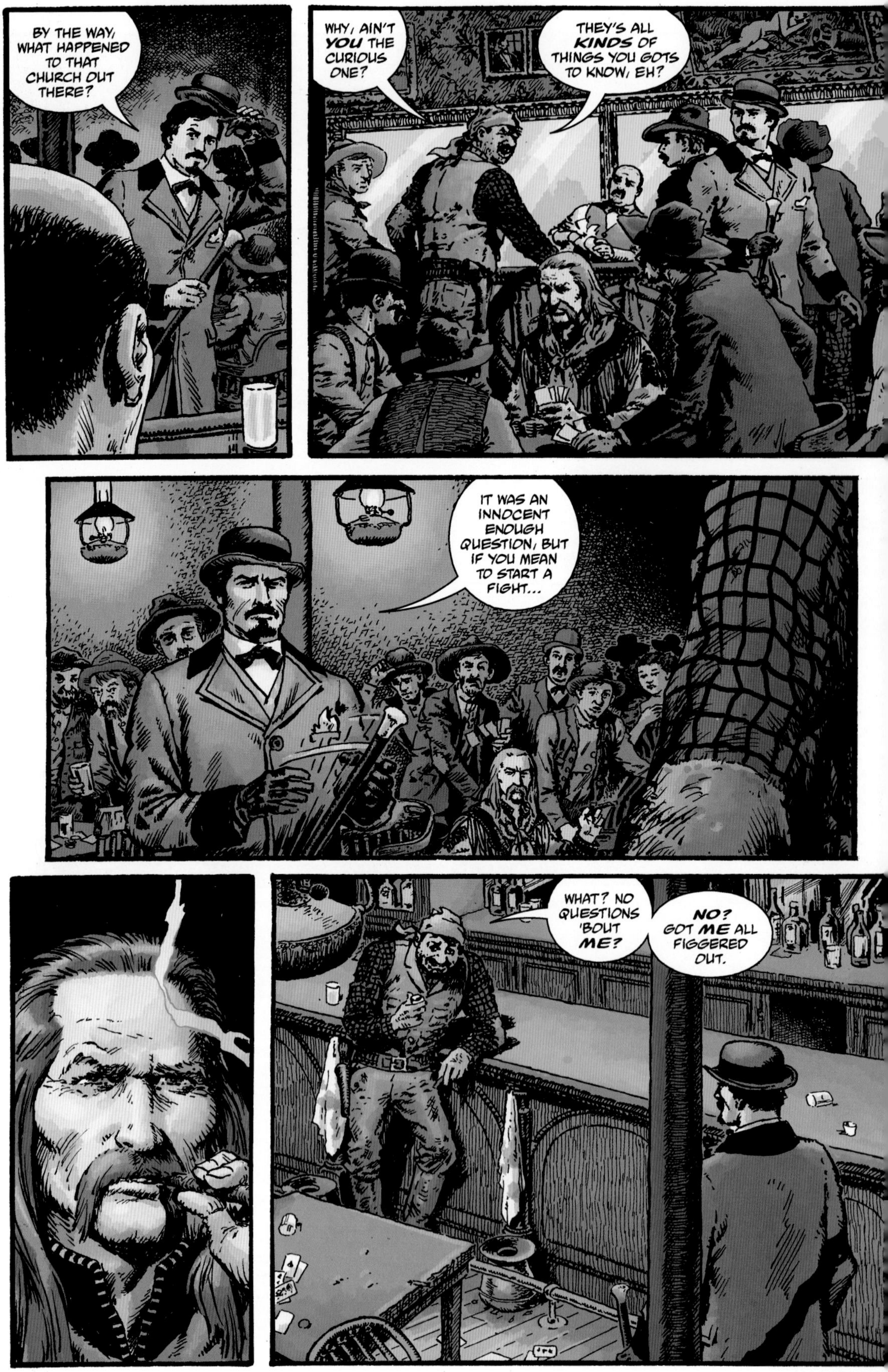
BY THE WAY, WHAT HAPPENED TO THAT CHURCH OUT THERE?
WHY, AIN'T YOU THE CURIOUS ONE?
THEY'S ALL KINDS OF THINGS YOU GOTS TO KNOW, EH?
IT WAS AN INNOCENT ENOUGH QUESTION, BUT IF YOU MEAN TO START A FIGHT...
WHAT? NO QUESTIONS 'BOUT ME?
NO? GOT ME ALL FIGGERED OUT.

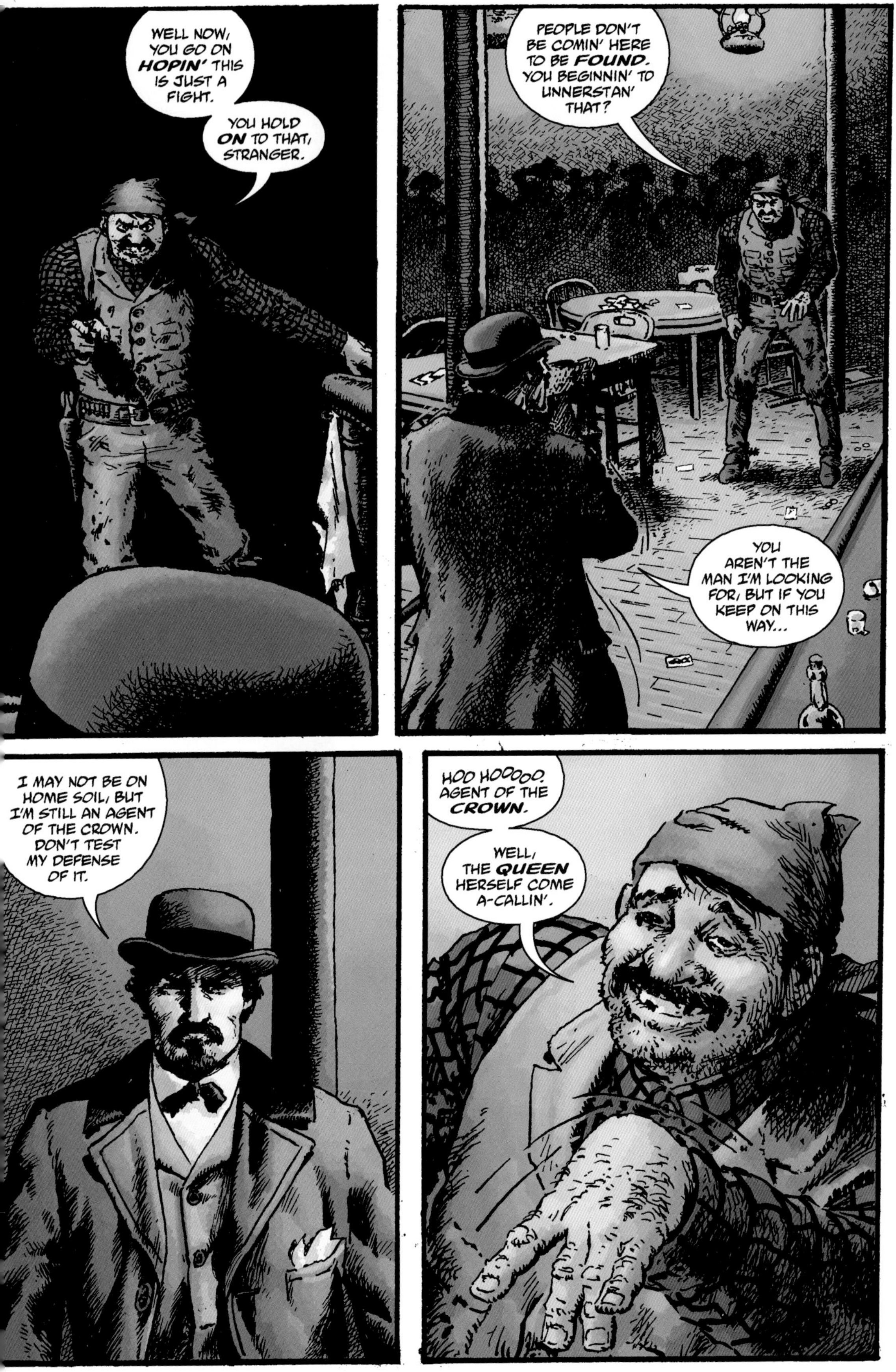

WELL NOW, YOU GO ON HOPIN' THIS IS JUST A FIGHT.
YOU HOLD ON TO THAT, STRANGER.
PEOPLE DON'T BE COMIN' HERE TO BE FOUND. YOU BEGINNIN' TO UNNERSTAN' THAT?
YOU AREN'T THE MAN I'M LOOKING FOR, BUT IF YOU KEEP ON THIS WAY...
I MAY NOT BE ON HOME SOIL, BUT I'M STILL AN AGENT OF THE CROWN. DON'T TEST MY DEFENSE OF IT.
HOO HOOOOO. AGENT OF THE CROWN.
WELL, THE QUEEN HERSELF COME A-CALLIN'.

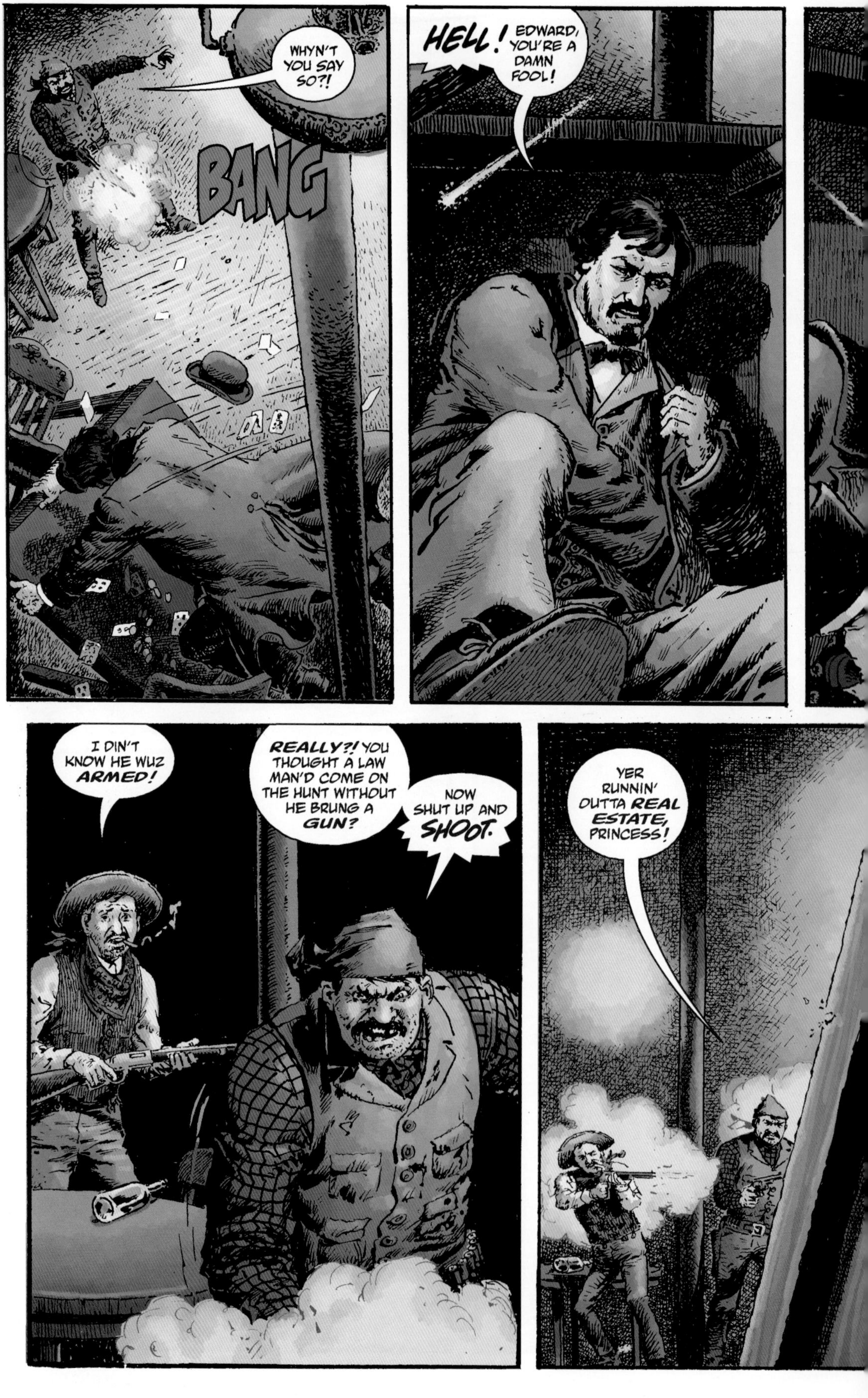
WHYN'T YOU SAY SO?!
BANG
HELL! EDWARD, YOU'RE A DAMN FOOL!
I DIN'T KNOW HE WUZ ARMED!
REALLY?! YOU THOUGHT A LAW MAN'D COME ON THE HUNT WITHOUT HE BRUNG A GUN?
NOW SHUT UP AND SHOOT.
YER RUNNIN' OUTTA REAL ESTATE, PRINCESS!

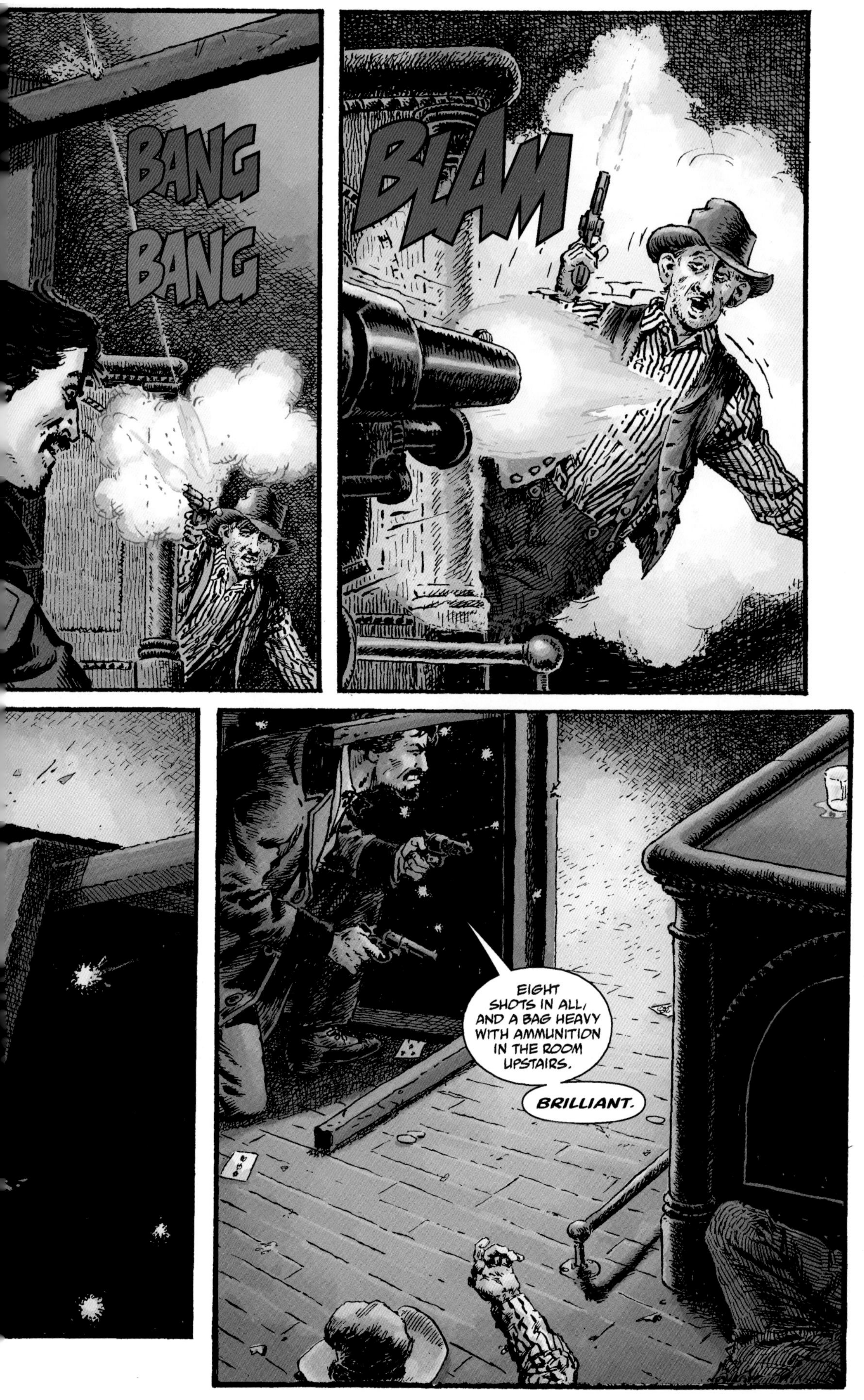
BANG
BANG
BLAM
EIGHT SHOTS IN ALL, AND A BAG HEAVY WITH AMMUNITION IN THE ROOM UPSTAIRS.
BRILLIANT.

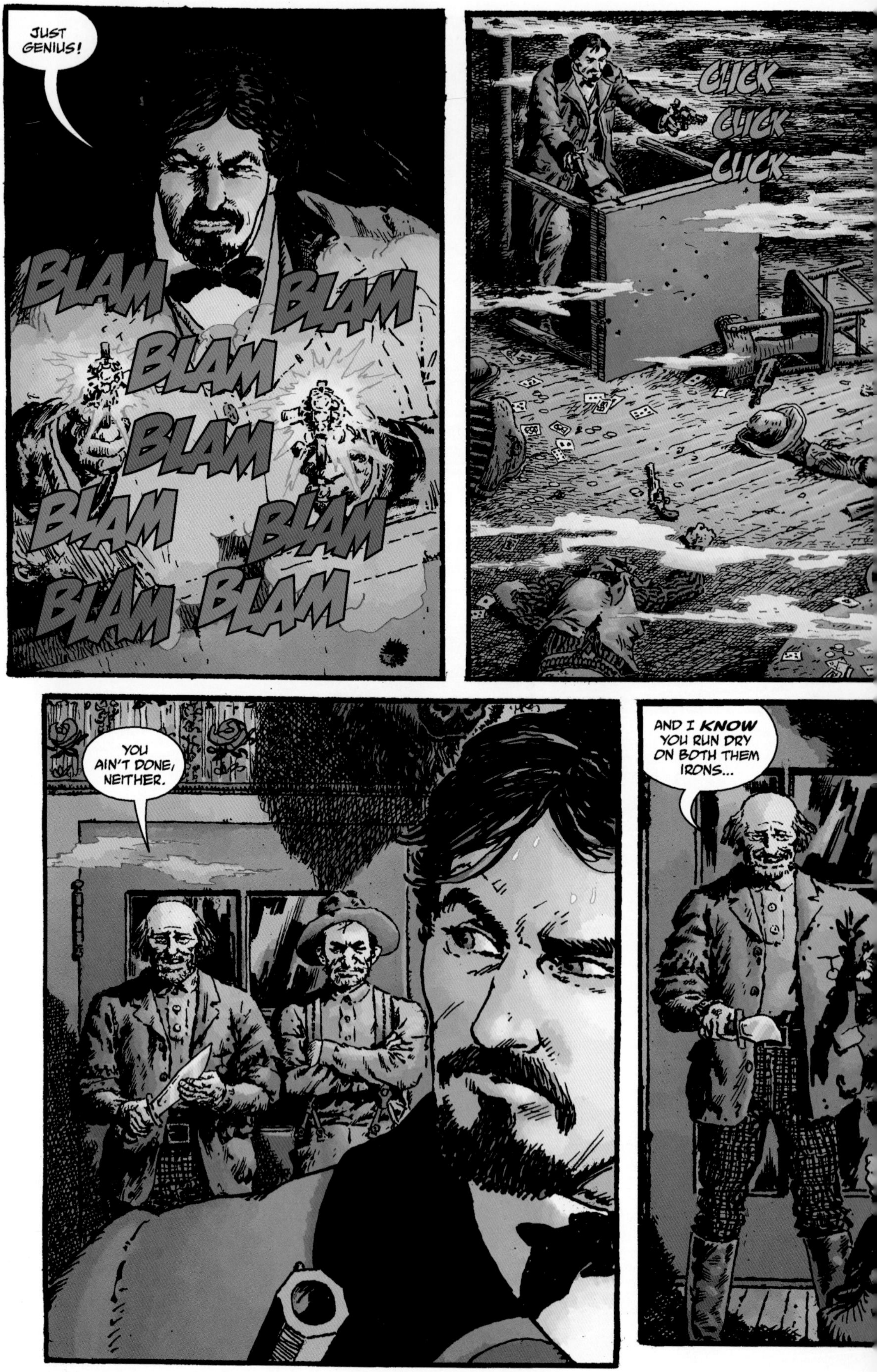

JUST GENIUS!
BLAM BLAM BLAM BLAM BLAM BLAM BLAM BLAM BLAM
CLICK CLICK CLICK
YOU AIN'T DONE, NEITHER.
AND I **KNOW** YOU RUN DRY ON BOTH THEM IRONS...

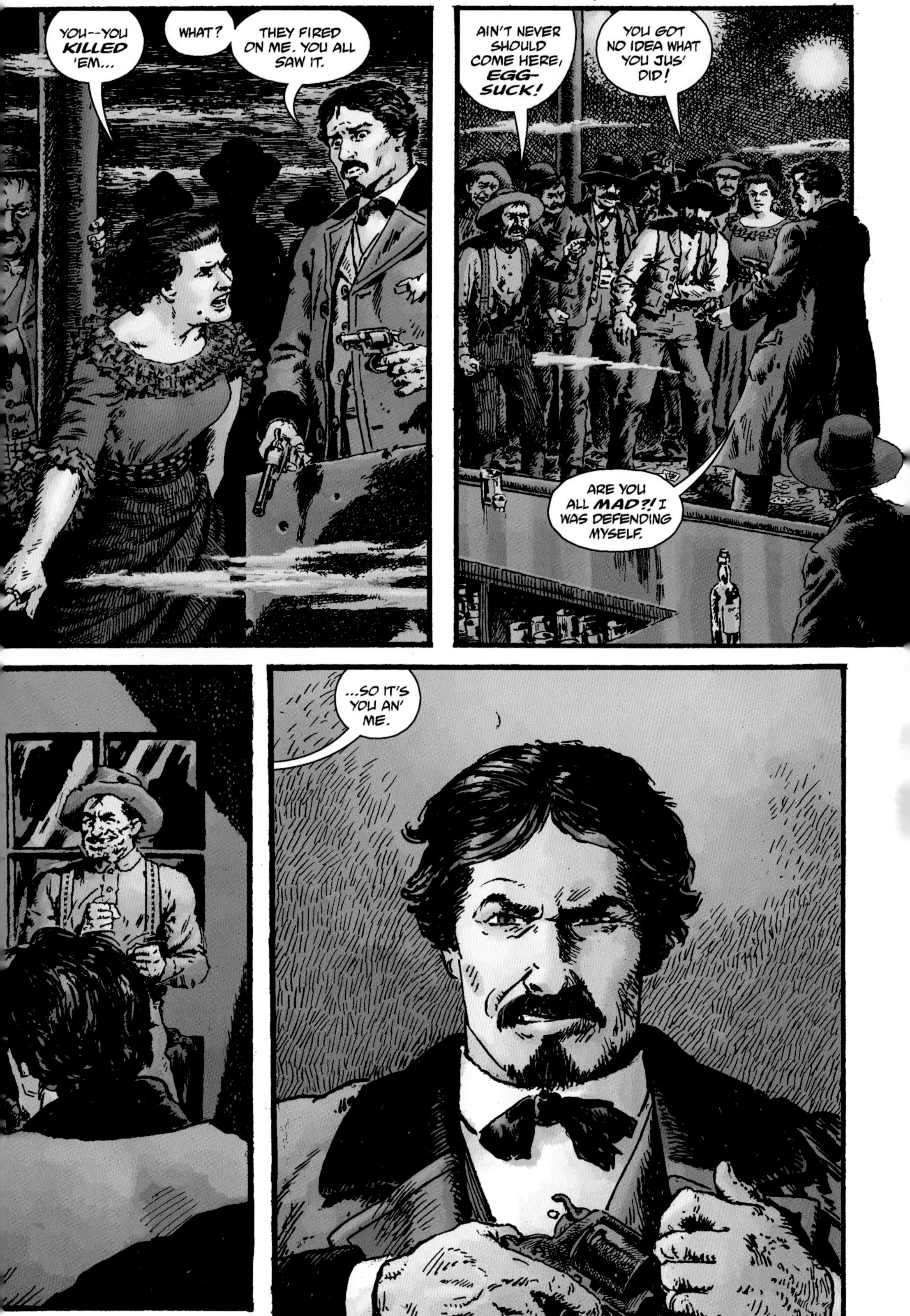
YOU--YOU KILLED 'EM...
WHAT?
THEY FIRED ON ME. YOU ALL SAW IT.
AIN'T NEVER SHOULD COME HERE, EGG-SUCK!
YOU GOT NO IDEA WHAT YOU JUS' DID!
ARE YOU ALL MAD?! I WAS DEFENDING MYSELF.
...SO IT'S YOU AN' ME.

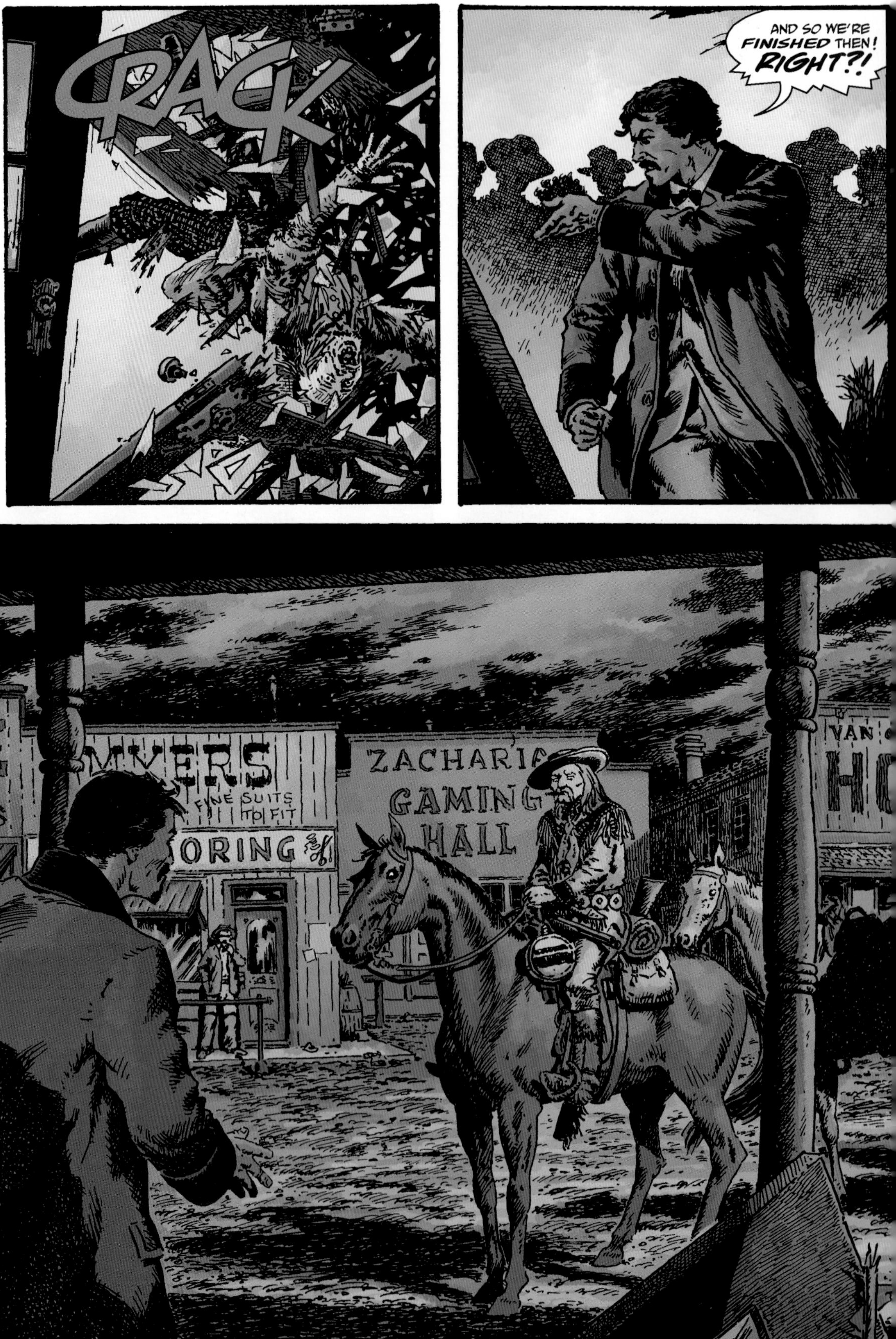
CRACK
AND SO WE'RE FINISHED THEN! RIGHT?!
MYERS
FINE SUITS TO FIT
ZACHARIA
GAMING HALL

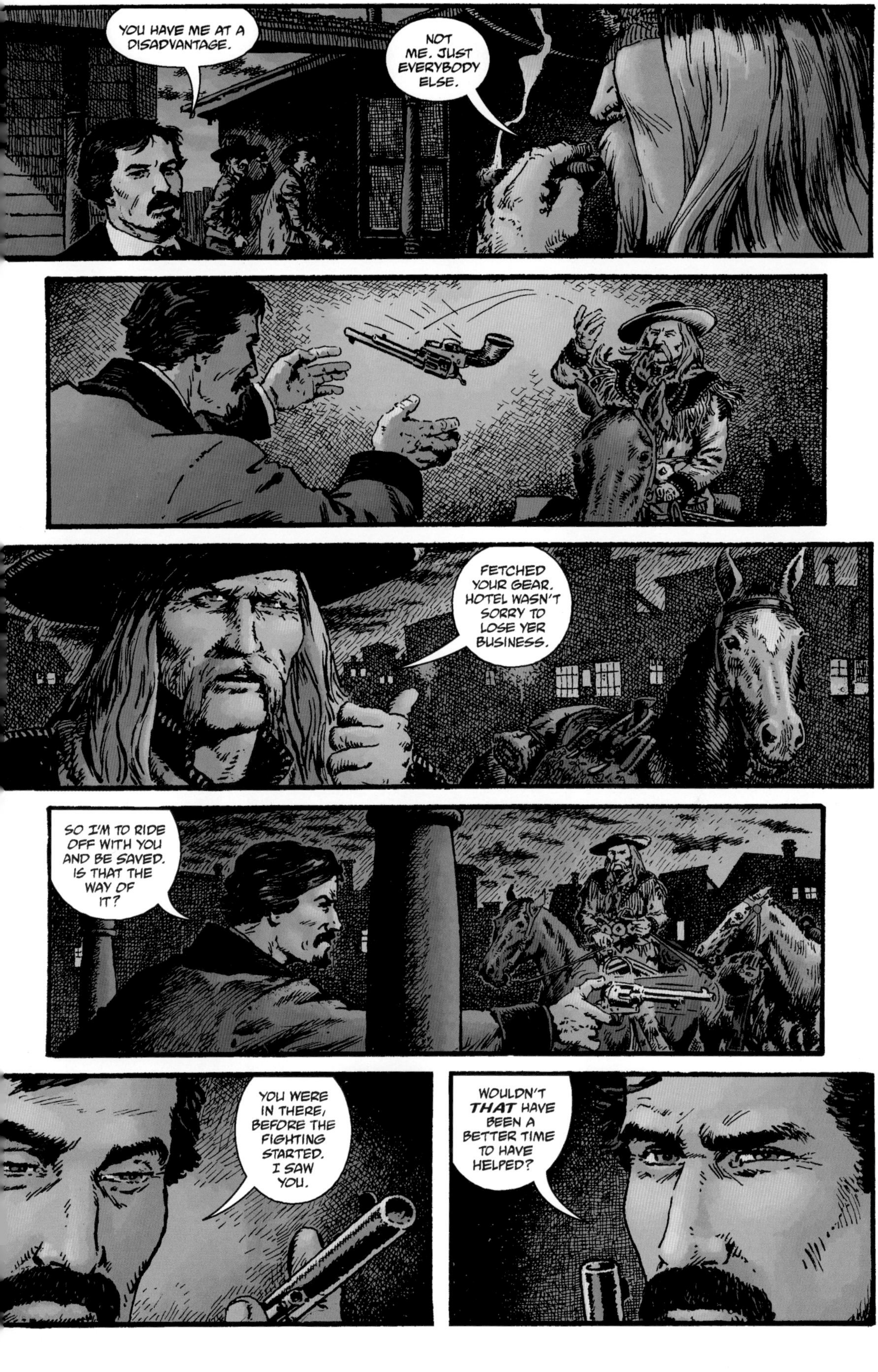
YOU HAVE ME AT A DISADVANTAGE.
NOT ME. JUST EVERYBODY ELSE.
FETCHED YOUR GEAR. HOTEL WASN'T SORRY TO LOSE YER BUSINESS.
SO I'M TO RIDE OFF WITH YOU AND BE SAVED. IS THAT THE WAY OF IT?
YOU WERE IN THERE, BEFORE THE FIGHTING STARTED. I SAW YOU.
WOULDN'T *THAT* HAVE BEEN A BETTER TIME TO HAVE HELPED?

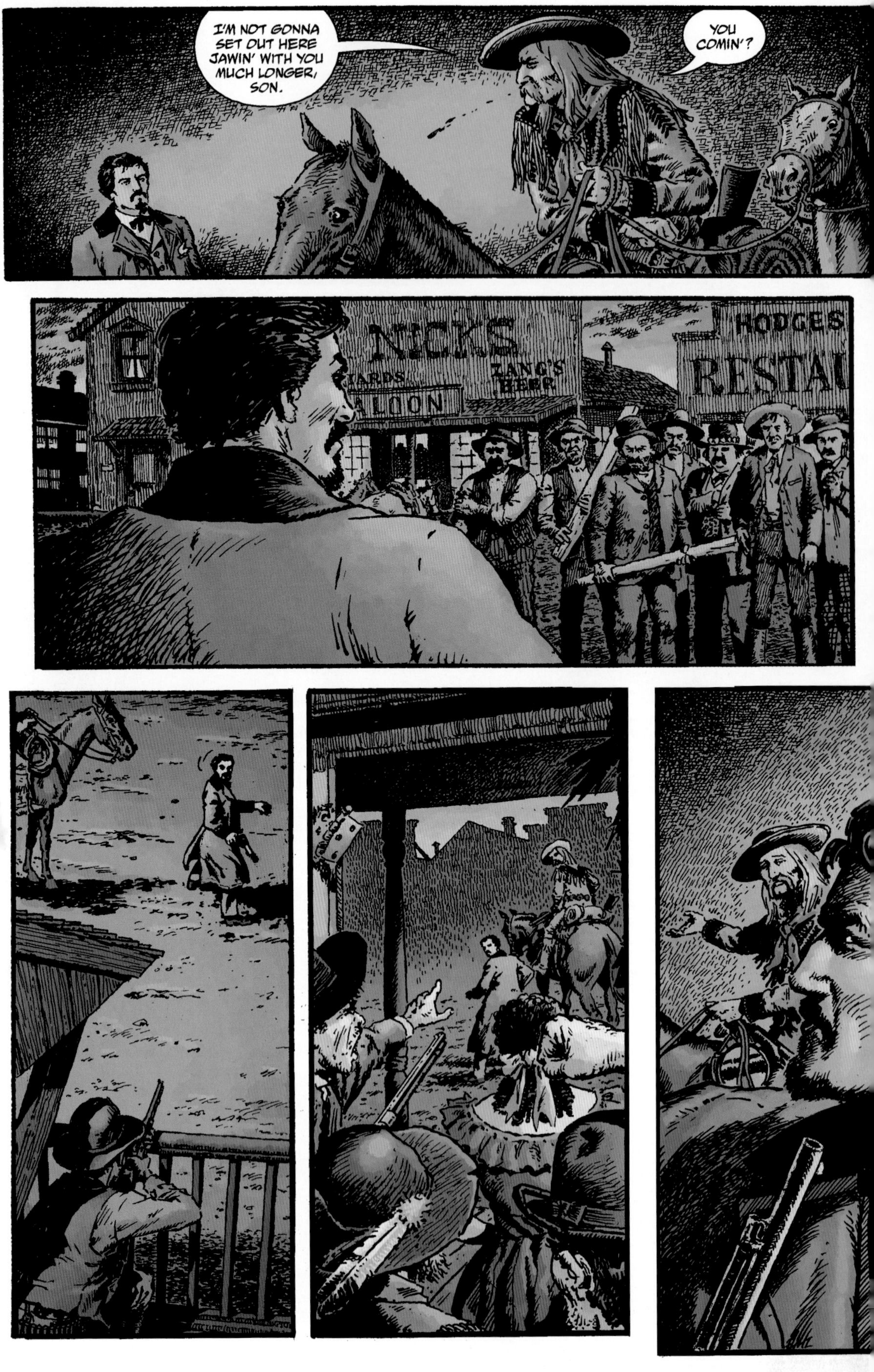
I'M NOT GONNA SET OUT HERE JAWIN' WITH YOU MUCH LONGER, SON.
YOU COMIN'?
NICKS
ZANG'S BEER
HODGES

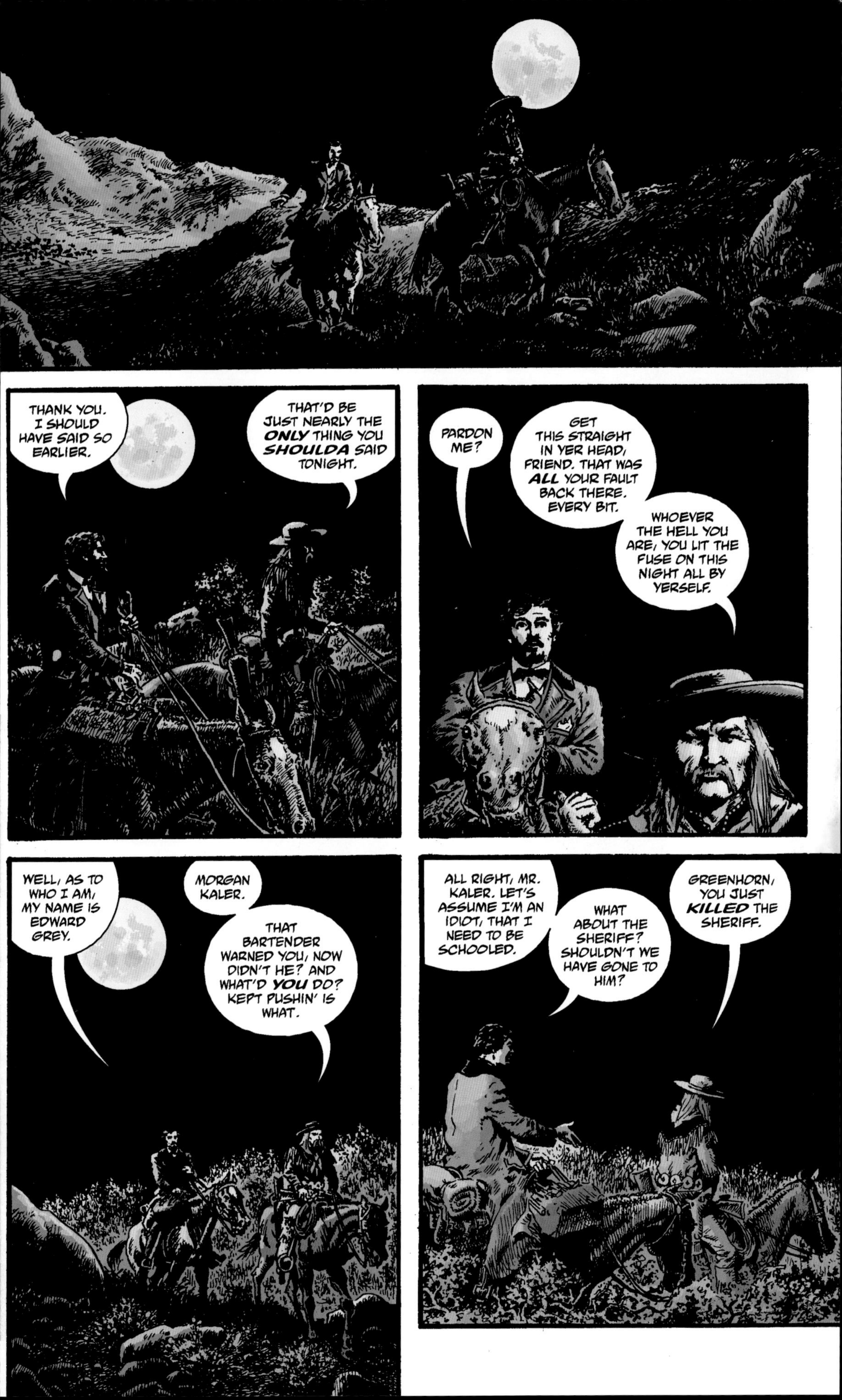
THANK YOU. I SHOULD HAVE SAID SO EARLIER.
THAT'D BE JUST NEARLY THE ONLY THING YOU SHOULDA SAID TONIGHT.
PARDON ME?
GET THIS STRAIGHT IN YER HEAD, FRIEND. THAT WAS ALL YOUR FAULT BACK THERE. EVERY BIT.
WHOEVER THE HELL YOU ARE, YOU LIT THE FUSE ON THIS NIGHT ALL BY YERSELF.
WELL, AS TO WHO I AM, MY NAME IS EDWARD GREY.
MORGAN KALER.
THAT BARTENDER WARNED YOU, NOW DIDN'T HE? AND WHAT'D YOU DO? KEPT PUSHIN' IS WHAT.
ALL RIGHT, MR. KALER. LET'S ASSUME I'M AN IDIOT, THAT I NEED TO BE SCHOOLED.
WHAT ABOUT THE SHERIFF? SHOULDN'T WE HAVE GONE TO HIM?
GREENHORN, YOU JUST KILLED THE SHERIFF.

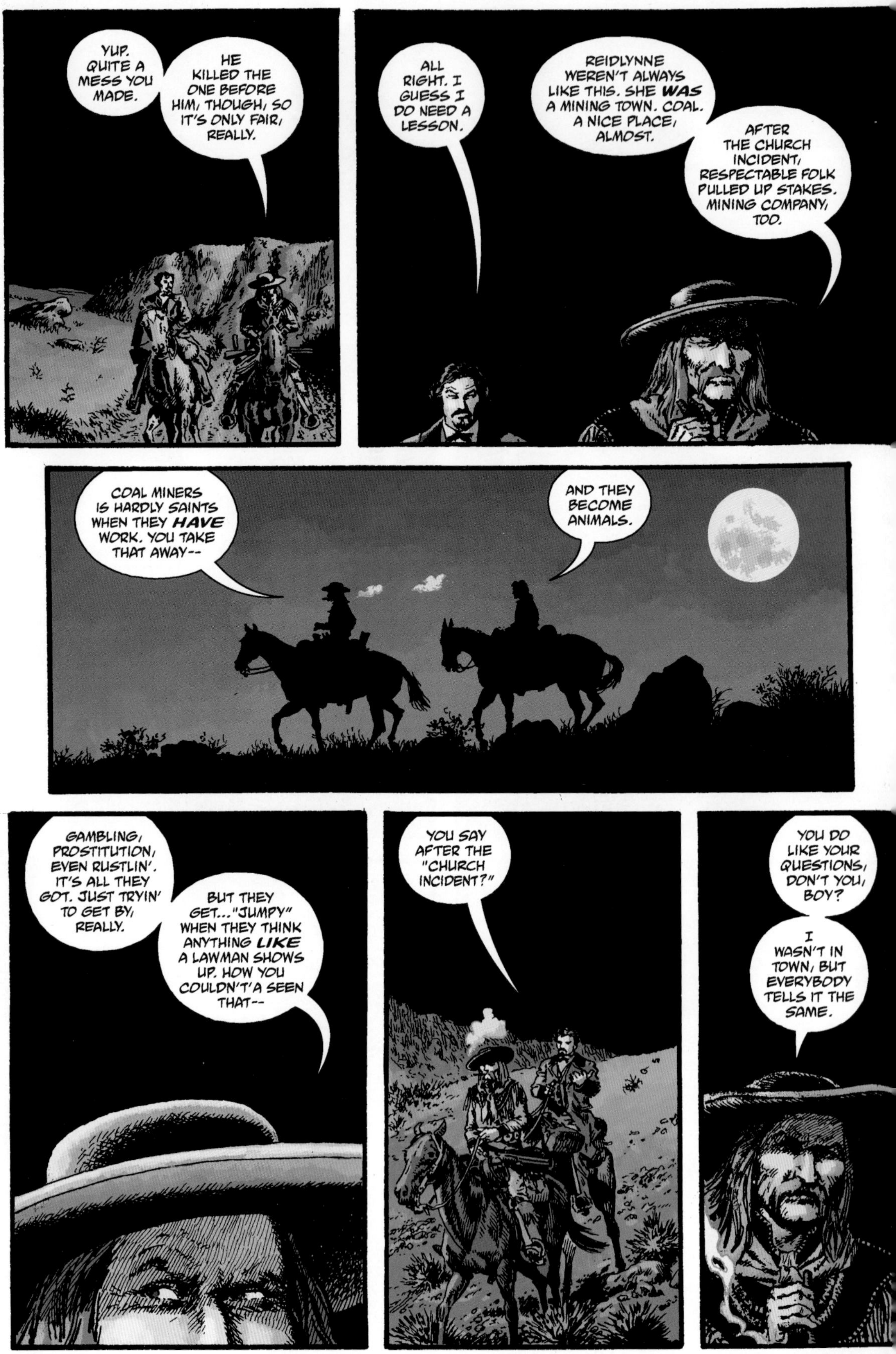
YUP. QUITE A MESS YOU MADE.
HE KILLED THE ONE BEFORE HIM, THOUGH, SO IT'S ONLY FAIR, REALLY.
ALL RIGHT. I GUESS I DO NEED A LESSON.
REIDLYNNE WEREN'T ALWAYS LIKE THIS. SHE WAS A MINING TOWN. COAL. A NICE PLACE, ALMOST.
AFTER THE CHURCH INCIDENT, RESPECTABLE FOLK PULLED UP STAKES. MINING COMPANY, TOO.
COAL MINERS IS HARDLY SAINTS WHEN THEY HAVE WORK. YOU TAKE THAT AWAY--
AND THEY BECOME ANIMALS.
GAMBLING, PROSTITUTION, EVEN RUSTLIN'. IT'S ALL THEY GOT. JUST TRYIN' TO GET BY, REALLY.
BUT THEY GET... "JUMPY" WHEN THEY THINK ANYTHING LIKE A LAWMAN SHOWS UP. HOW YOU COULDN'T'A SEEN THAT--
YOU SAY AFTER THE "CHURCH INCIDENT?"
YOU DO LIKE YOUR QUESTIONS, DON'T YOU, BOY?
I WASN'T IN TOWN, BUT EVERYBODY TELLS IT THE SAME.

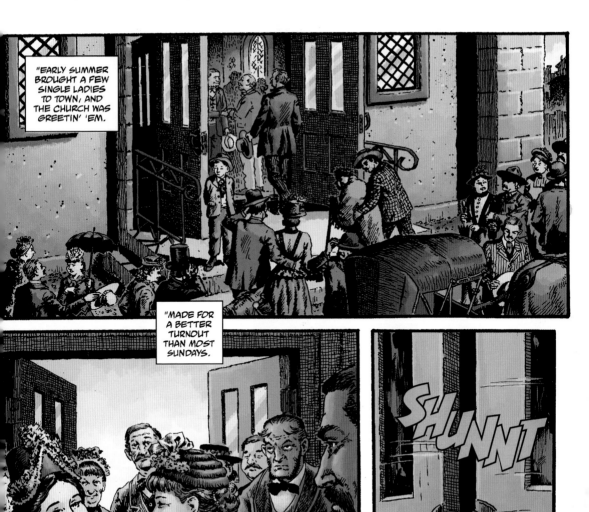

"EARLY SUMMER BROUGHT A FEW SINGLE LADIES TO TOWN, AND THE CHURCH WAS GREETIN' 'EM.

"MADE FOR A BETTER TURNOUT THAN MOST SUNDAYS.

SHUNNT

"DOORS WEREN'T CLOSED TWO SECONDS WHEN SCREAMS CAME POURIN' OUT. HORRIBLE SCREAMS.

"LIKE TO DRIVE THE SOUL FROM MAN AND BEAST.

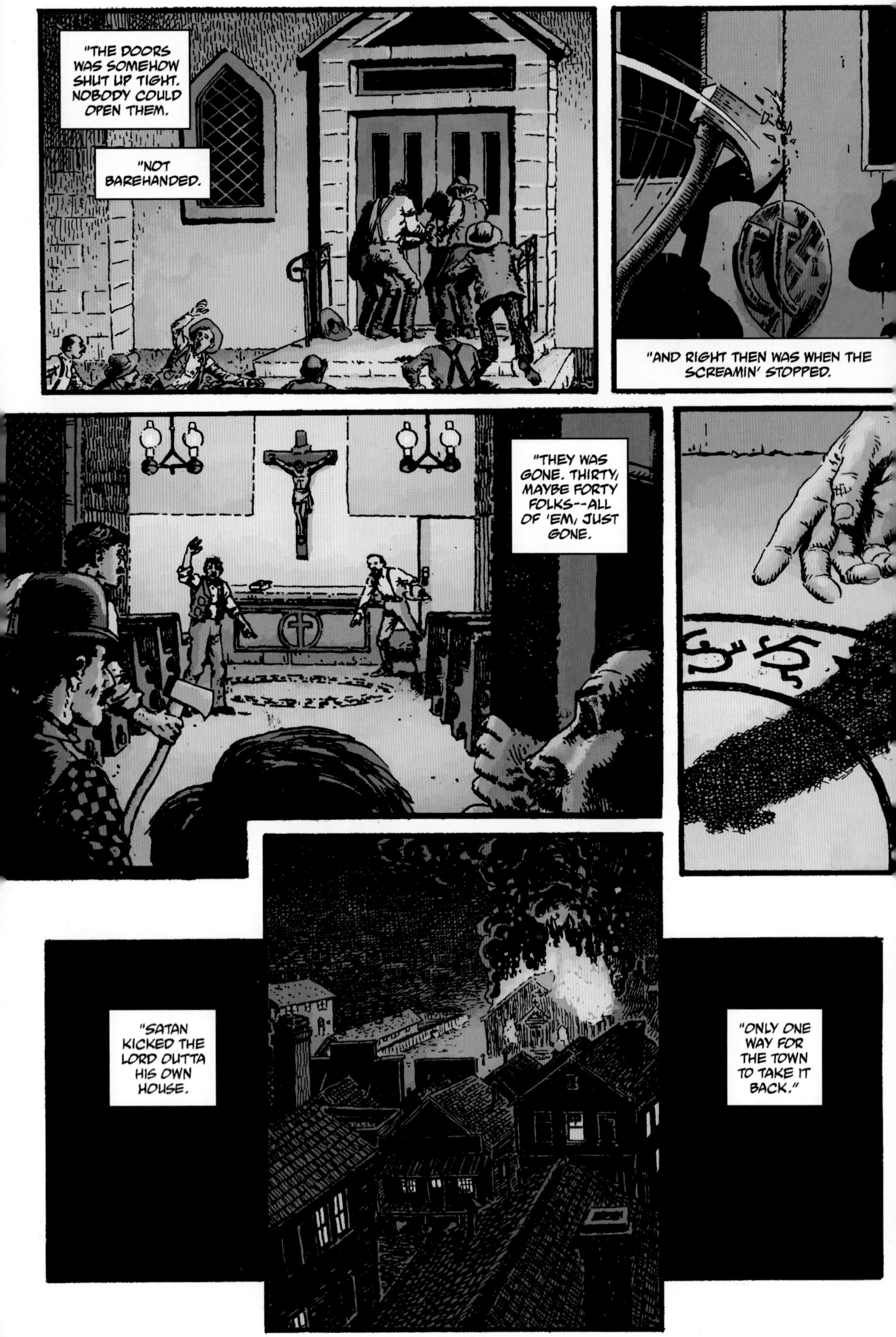
"THE DOORS WAS SOMEHOW SHUT UP TIGHT. NOBODY COULD OPEN THEM.
"NOT BAREHANDED.
"AND RIGHT THEN WAS WHEN THE SCREAMIN' STOPPED.
"THEY WAS GONE. THIRTY, MAYBE FORTY FOLKS--ALL OF 'EM, JUST GONE.
"SATAN KICKED THE LORD OUTTA HIS OWN HOUSE.
"ONLY ONE WAY FOR THE TOWN TO TAKE IT BACK."

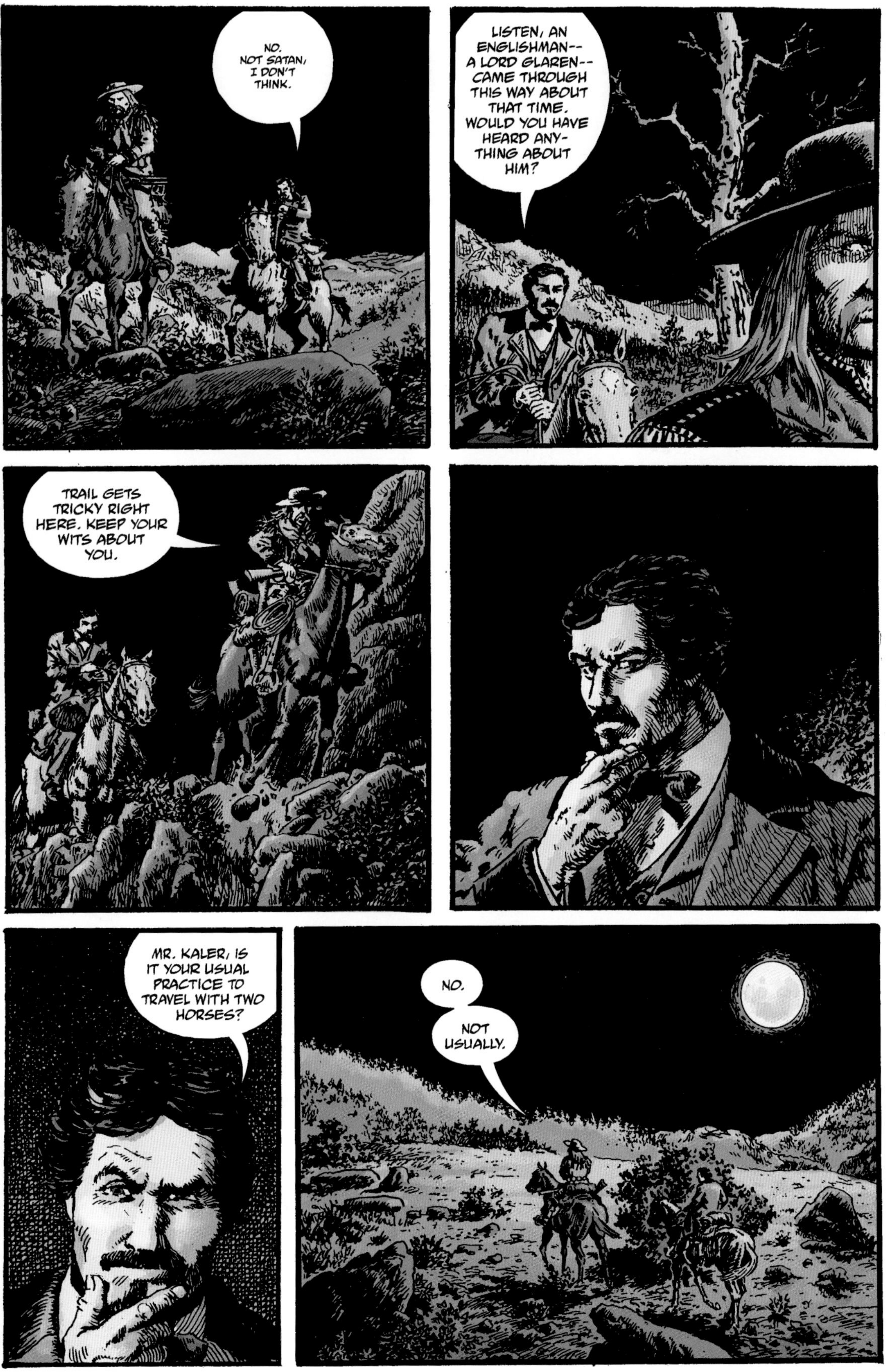
NO. NOT SATAN, I DON'T THINK.
LISTEN, AN ENGLISHMAN-- A LORD GLAREN-- CAME THROUGH THIS WAY ABOUT THAT TIME. WOULD YOU HAVE HEARD ANYTHING ABOUT HIM?
TRAIL GETS TRICKY RIGHT HERE. KEEP YOUR WITS ABOUT YOU.
MR. KALER, IS IT YOUR USUAL PRACTICE TO TRAVEL WITH TWO HORSES?
NO.
NOT USUALLY.

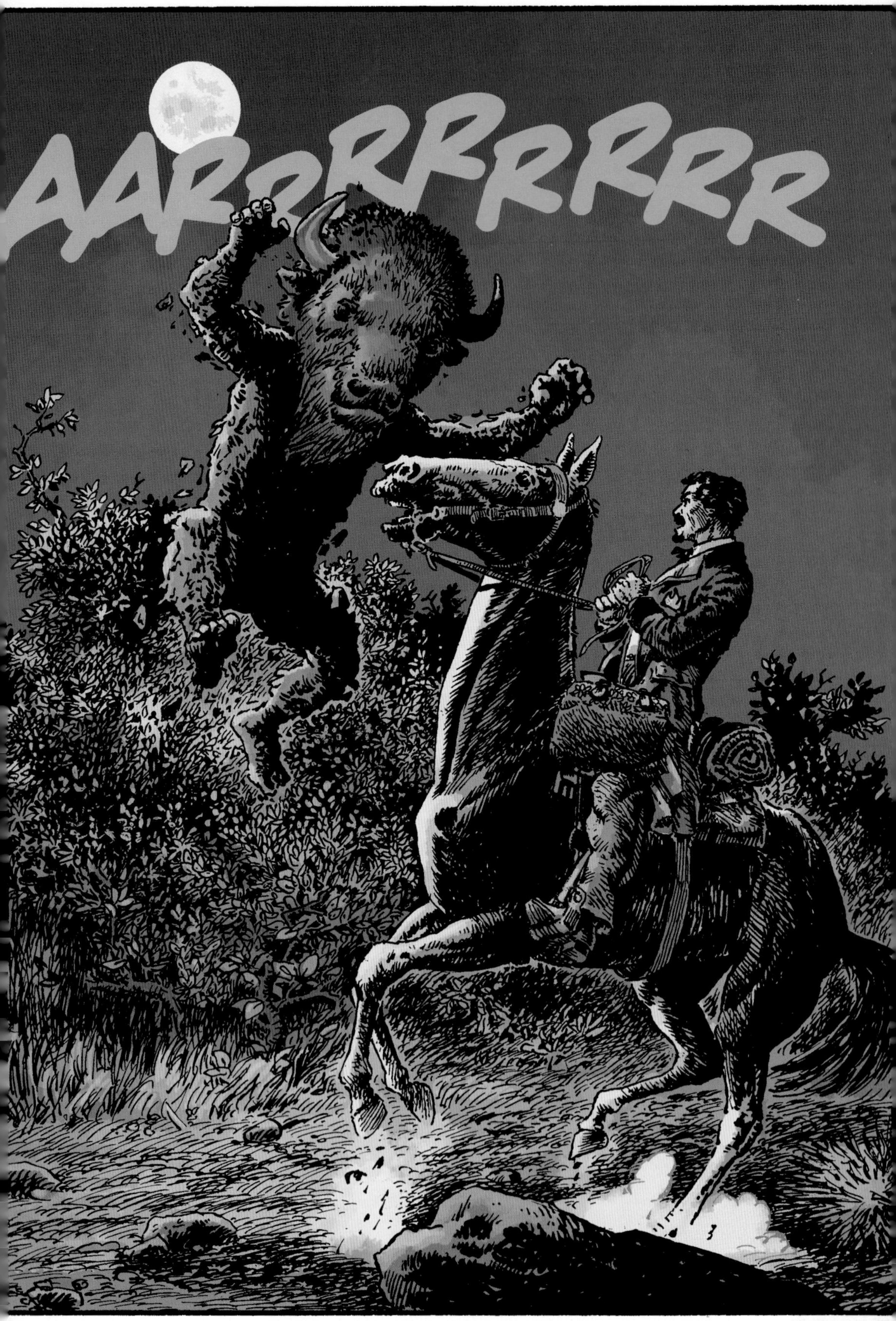
AARRRRRRRR

CHAPTER TWO

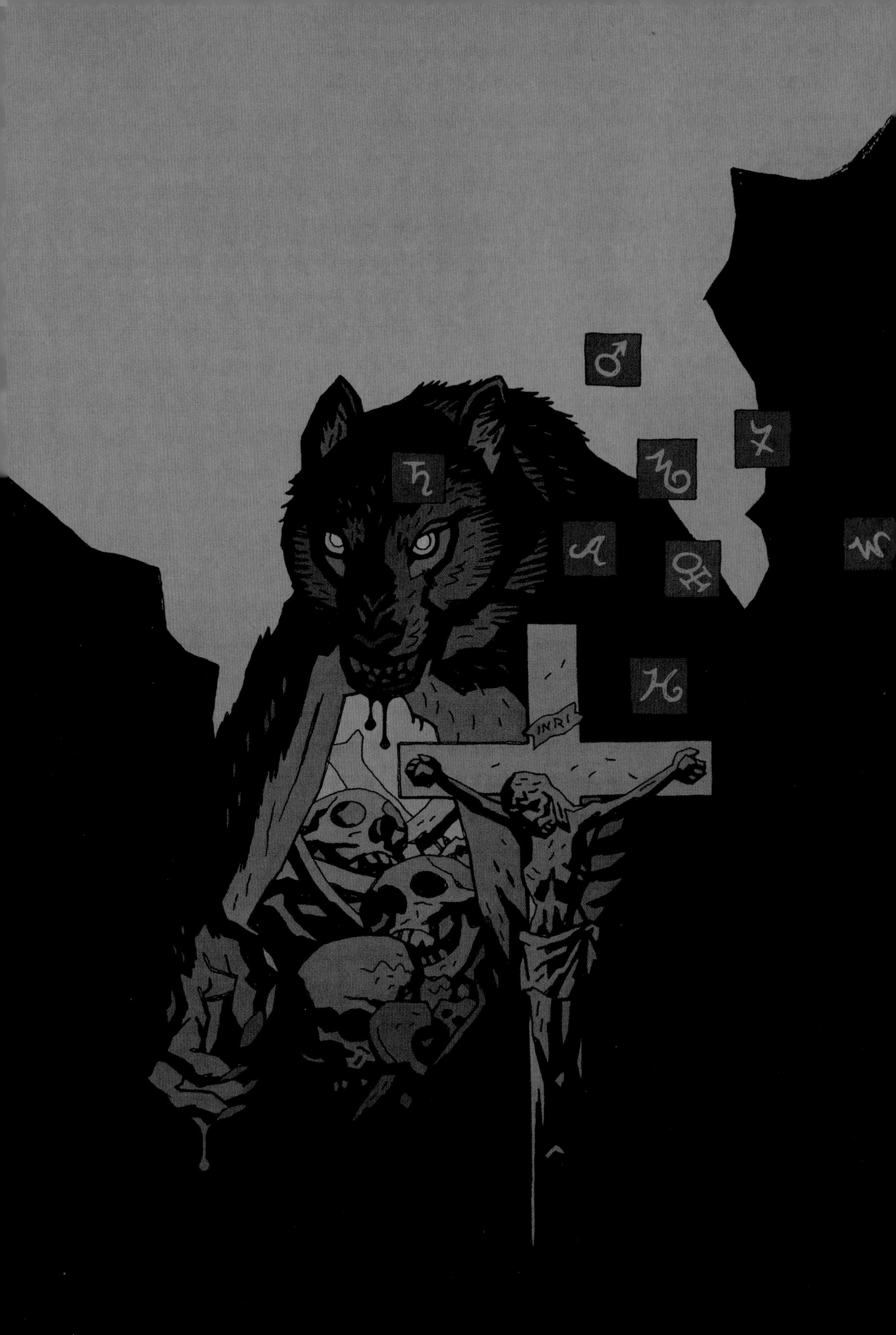
INRI

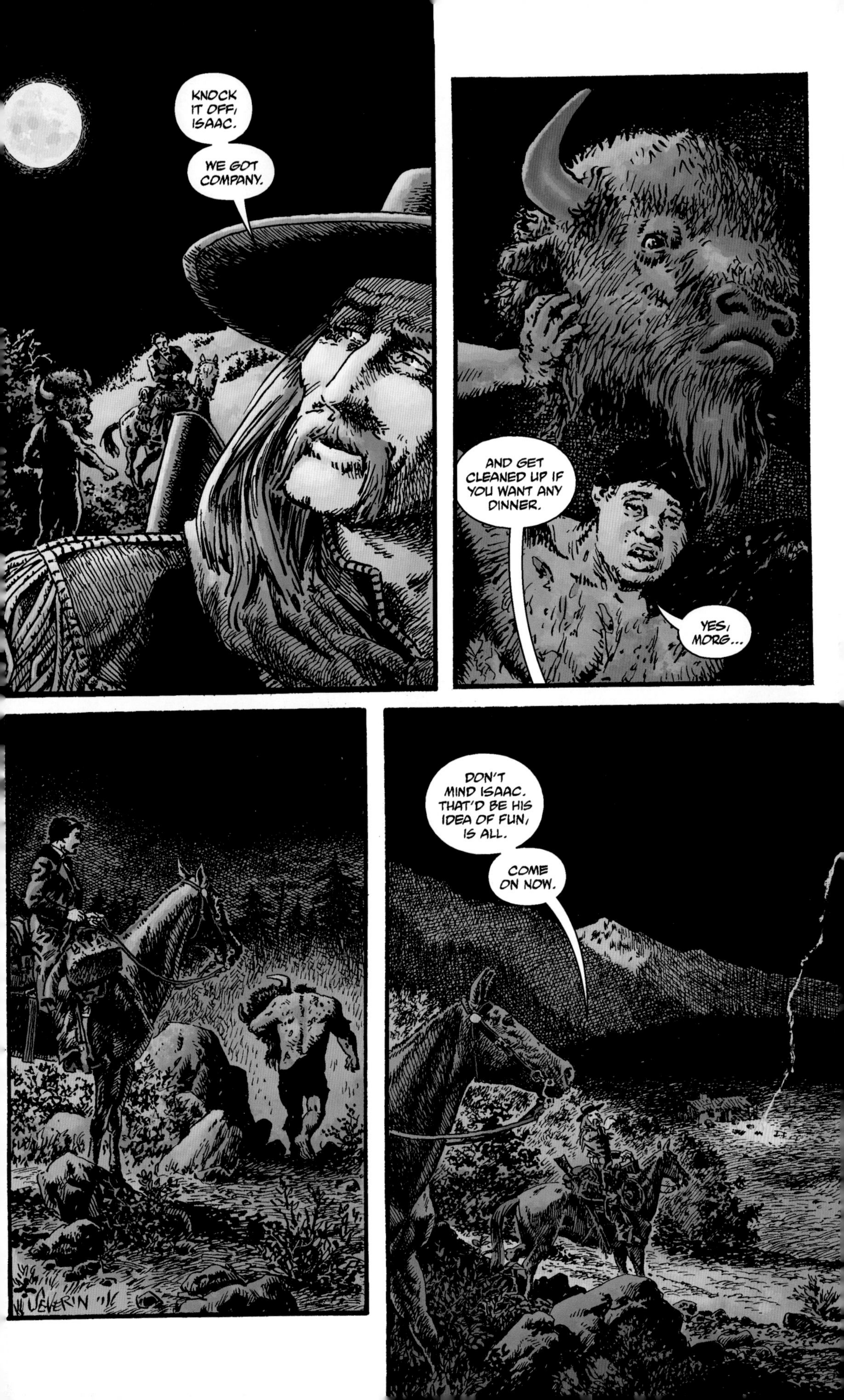
KNOCK IT OFF, ISAAC.
WE GOT COMPANY.
AND GET CLEANED UP IF YOU WANT ANY DINNER.
YES, MORG...
SEVERIN '11
DON'T MIND ISAAC. THAT'D BE HIS IDEA OF FUN, IS ALL.
COME ON NOW.

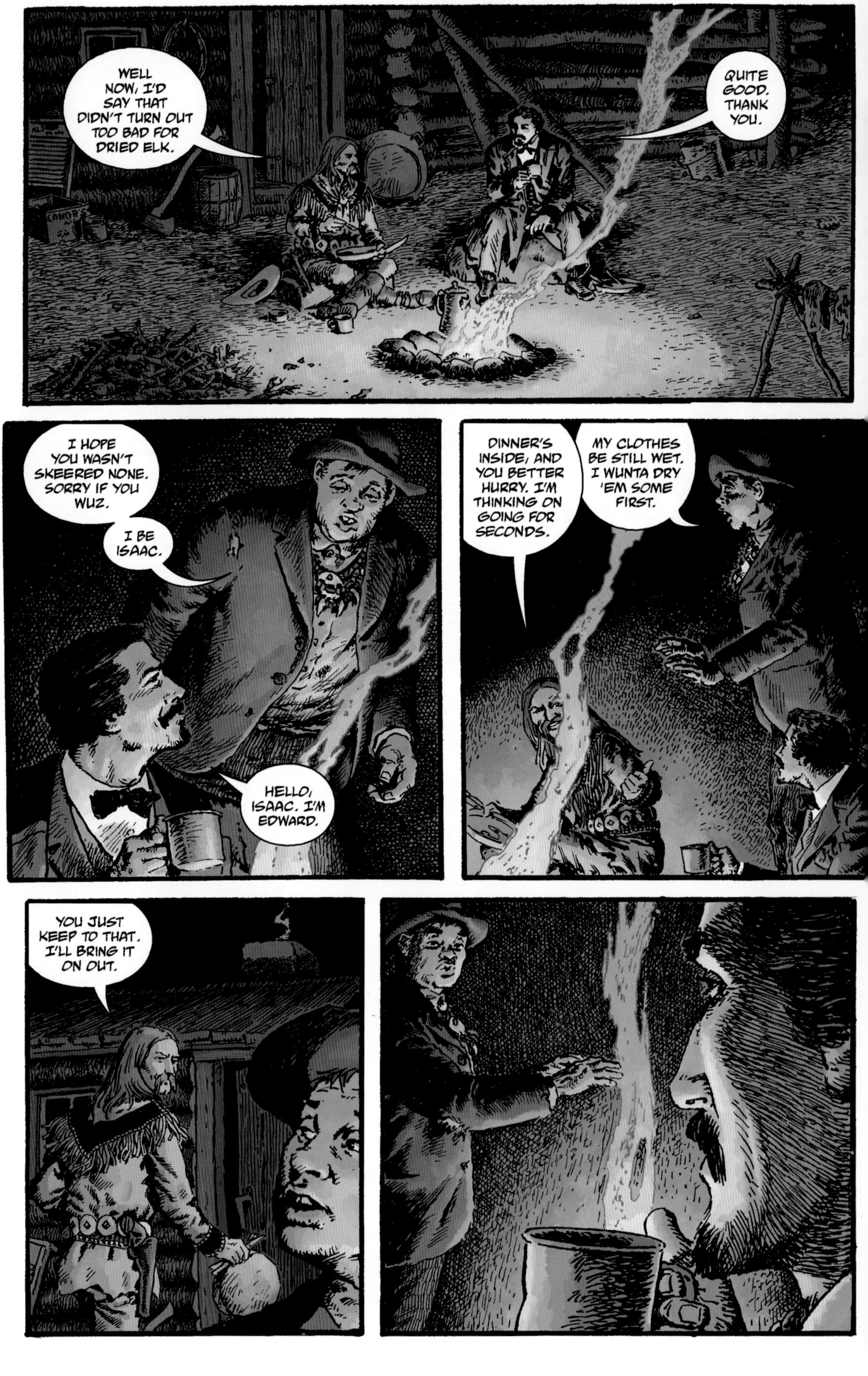
WELL NOW, I'D SAY THAT DIDN'T TURN OUT TOO BAD FOR DRIED ELK.
QUITE GOOD. THANK YOU.
I HOPE YOU WASN'T SKEERED NONE. SORRY IF YOU WUZ.
I BE ISAAC.
HELLO, ISAAC. I'M EDWARD.
DINNER'S INSIDE, AND YOU BETTER HURRY. I'M THINKING ON GOING FOR SECONDS.
MY CLOTHES BE STILL WET. I WUNTA DRY 'EM SOME FIRST.
YOU JUST KEEP TO THAT. I'LL BRING IT ON OUT.

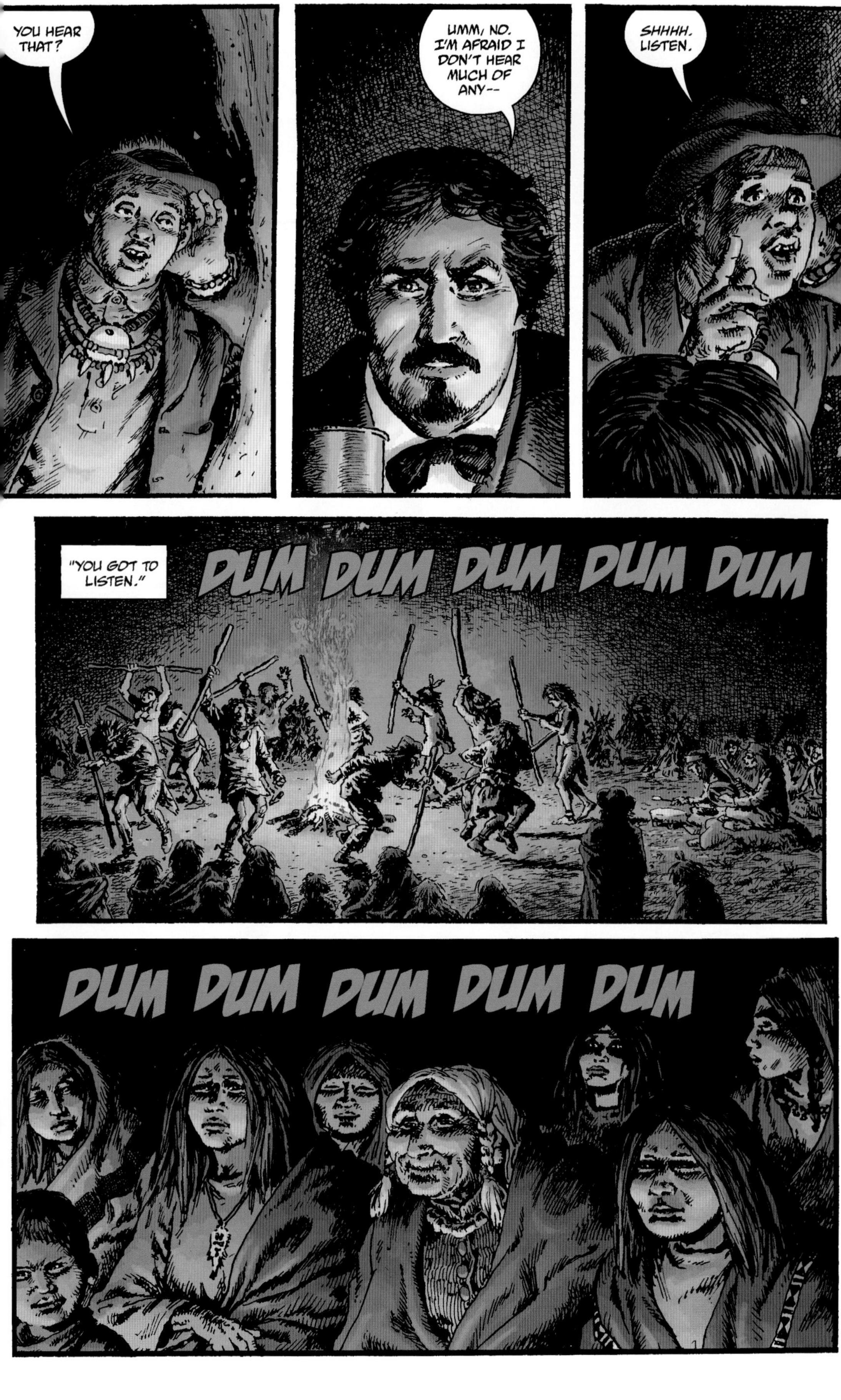
YOU HEAR THAT?
UMM, NO. I'M AFRAID I DON'T HEAR MUCH OF ANY--
SHHHH. LISTEN.
"YOU GOT TO LISTEN."
DUM DUM DUM DUM DUM
DUM DUM DUM DUM DUM

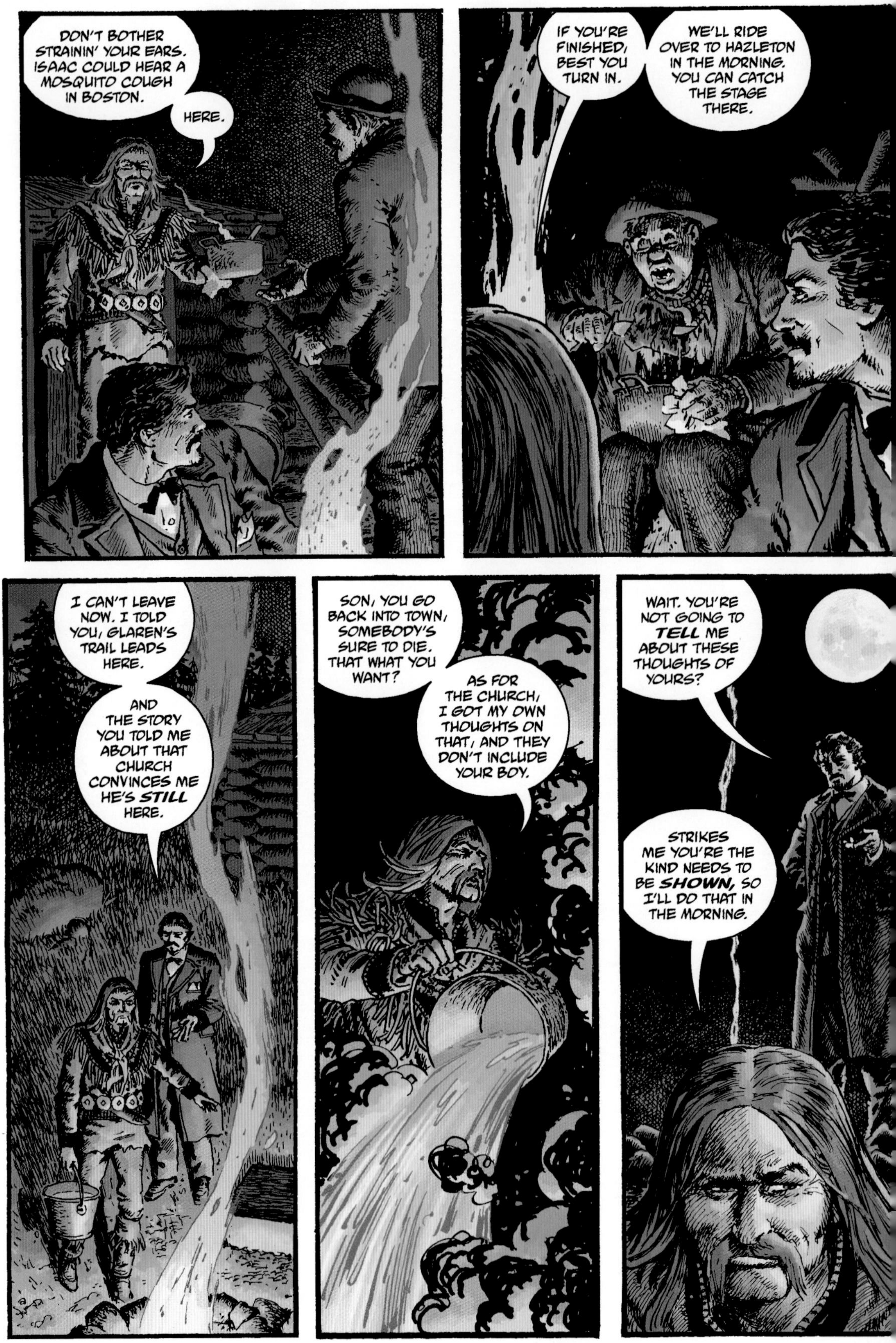
DON'T BOTHER STRAININ' YOUR EARS. ISAAC COULD HEAR A MOSQUITO COUGH IN BOSTON.
HERE.
IF YOU'RE FINISHED, BEST YOU TURN IN.
WE'LL RIDE OVER TO HAZLETON IN THE MORNING. YOU CAN CATCH THE STAGE THERE.
I CAN'T LEAVE NOW. I TOLD YOU, GLAREN'S TRAIL LEADS HERE.
AND THE STORY YOU TOLD ME ABOUT THAT CHURCH CONVINCES ME HE'S STILL HERE.
SON, YOU GO BACK INTO TOWN, SOMEBODY'S SURE TO DIE. THAT WHAT YOU WANT?
AS FOR THE CHURCH, I GOT MY OWN THOUGHTS ON THAT, AND THEY DON'T INCLUDE YOUR BOY.
WAIT. YOU'RE NOT GOING TO TELL ME ABOUT THESE THOUGHTS OF YOURS?
STRIKES ME YOU'RE THE KIND NEEDS TO BE SHOWN, SO I'LL DO THAT IN THE MORNING.

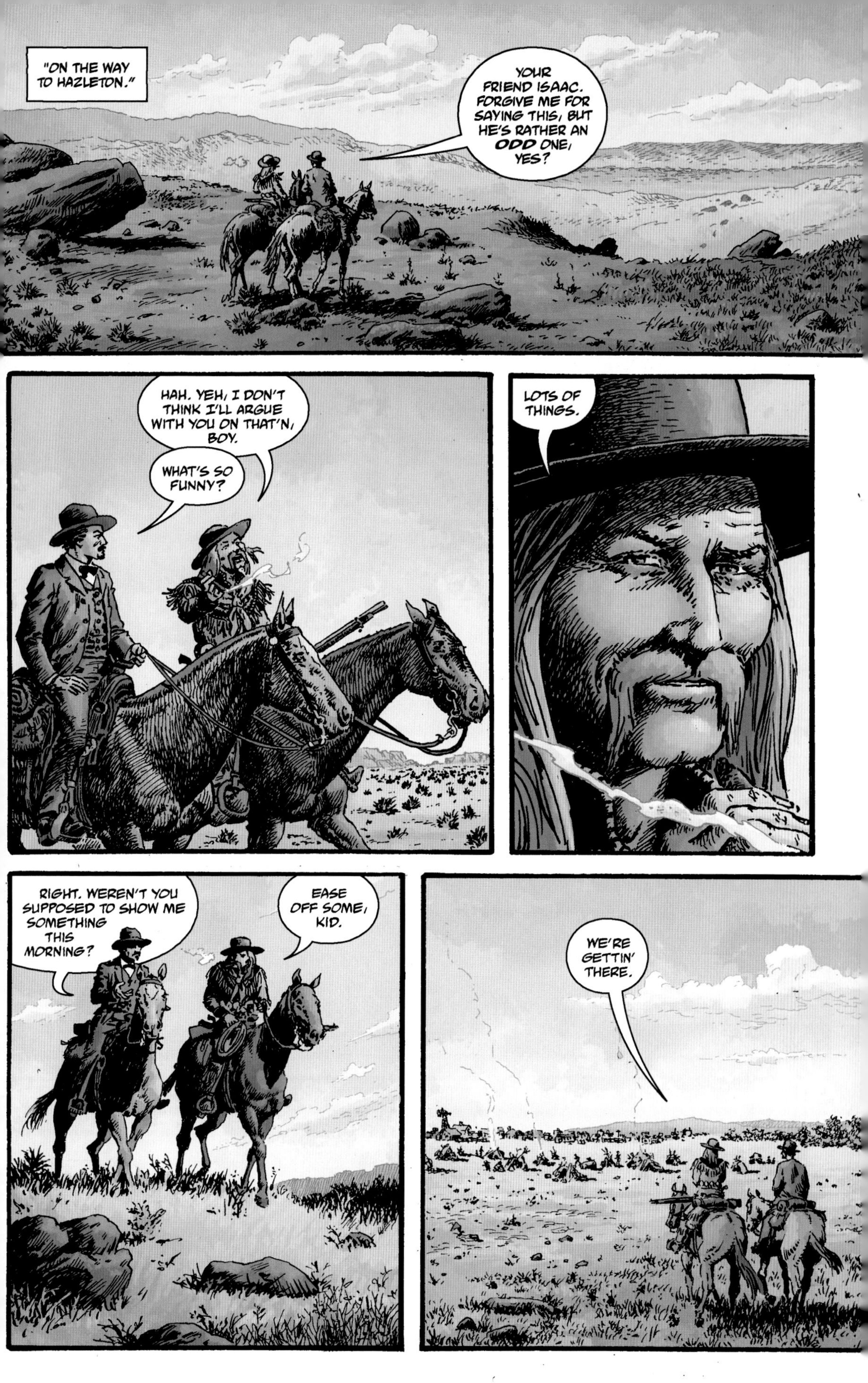
"ON THE WAY TO HAZLETON."
YOUR FRIEND ISAAC. FORGIVE ME FOR SAYING THIS, BUT HE'S RATHER AN ODD ONE, YES?
HAH. YEH, I DON'T THINK I'LL ARGUE WITH YOU ON THAT'N, BOY.
WHAT'S SO FUNNY?
LOTS OF THINGS.
RIGHT. WEREN'T YOU SUPPOSED TO SHOW ME SOMETHING THIS MORNING?
EASE OFF SOME, KID.
WE'RE GETTIN' THERE.

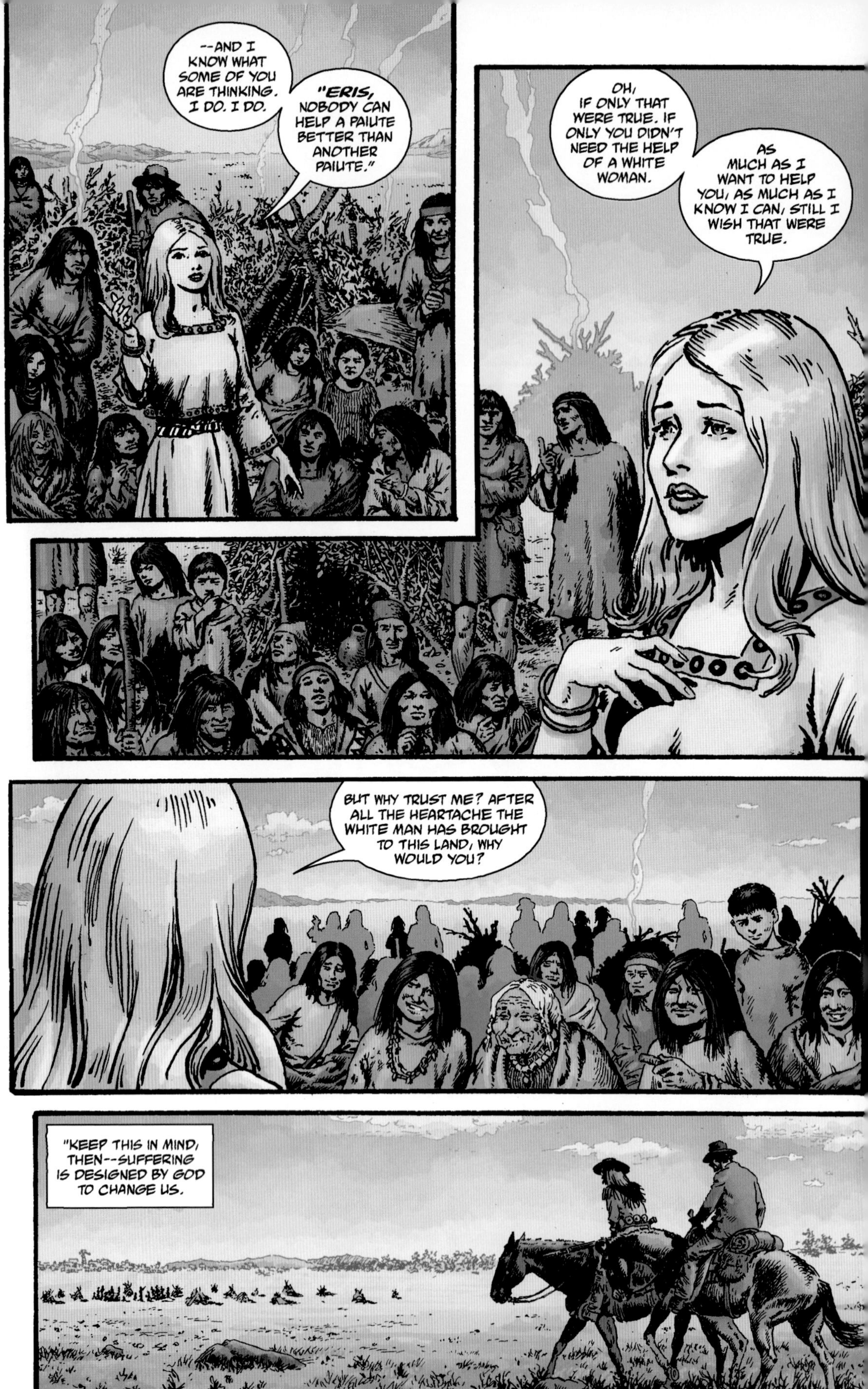
--AND I KNOW WHAT SOME OF YOU ARE THINKING. I DO. I DO.
"ERIS, NOBODY CAN HELP A PAIUTE BETTER THAN ANOTHER PAIUTE."
OH, IF ONLY THAT WERE TRUE. IF ONLY YOU DIDN'T NEED THE HELP OF A WHITE WOMAN.
AS MUCH AS I WANT TO HELP YOU, AS MUCH AS I KNOW I CAN, STILL I WISH THAT WERE TRUE.
BUT WHY TRUST ME? AFTER ALL THE HEARTACHE THE WHITE MAN HAS BROUGHT TO THIS LAND, WHY WOULD YOU?
"KEEP THIS IN MIND, THEN--SUFFERING IS DESIGNED BY GOD TO CHANGE US.

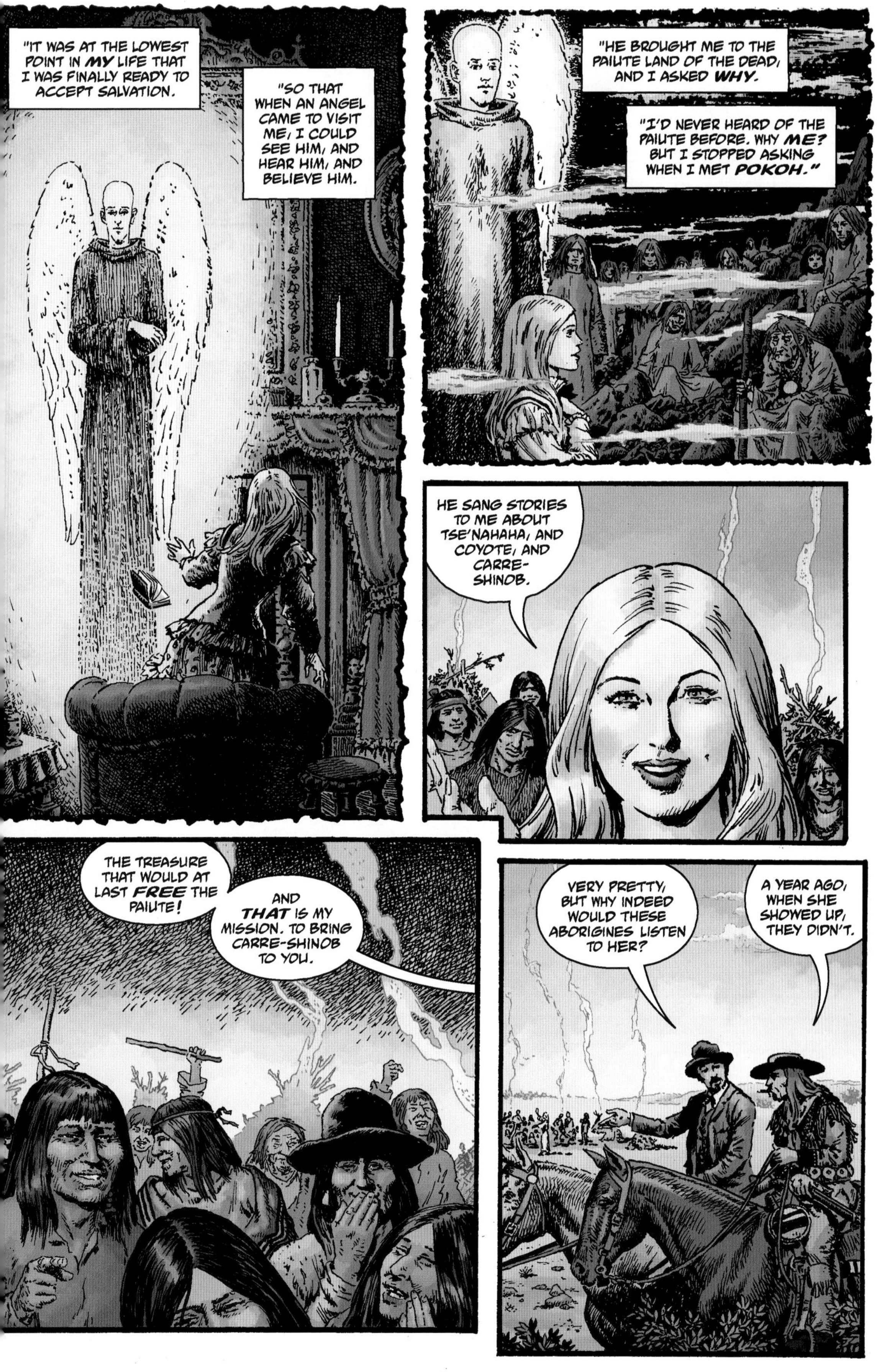
"IT WAS AT THE LOWEST POINT IN MY LIFE THAT I WAS FINALLY READY TO ACCEPT SALVATION.
"SO THAT WHEN AN ANGEL CAME TO VISIT ME, I COULD SEE HIM, AND HEAR HIM, AND BELIEVE HIM.
"HE BROUGHT ME TO THE PAIUTE LAND OF THE DEAD, AND I ASKED WHY.
"I'D NEVER HEARD OF THE PAIUTE BEFORE. WHY ME? BUT I STOPPED ASKING WHEN I MET POKOH."
HE SANG STORIES TO ME ABOUT TSE'NAHAHA, AND COYOTE, AND CARRE-SHINOB.
THE TREASURE THAT WOULD AT LAST FREE THE PAIUTE!
AND THAT IS MY MISSION. TO BRING CARRE-SHINOB TO YOU.
VERY PRETTY, BUT WHY INDEED WOULD THESE ABORIGINES LISTEN TO HER?
A YEAR AGO, WHEN SHE SHOWED UP, THEY DIDN'T.

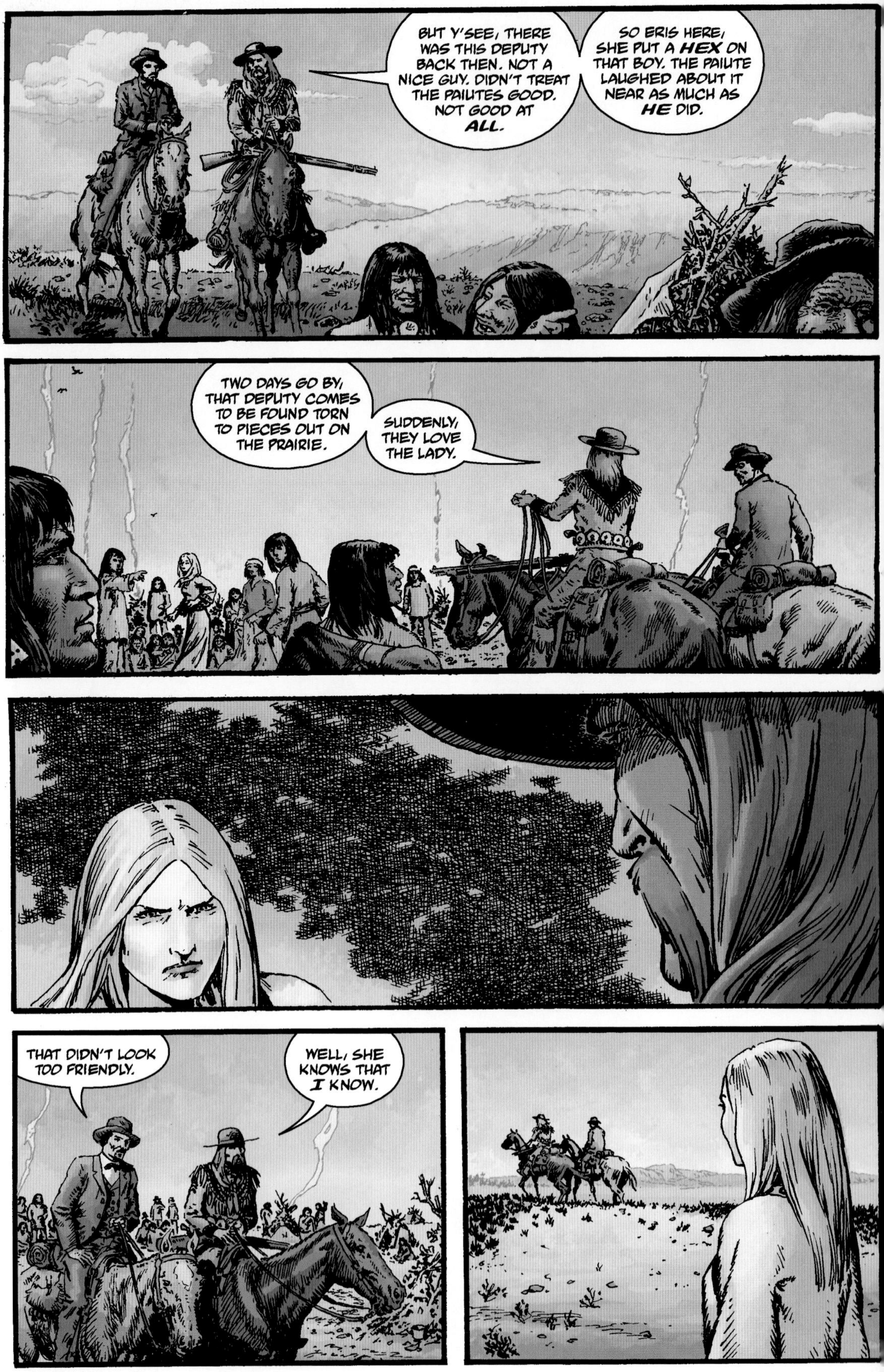
BUT Y'SEE, THERE WAS THIS DEPUTY BACK THEN. NOT A NICE GUY. DIDN'T TREAT THE PAIUTES GOOD. NOT GOOD AT ALL.
SO ERIS HERE, SHE PUT A HEX ON THAT BOY. THE PAIUTE LAUGHED ABOUT IT NEAR AS MUCH AS HE DID.
TWO DAYS GO BY, THAT DEPUTY COMES TO BE FOUND TORN TO PIECES OUT ON THE PRAIRIE.
SUDDENLY, THEY LOVE THE LADY.
THAT DIDN'T LOOK TOO FRIENDLY.
WELL, SHE KNOWS THAT I KNOW.

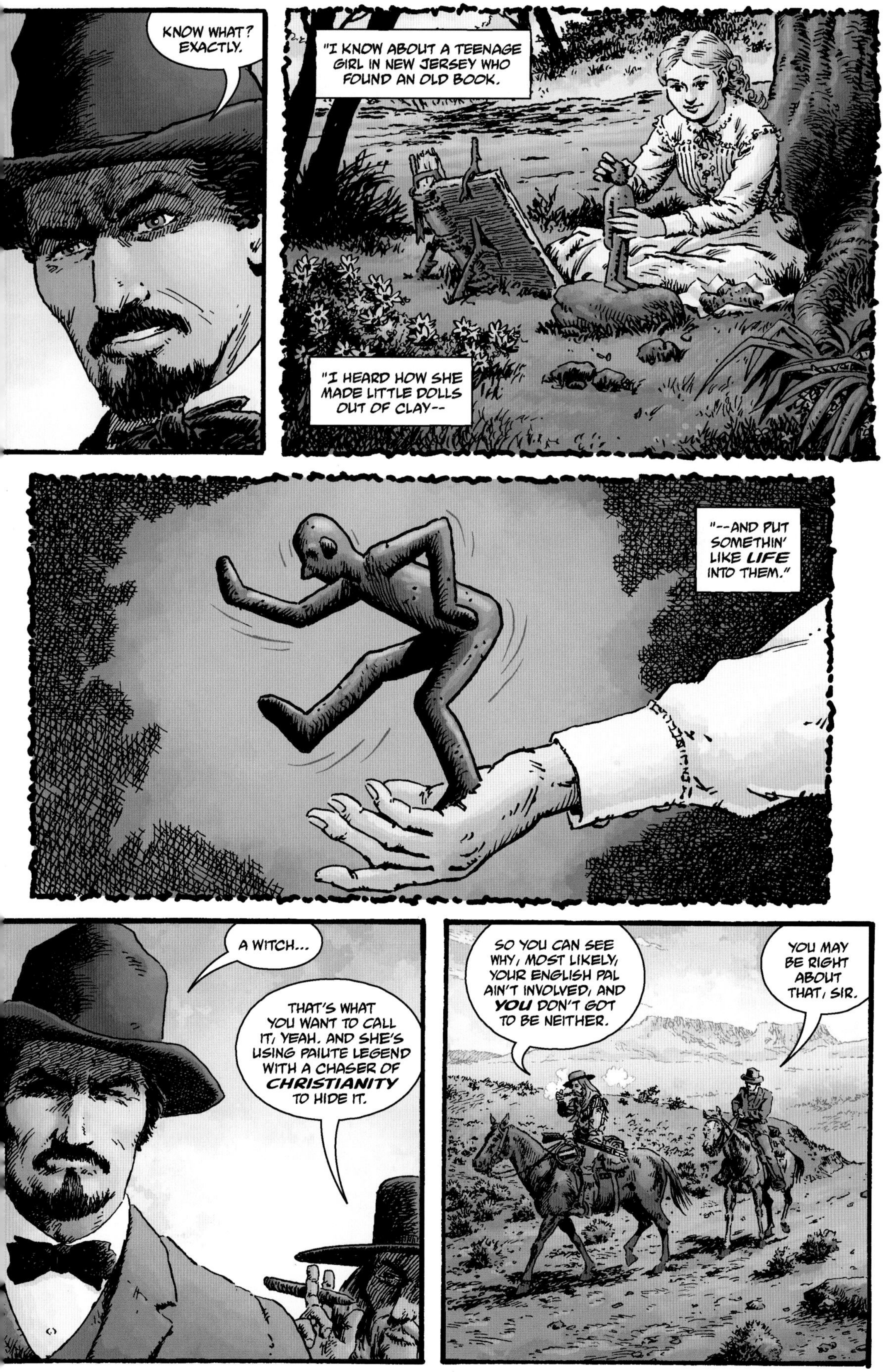
KNOW WHAT? EXACTLY.
"I KNOW ABOUT A TEENAGE GIRL IN NEW JERSEY WHO FOUND AN OLD BOOK.
"I HEARD HOW SHE MADE LITTLE DOLLS OUT OF CLAY--
"--AND PUT SOMETHIN' LIKE *LIFE* INTO THEM."
A WITCH...
THAT'S WHAT YOU WANT TO CALL IT, YEAH. AND SHE'S USING PAIUTE LEGEND WITH A CHASER OF *CHRISTIANITY* TO HIDE IT.
SO YOU CAN SEE WHY, MOST LIKELY, YOUR ENGLISH PAL AIN'T INVOLVED, AND *YOU* DON'T GOT TO BE NEITHER.
YOU MAY BE RIGHT ABOUT THAT, SIR.

I'M IN NO HURRY TO LEAVE, THOUGH. THIS COUNTRY MAKES ME NOSTALGIC FOR HOME, SOMEHOW.

HOME? I AIN'T NEVER BEEN TO LONDON, BUT I HAVE SEEN ME A FEW PICTURES.

NOT ALL ENGLISHMEN ARE BORN IN LONDON.

WHERE I'M FROM IS NOT SO EXPANSIVE AS ALL THIS, BUT STILL.

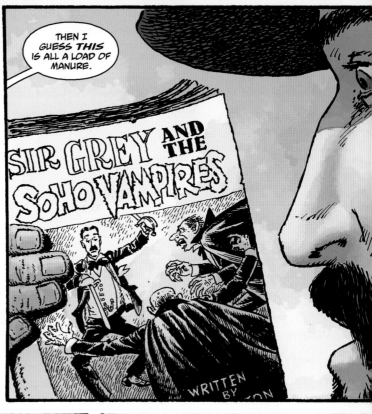

THEN I GUESS THIS IS ALL A LOAD OF MANURE.

SIR GREY AND THE SOHO VAMPIRES

WRITTEN BY

ISAAC LOVES THOSE STORIES.

SO, YOU KNEW WHO I WAS ALL ALONG.

OR YOU THOUGHT YOU DID. "A LOAD OF MANURE"?

DOUBTLESS YOU'D BE INTERESTED A GREAT DEAL MORE IN SOME TRUTH.

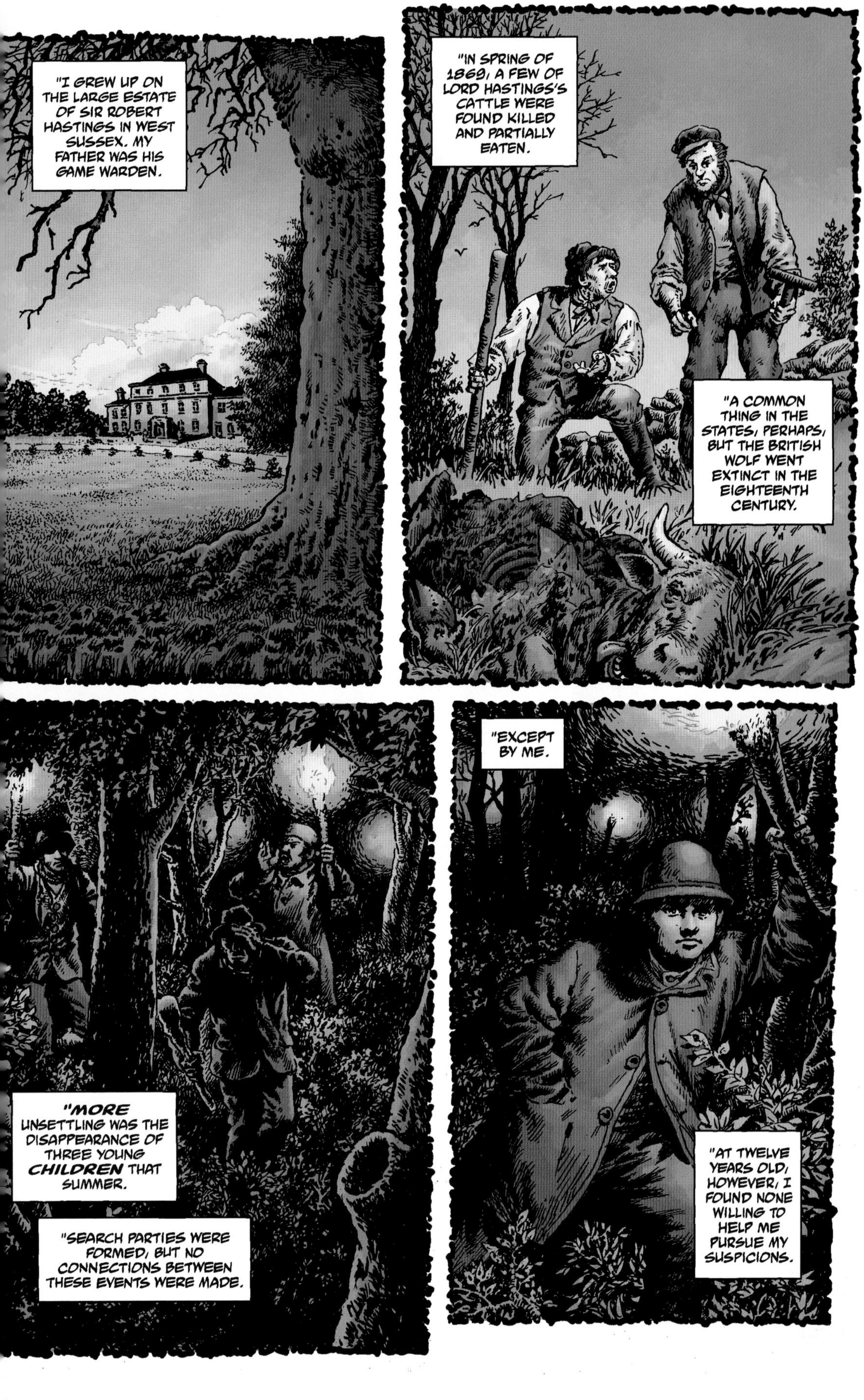
"I GREW UP ON THE LARGE ESTATE OF SIR ROBERT HASTINGS IN WEST SUSSEX. MY FATHER WAS HIS GAME WARDEN.
"IN SPRING OF 1869, A FEW OF LORD HASTINGS'S CATTLE WERE FOUND KILLED AND PARTIALLY EATEN.
"A COMMON THING IN THE STATES, PERHAPS, BUT THE BRITISH WOLF WENT EXTINCT IN THE EIGHTEENTH CENTURY.
"MORE UNSETTLING WAS THE DISAPPEARANCE OF THREE YOUNG CHILDREN THAT SUMMER.
"SEARCH PARTIES WERE FORMED, BUT NO CONNECTIONS BETWEEN THESE EVENTS WERE MADE.
"EXCEPT BY ME.
"AT TWELVE YEARS OLD, HOWEVER, I FOUND NONE WILLING TO HELP ME PURSUE MY SUSPICIONS.

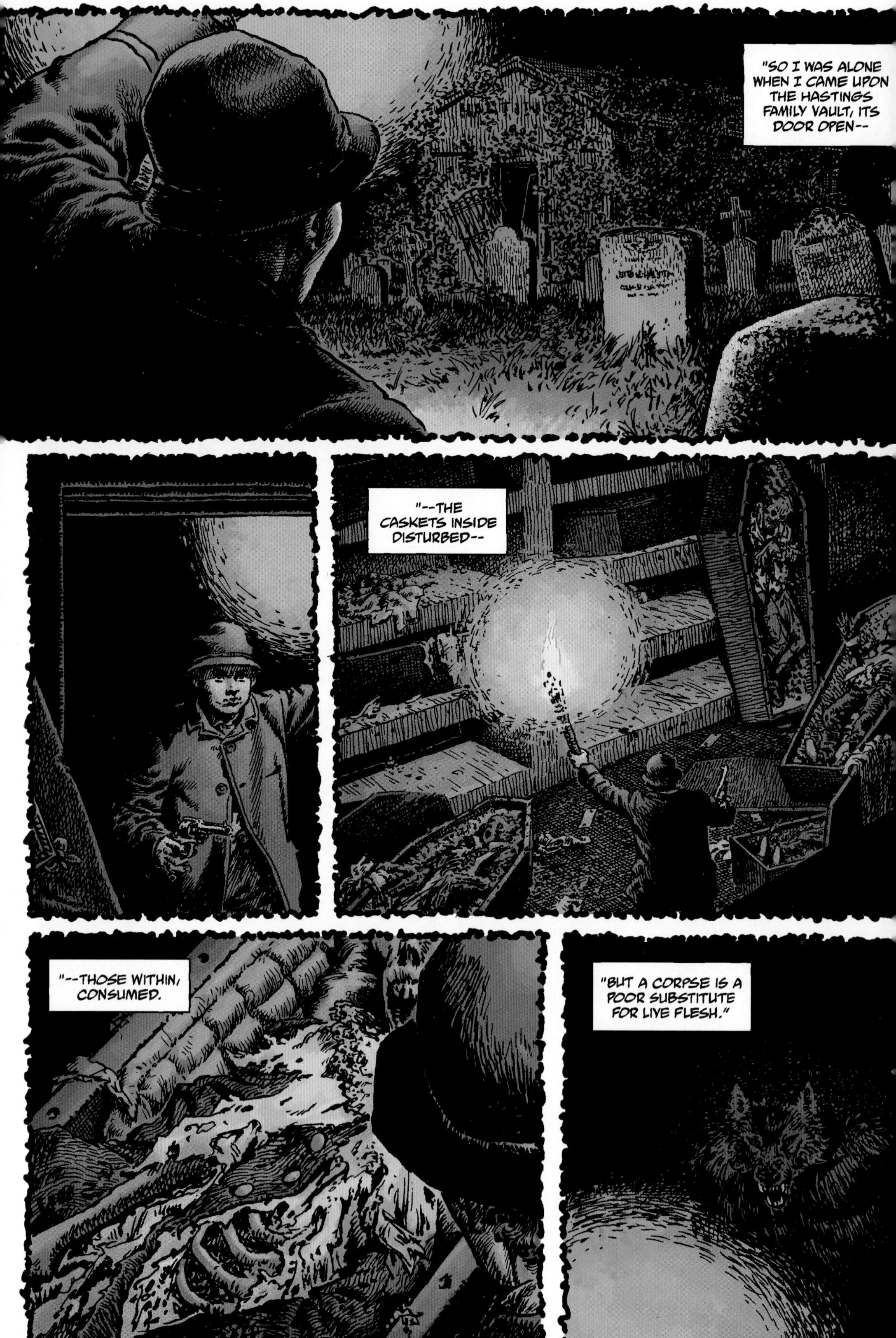
"SO I WAS ALONE WHEN I CAME UPON THE HASTINGS FAMILY VAULT, ITS DOOR OPEN--
"--THE CASKETS INSIDE DISTURBED--
"--THOSE WITHIN, CONSUMED.
"BUT A CORPSE IS A POOR SUBSTITUTE FOR LIVE FLESH."

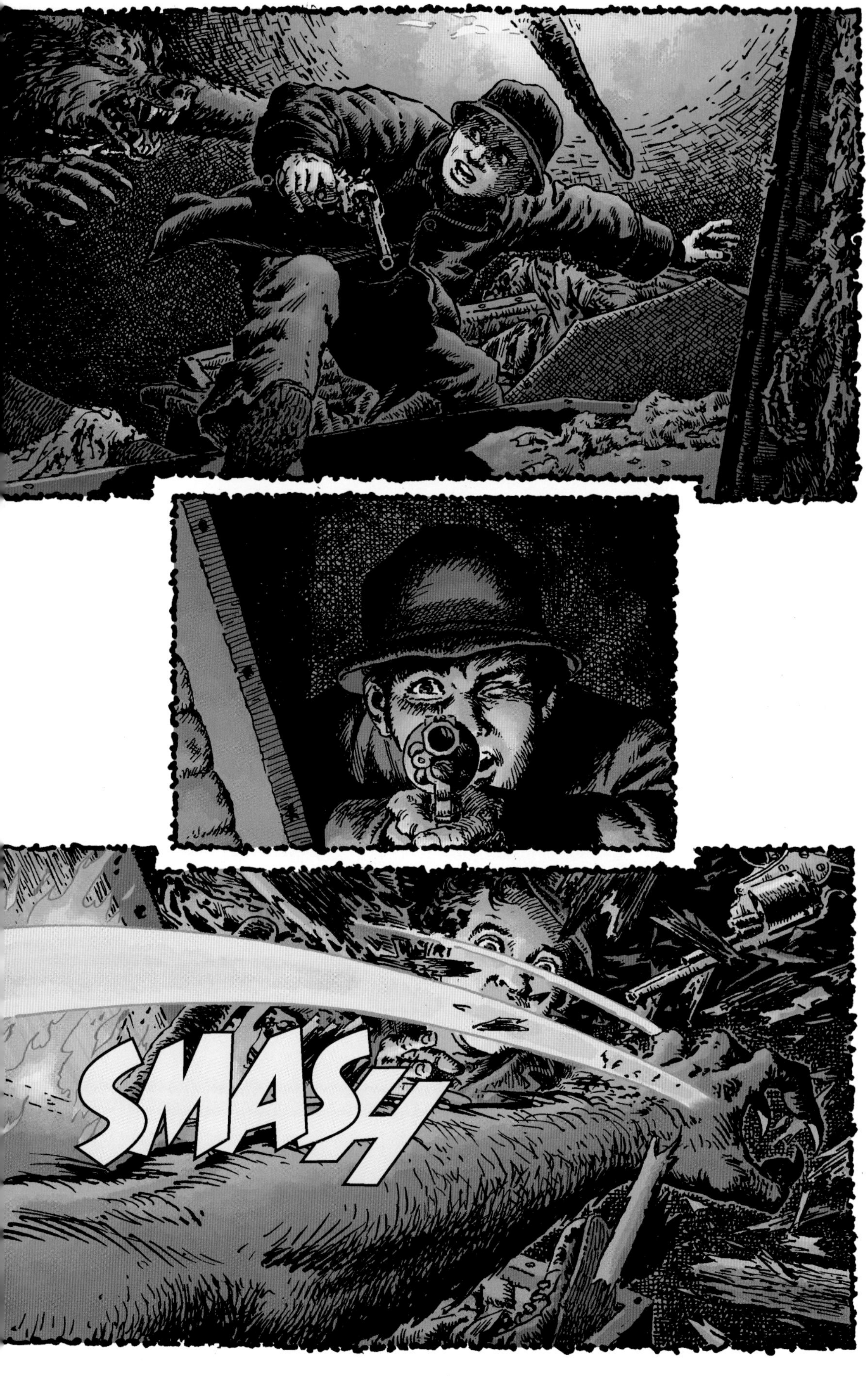
SMASH

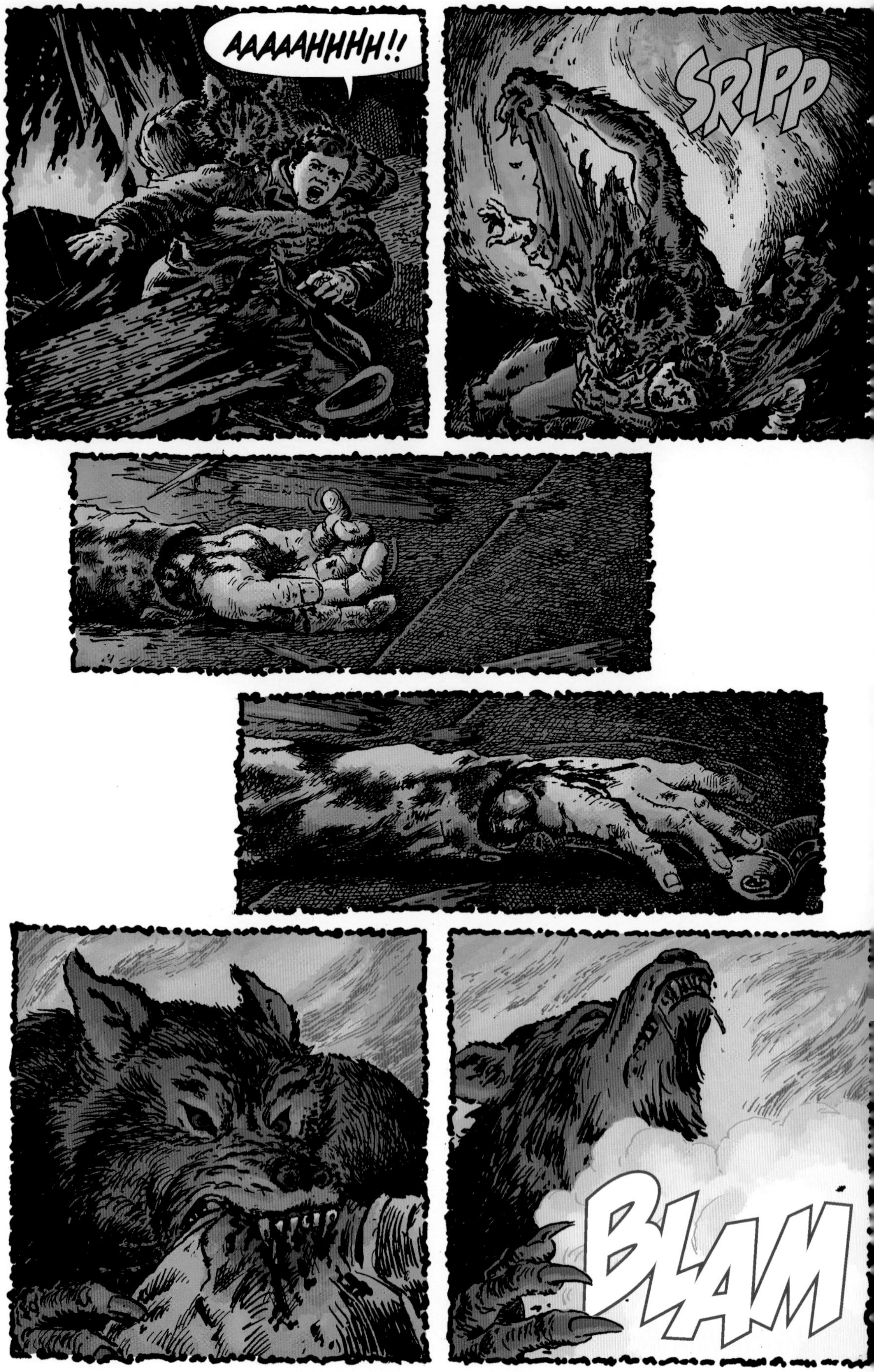

AAAAAHHHH!!
SRIPP
BLAM

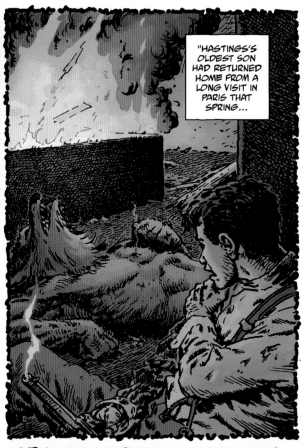

"HASTINGS'S OLDEST SON HAD RETURNED HOME FROM A LONG VISIT IN PARIS THAT SPRING...

"...JUST WEEKS BEFORE THE TROUBLES STARTED.

"THEY FOUND RAW MEAT IN HIS STOMACH-- ALONG WITH A CHILD'S LOCKET.

ABRAHAM E. POWERS

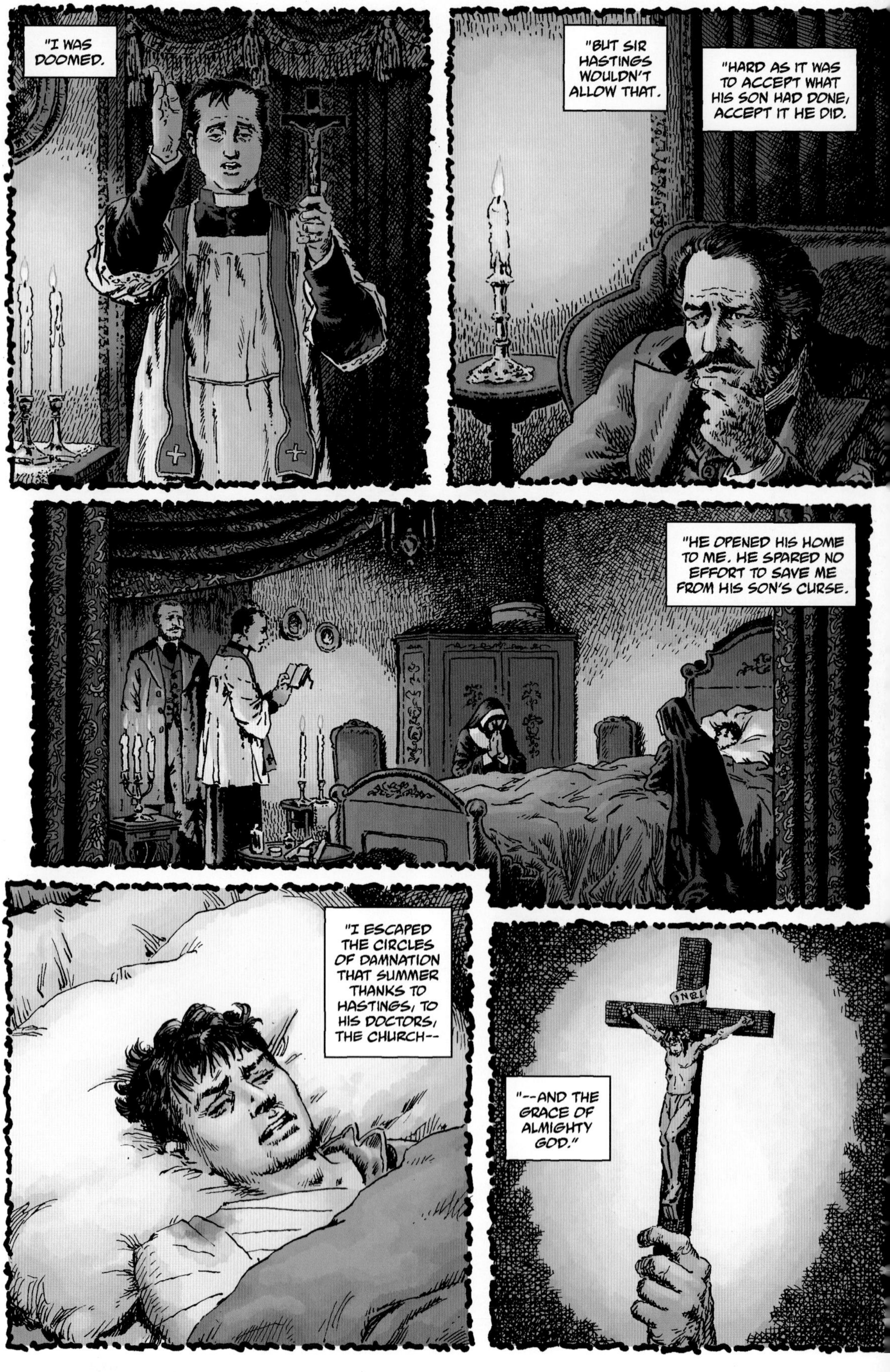

"I WAS DOOMED.
"BUT SIR HASTINGS WOULDN'T ALLOW THAT.
"HARD AS IT WAS TO ACCEPT WHAT HIS SON HAD DONE, ACCEPT IT HE DID.
"HE OPENED HIS HOME TO ME. HE SPARED NO EFFORT TO SAVE ME FROM HIS SON'S CURSE.
"I ESCAPED THE CIRCLES OF DAMNATION THAT SUMMER THANKS TO HASTINGS, TO HIS DOCTORS, THE CHURCH--
"--AND THE GRACE OF ALMIGHTY GOD."

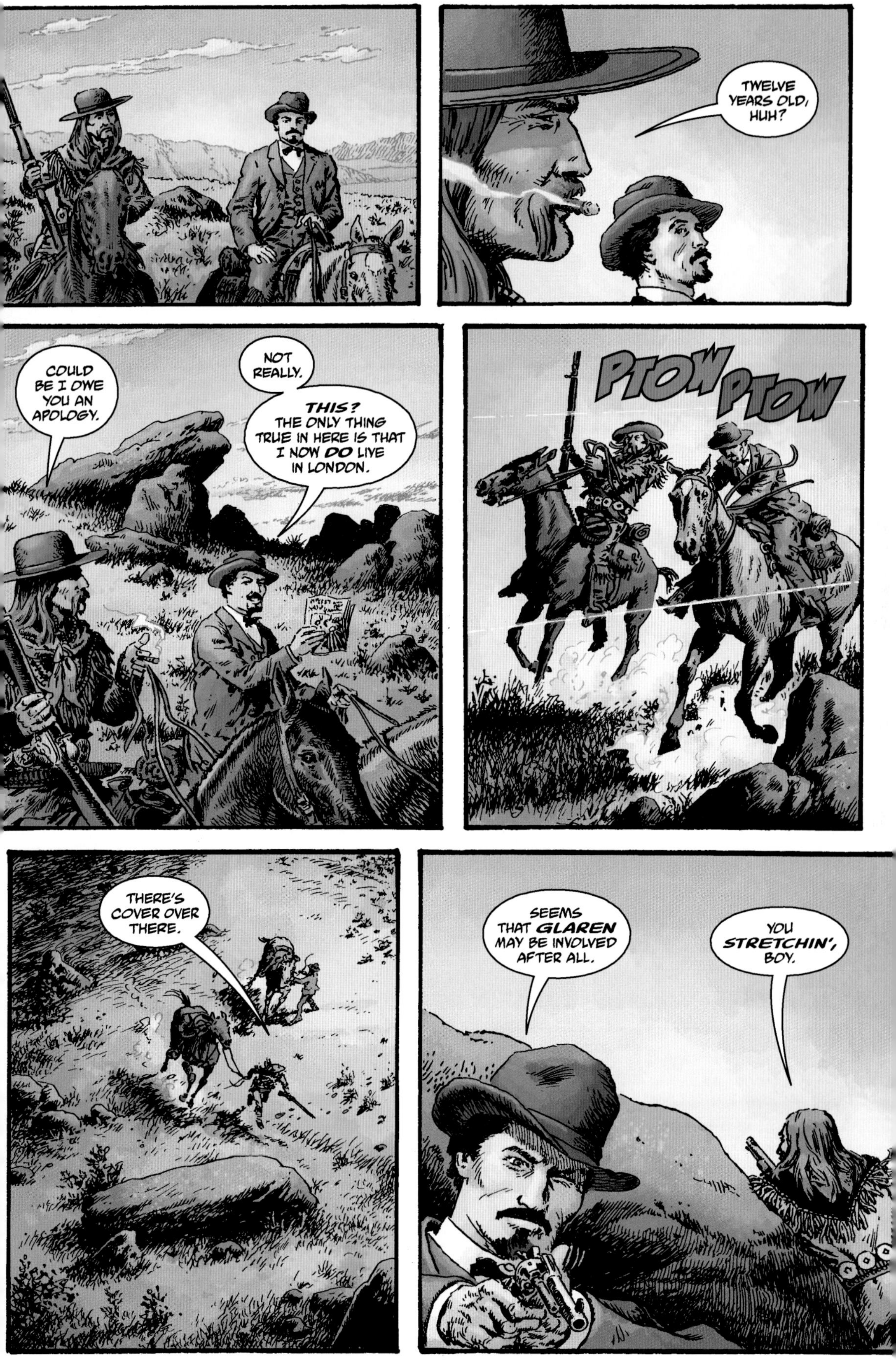
TWELVE YEARS OLD, HUH?
COULD BE I OWE YOU AN APOLOGY.
NOT REALLY.
THIS? THE ONLY THING TRUE IN HERE IS THAT I NOW DO LIVE IN LONDON.
PTOW PTOW
THERE'S COVER OVER THERE.
SEEMS THAT GLAREN MAY BE INVOLVED AFTER ALL.
YOU STRETCHIN', BOY.

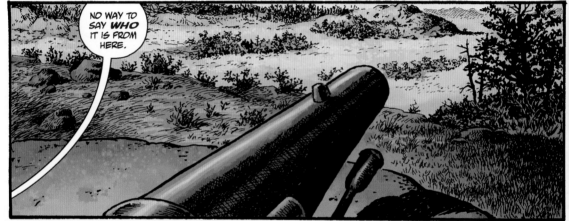

NO WAY TO SAY **WHO** IT IS FROM HERE.

BUT WE'LL FIGURE **THAT** OUT AFTER WE CHASE THE **BUZZARDS** OFF HIS **BODY.**

BOOM

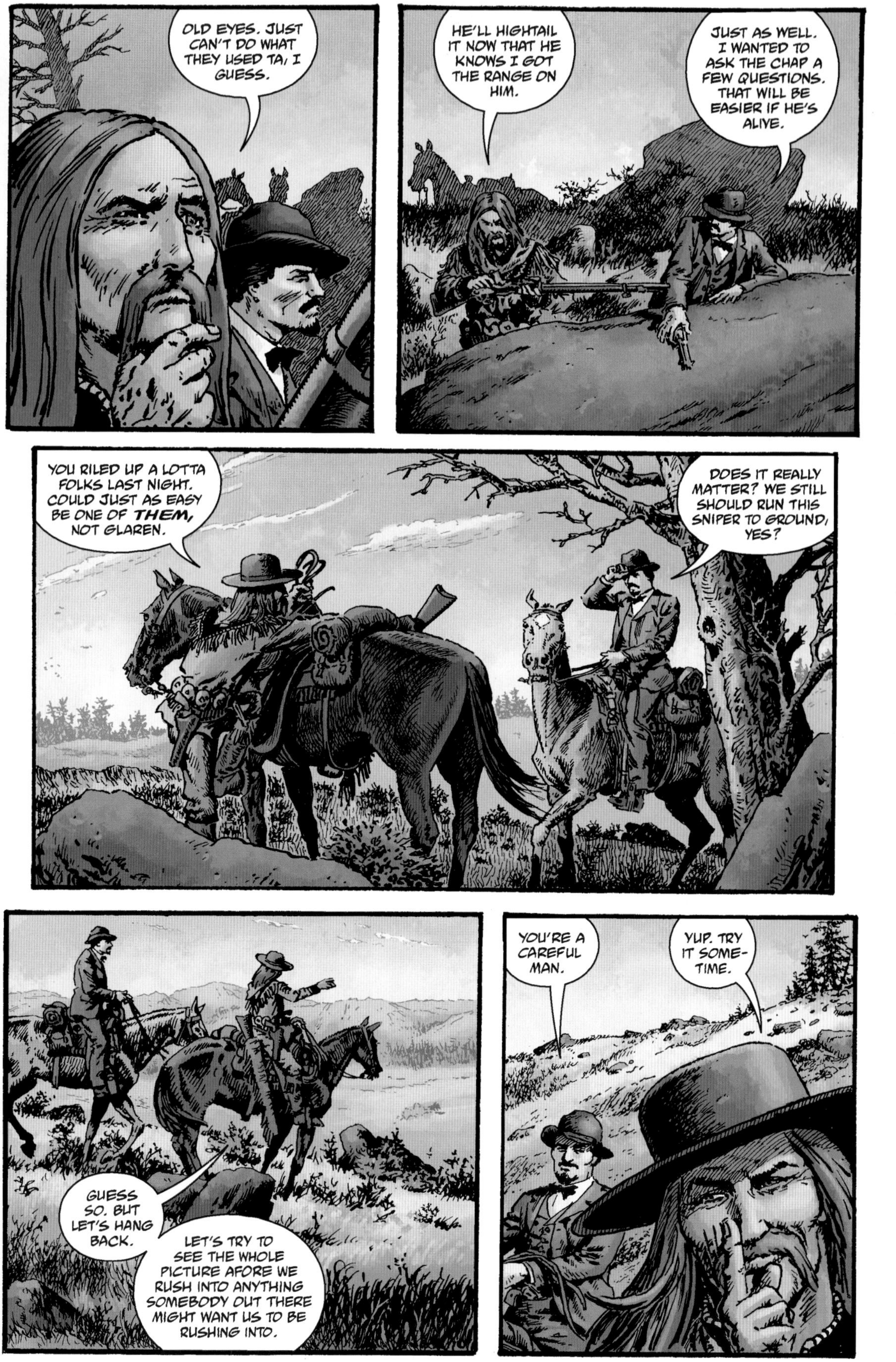
OLD EYES. JUST CAN'T DO WHAT THEY USED TA, I GUESS.
HE'LL HIGHTAIL IT NOW THAT HE KNOWS I GOT THE RANGE ON HIM.
JUST AS WELL. I WANTED TO ASK THE CHAP A FEW QUESTIONS. THAT WILL BE EASIER IF HE'S ALIVE.
YOU RILED UP A LOTTA FOLKS LAST NIGHT. COULD JUST AS EASY BE ONE OF THEM, NOT GLAREN.
DOES IT REALLY MATTER? WE STILL SHOULD RUN THIS SNIPER TO GROUND, YES?
GUESS SO. BUT LET'S HANG BACK.
LET'S TRY TO SEE THE WHOLE PICTURE AFORE WE RUSH INTO ANYTHING SOMEBODY OUT THERE MIGHT WANT US TO BE RUSHING INTO.
YOU'RE A CAREFUL MAN.
YUP. TRY IT SOME-TIME.

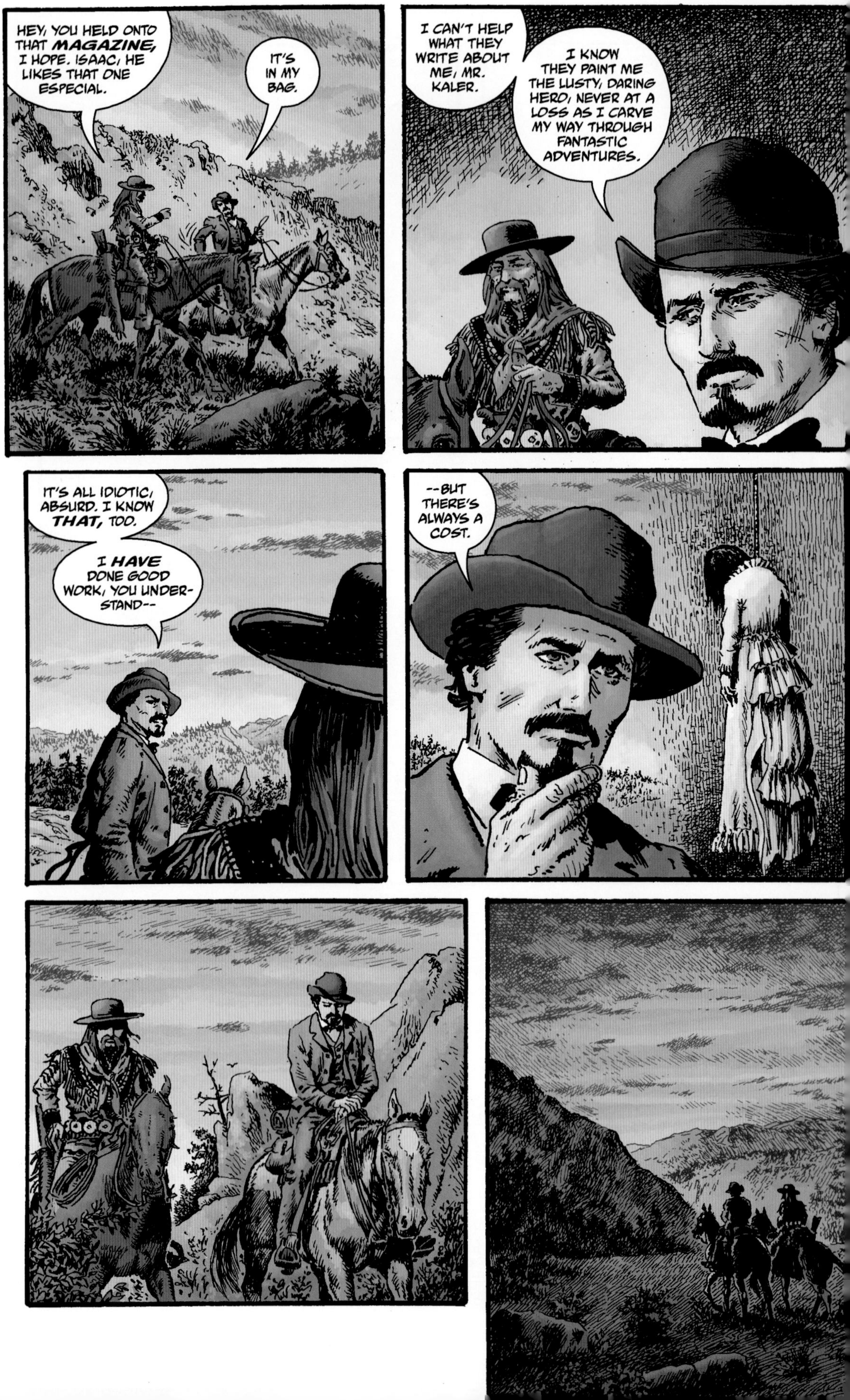
HEY, YOU HELD ONTO THAT **MAGAZINE,** I HOPE. ISAAC, HE LIKES THAT ONE ESPECIAL.
IT'S IN MY BAG.
I CAN'T HELP WHAT THEY WRITE ABOUT ME, MR. KALER.
I KNOW THEY PAINT ME THE LUSTY, DARING HERO, NEVER AT A LOSS AS I CARVE MY WAY THROUGH FANTASTIC ADVENTURES.
IT'S ALL IDIOTIC, ABSURD. I KNOW **THAT,** TOO.
I **HAVE** DONE GOOD WORK, YOU UNDER-STAND--
--BUT THERE'S ALWAYS A COST.

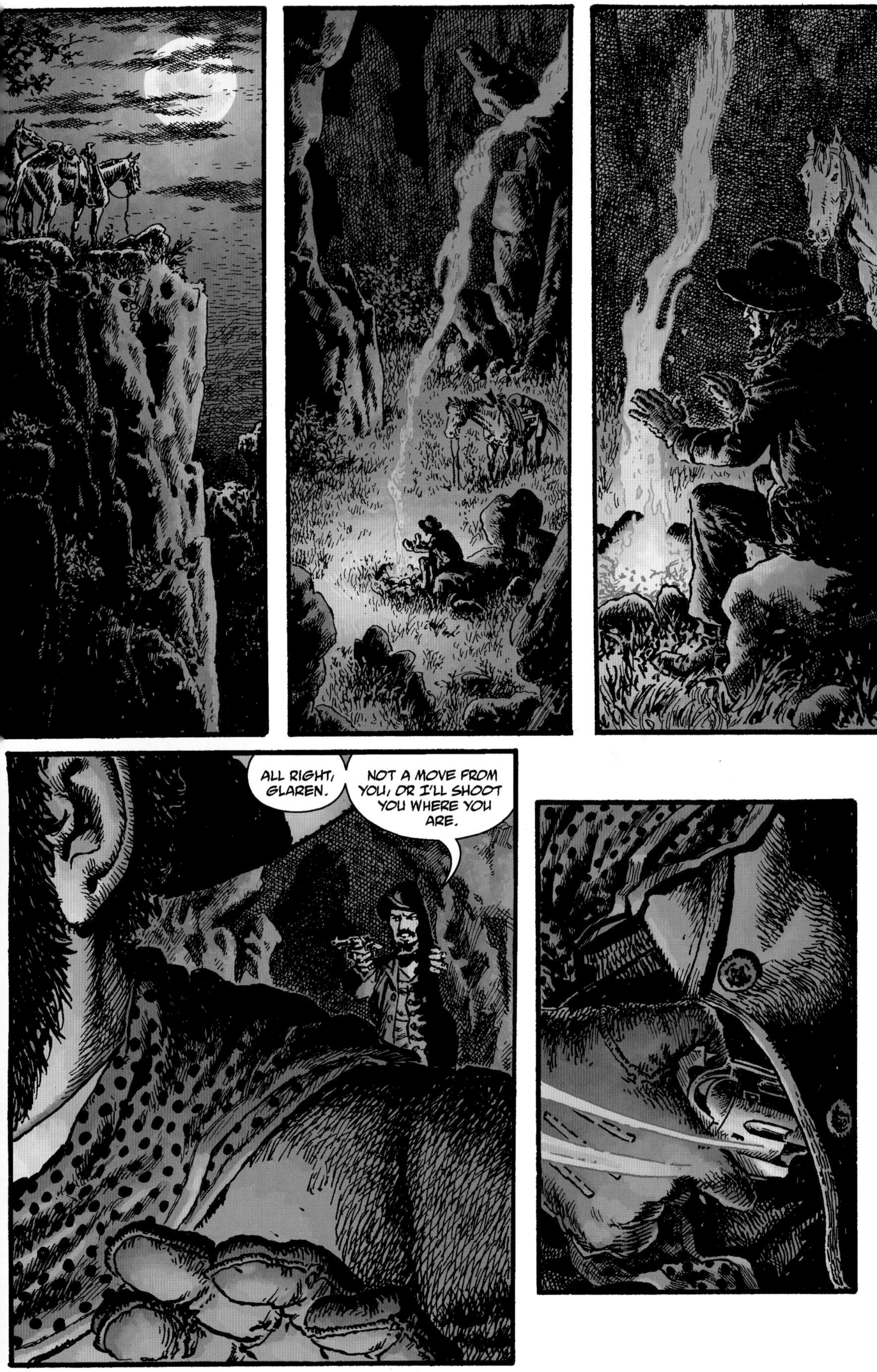
ALL RIGHT, GLAREN.
NOT A MOVE FROM YOU, OR I'LL SHOOT YOU WHERE YOU ARE.

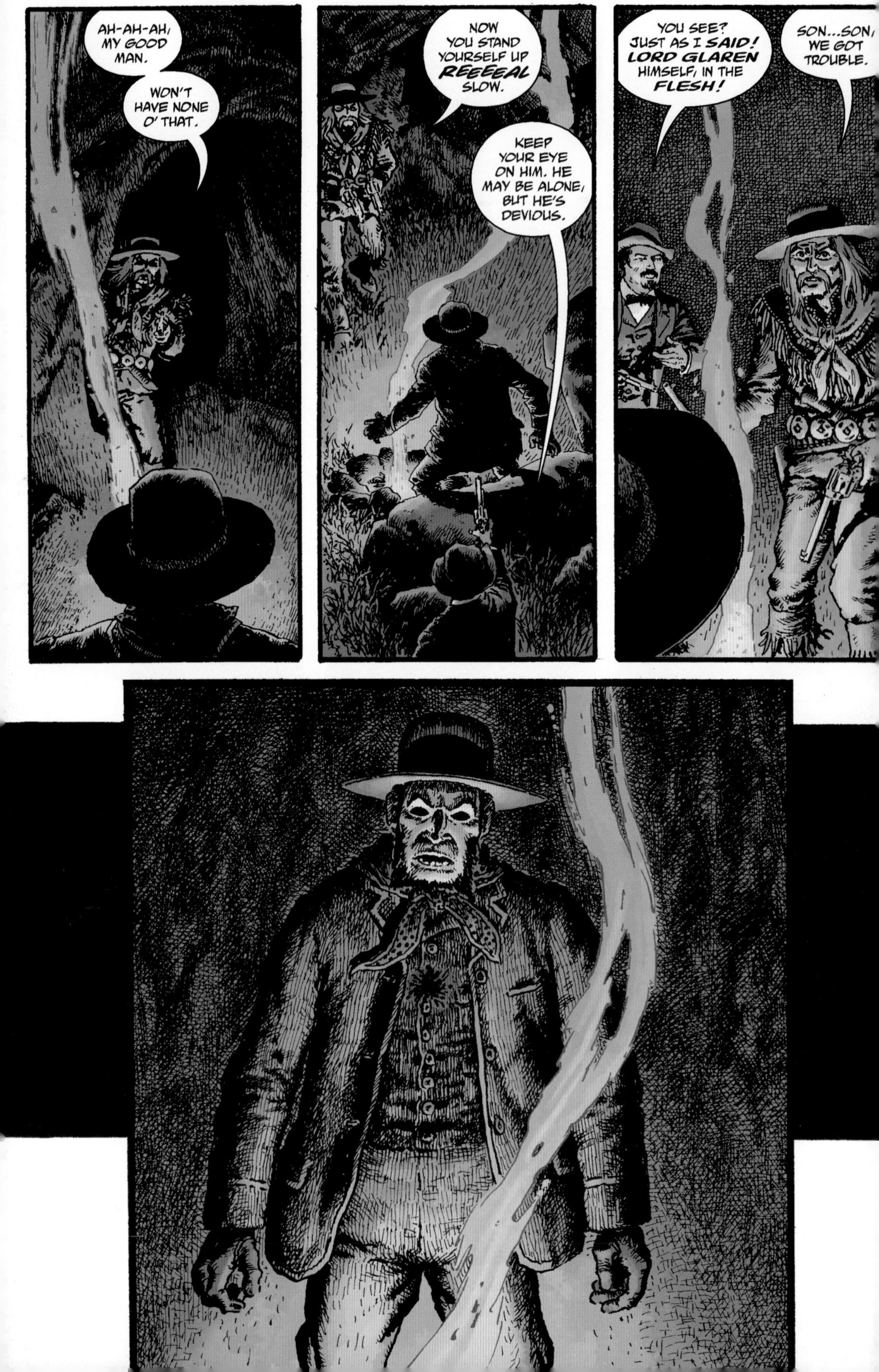
AH-AH-AH, MY GOOD MAN.
WON'T HAVE NONE O' THAT.
NOW YOU STAND YOURSELF UP **REEEEAL** SLOW.
KEEP YOUR EYE ON HIM. HE MAY BE ALONE, BUT HE'S DEVIOUS.
YOU SEE? JUST AS I **SAID! LORD GLAREN** HIMSELF, IN THE **FLESH!**
SON...SON, WE GOT TROUBLE.

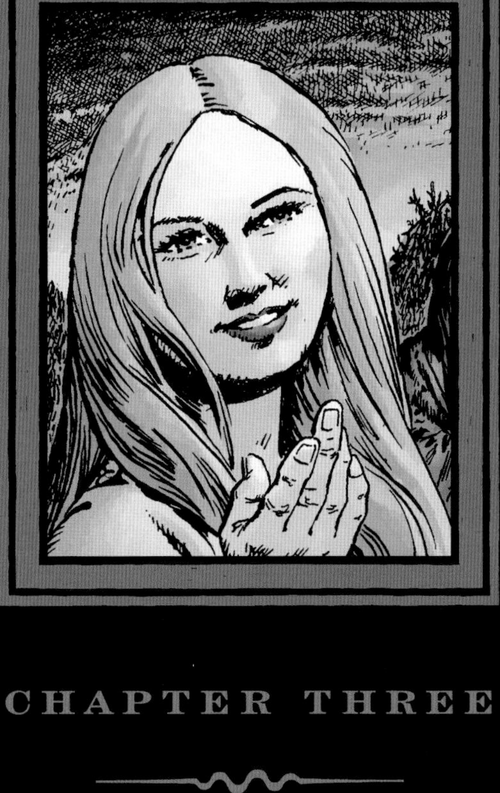

CHAPTER THREE

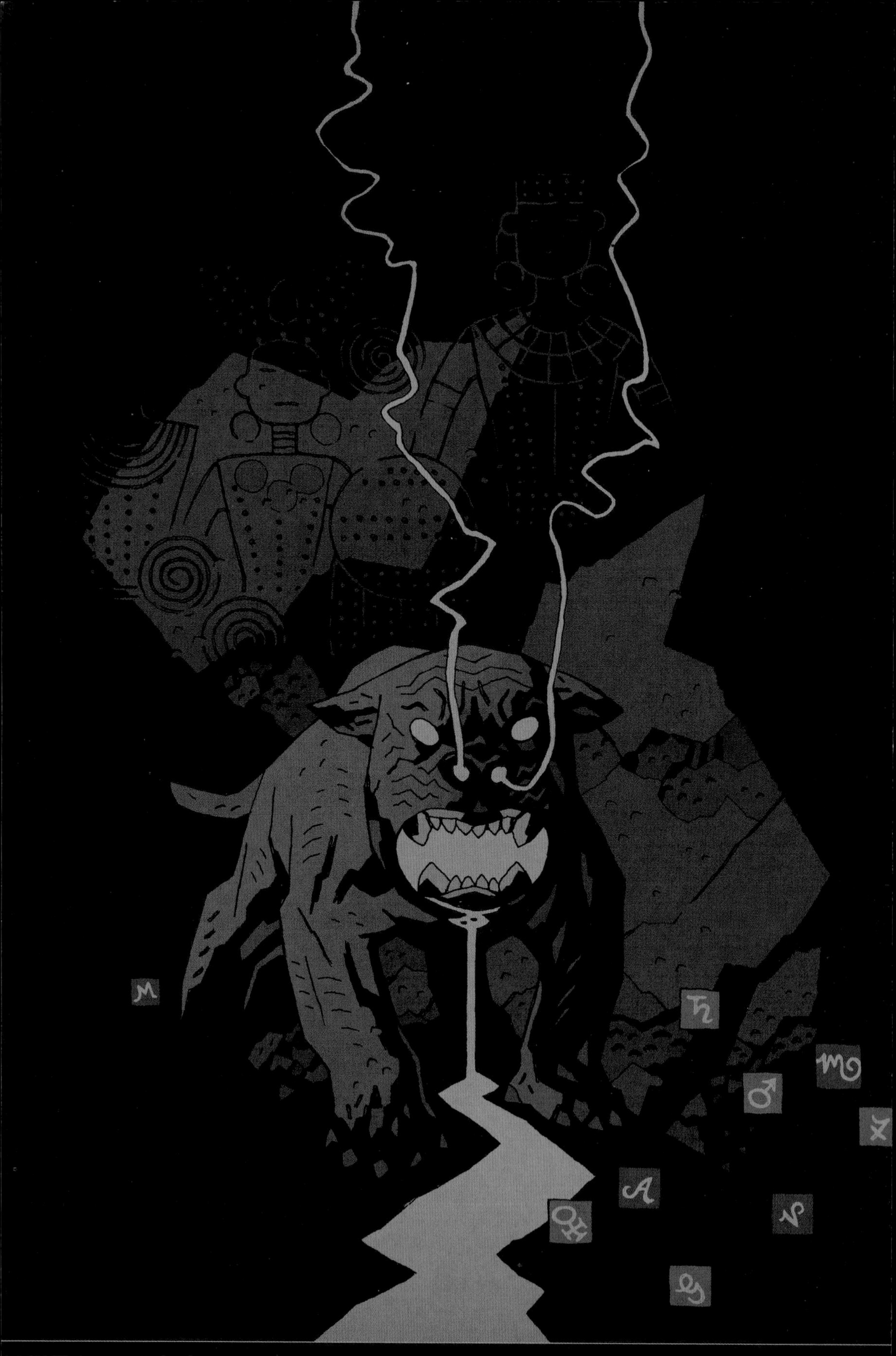

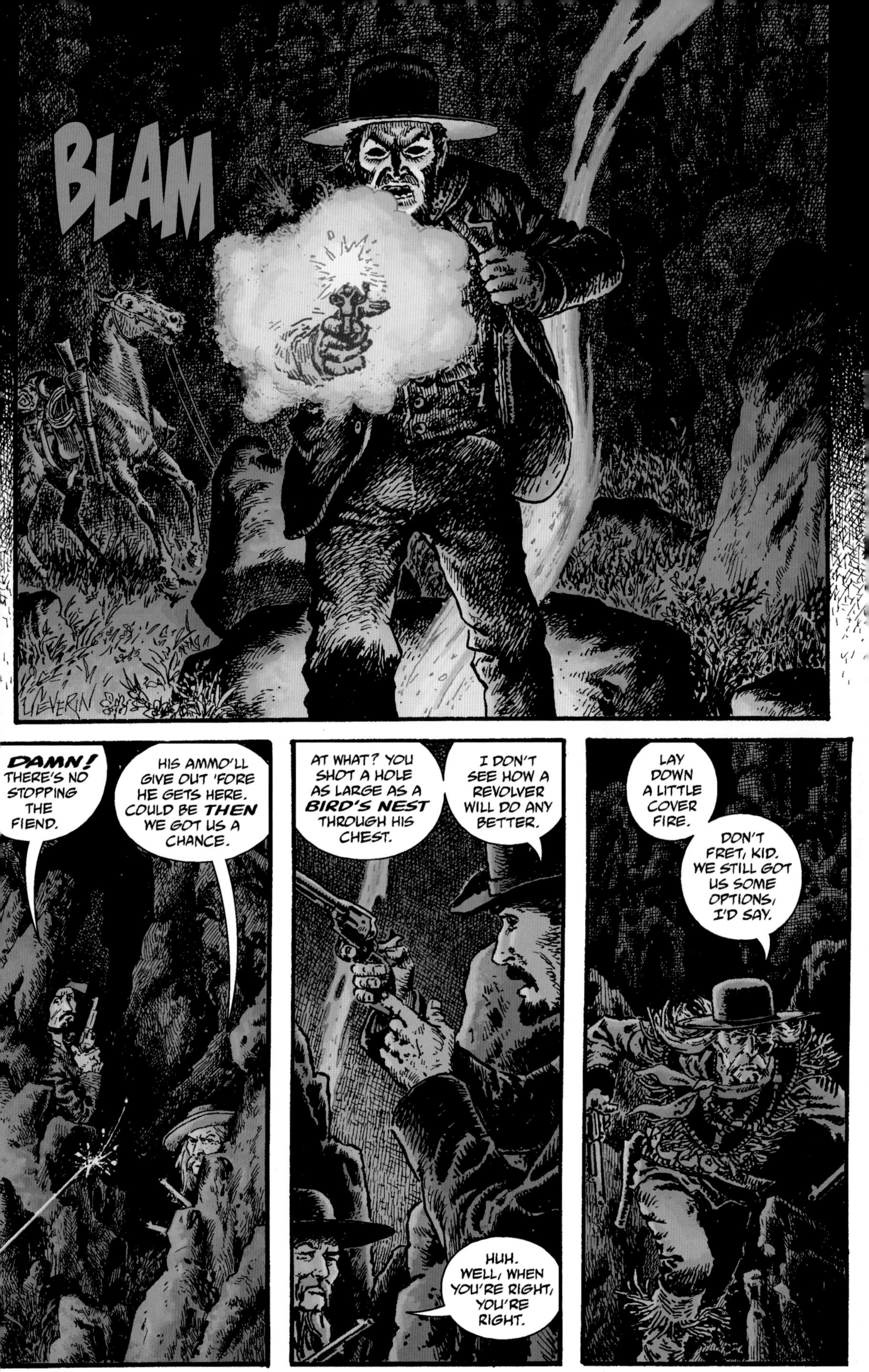
BLAM
LIEVERIN
DAMN! THERE'S NO STOPPING THE FIEND.
HIS AMMO'LL GIVE OUT 'FORE HE GETS HERE. COULD BE THEN WE GOT US A CHANCE.
AT WHAT? YOU SHOT A HOLE AS LARGE AS A BIRD'S NEST THROUGH HIS CHEST.
I DON'T SEE HOW A REVOLVER WILL DO ANY BETTER.
HUH. WELL, WHEN YOU'RE RIGHT, YOU'RE RIGHT.
LAY DOWN A LITTLE COVER FIRE.
DON'T FRET, KID. WE STILL GOT US SOME OPTIONS, I'D SAY.

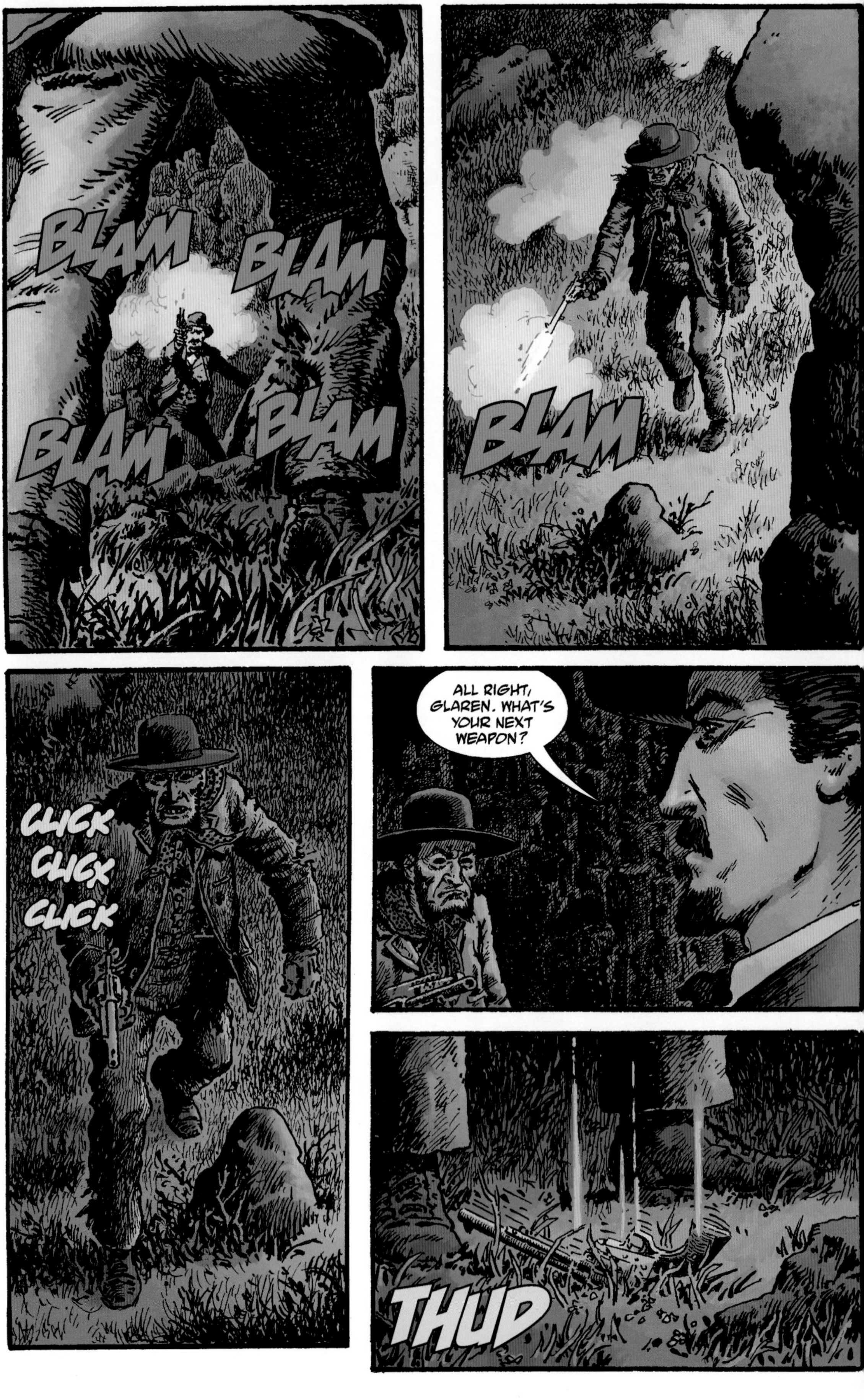
BLAM
BLAM
BLAM
BLAM
BLAM
CLICK
CLICK
CLICK
ALL RIGHT, GLAREN. WHAT'S YOUR NEXT WEAPON?
THUD

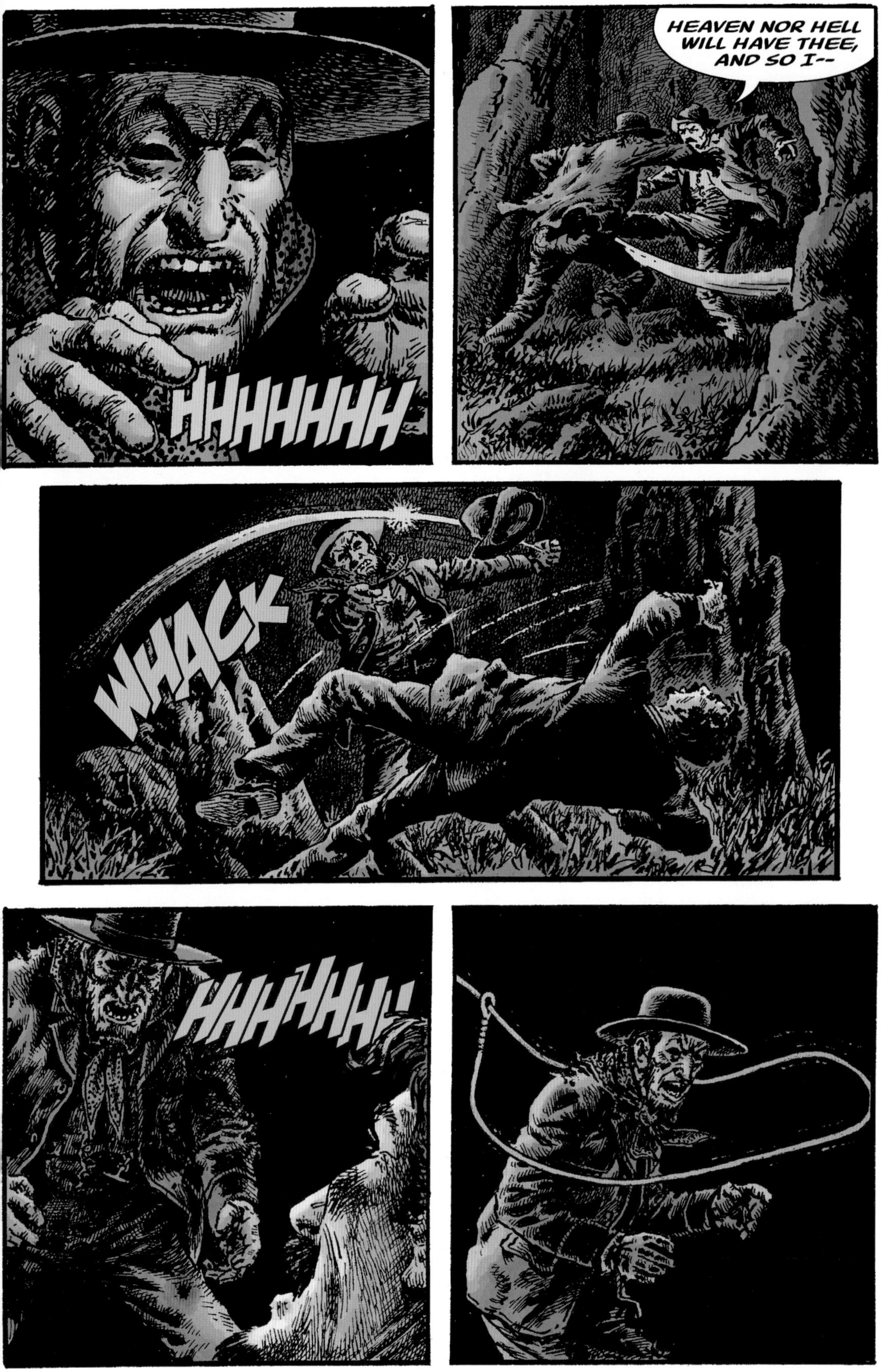
HHHHHHH
HEAVEN NOR HELL WILL HAVE THEE, AND SO I--
WHACK
HHHHHH

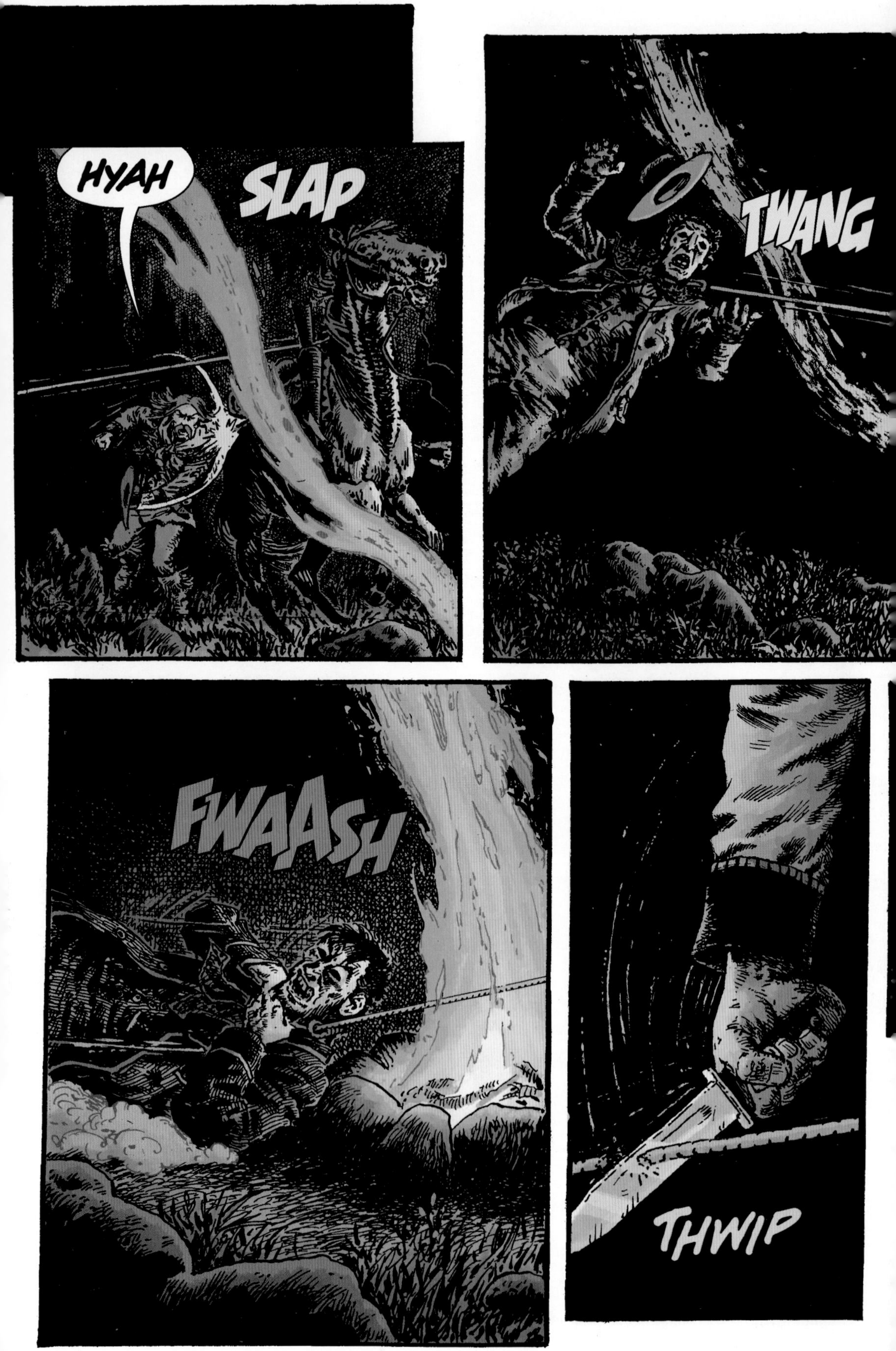
HYAH
SLAP
TWANG
FWAASH
THWIP

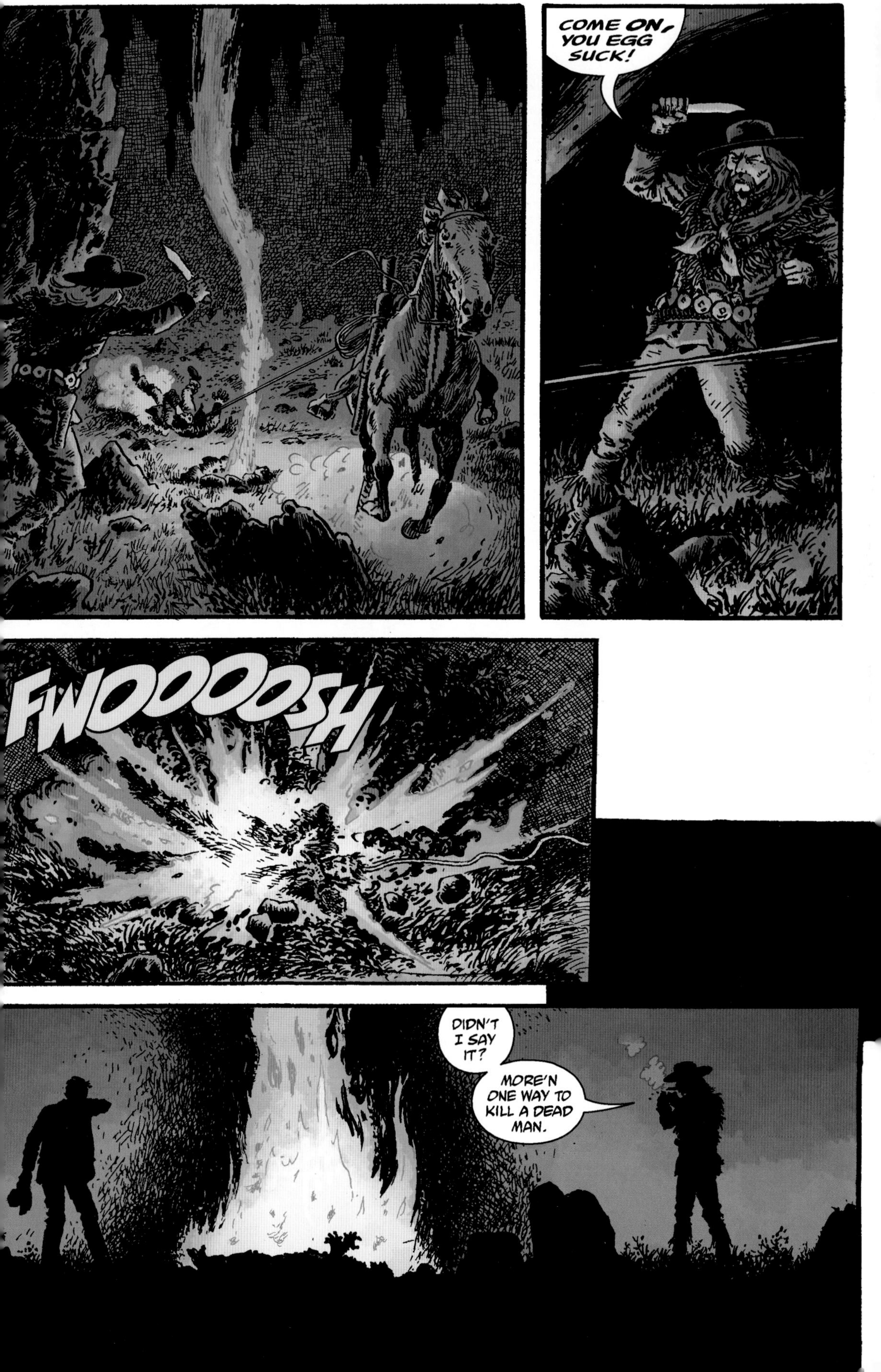
COME ON, YOU EGG SUCK!
FWOOOOSH
DIDN'T I SAY IT?
MORE'N ONE WAY TO KILL A DEAD MAN.

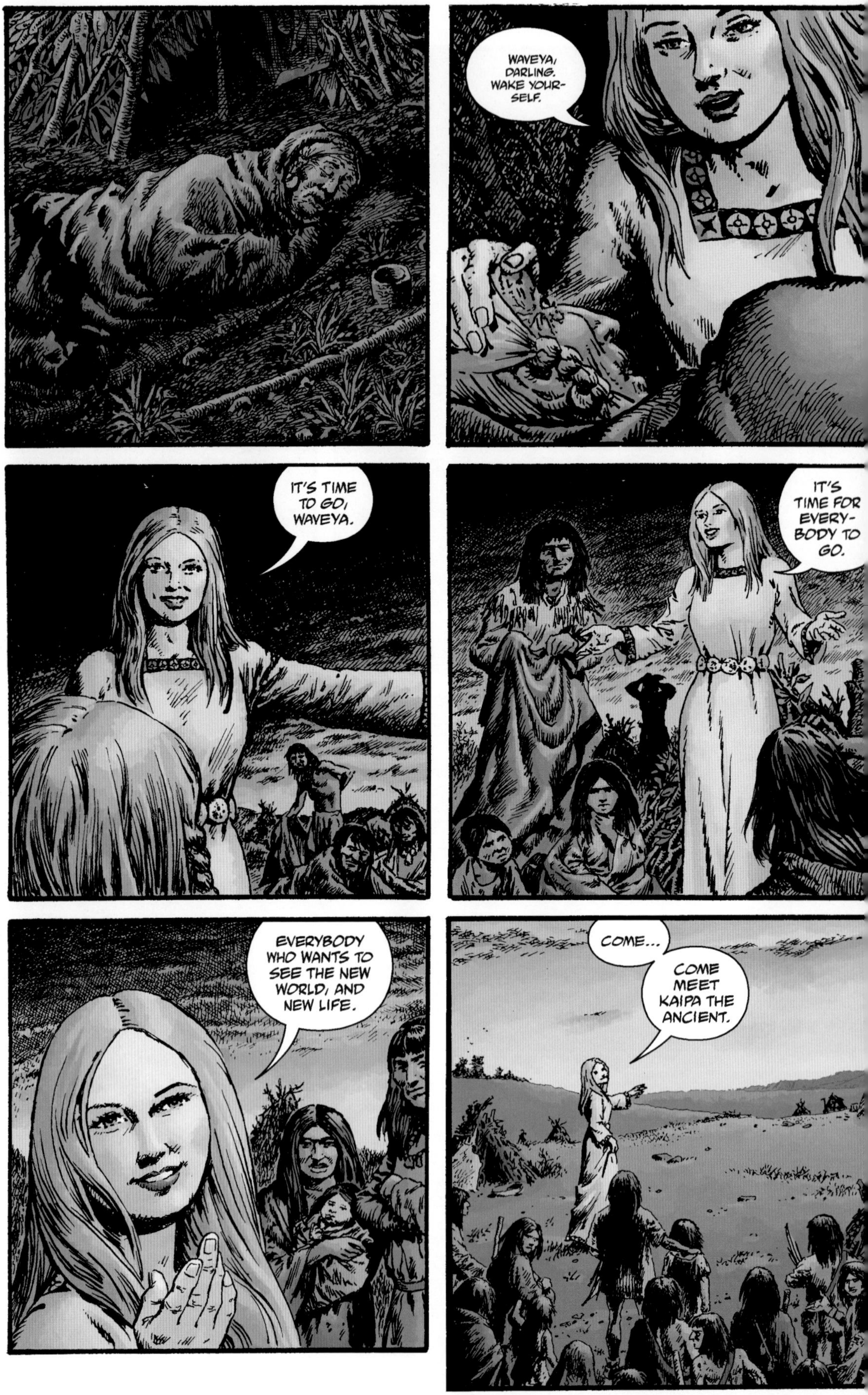
WAVEYA, DARLING. WAKE YOURSELF.
IT'S TIME TO GO, WAVEYA.
IT'S TIME FOR EVERYBODY TO GO.
EVERYBODY WHO WANTS TO SEE THE NEW WORLD, AND NEW LIFE.
COME...
COME MEET KAIPA THE ANCIENT.

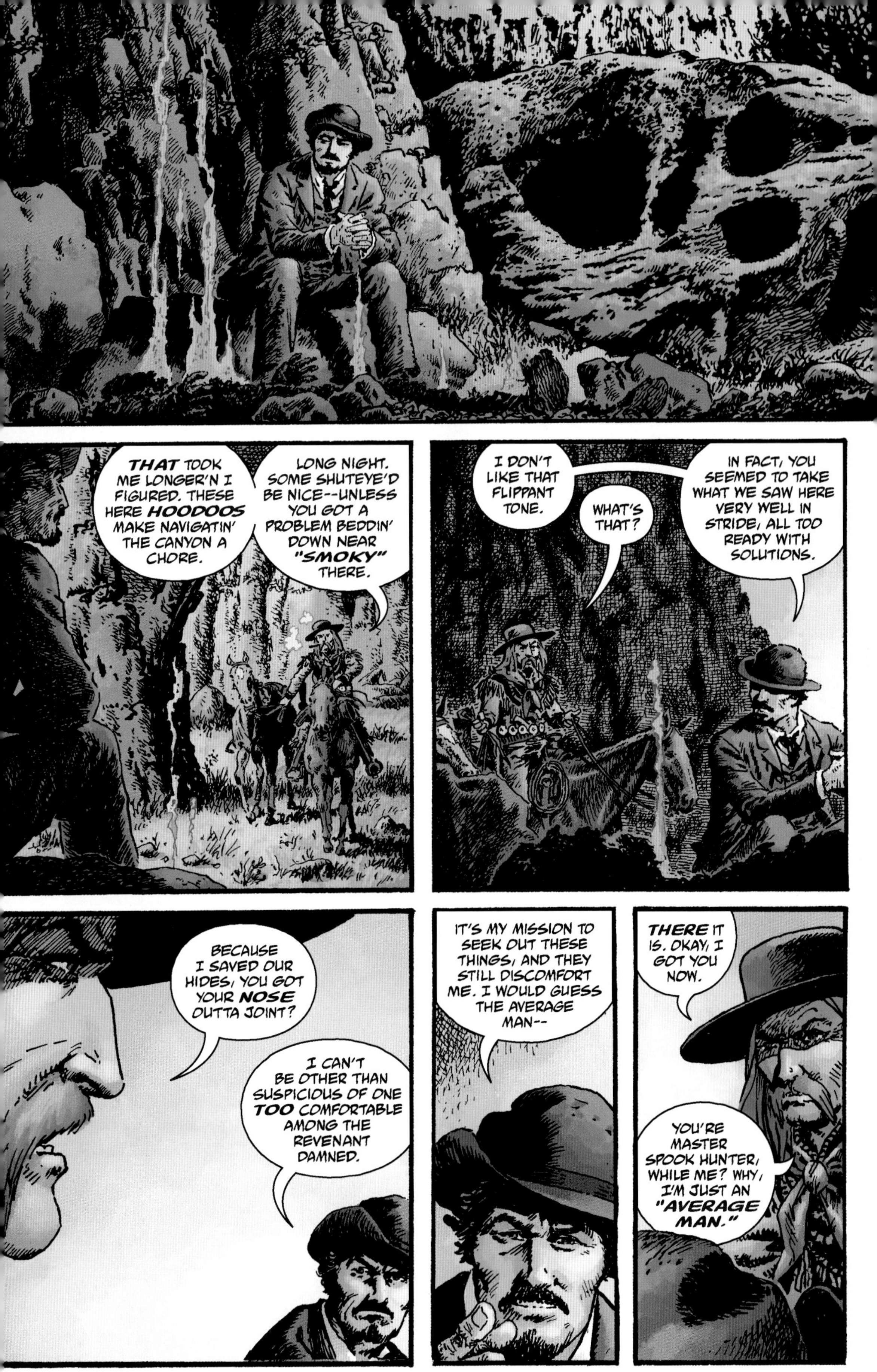
THAT TOOK ME LONGER'N I FIGURED. THESE HERE HOODOOS MAKE NAVIGATIN' THE CANYON A CHORE.
LONG NIGHT. SOME SHUTEYE'D BE NICE--UNLESS YOU GOT A PROBLEM BEDDIN' DOWN NEAR "SMOKY" THERE.
I DON'T LIKE THAT FLIPPANT TONE.
WHAT'S THAT?
IN FACT, YOU SEEMED TO TAKE WHAT WE SAW HERE VERY WELL IN STRIDE, ALL TOO READY WITH SOLUTIONS.
BECAUSE I SAVED OUR HIDES, YOU GOT YOUR NOSE OUTTA JOINT?
I CAN'T BE OTHER THAN SUSPICIOUS OF ONE TOO COMFORTABLE AMONG THE REVENANT DAMNED.
IT'S MY MISSION TO SEEK OUT THESE THINGS, AND THEY STILL DISCOMFORT ME. I WOULD GUESS THE AVERAGE MAN--
THERE IT IS. OKAY, I GOT YOU NOW.
YOU'RE MASTER SPOOK HUNTER, WHILE ME? WHY, I'M JUST AN "AVERAGE MAN."

I'VE BEEN AROUND FOR MORE THAN A LITTLE BIT, SON. I'VE SEEN SOME THINGS.

DON'T THINK I HAVEN'T.

YOU TAKE YOUR FRIEND. I DOUBT HE WAS A "REVENANT," WHATEVER THE HELL THAT MIGHT BE.

MORE LIKELY WE GOT HERE A ZONBI.

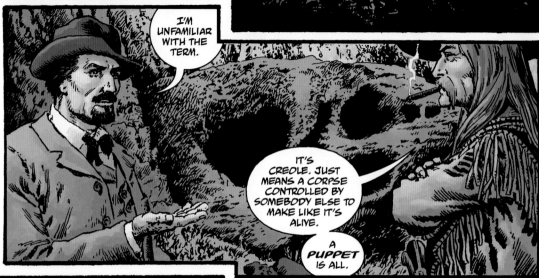

I'M UNFAMILIAR WITH THE TERM.

IT'S CREOLE. JUST MEANS A CORPSE CONTROLLED BY SOMEBODY ELSE TO MAKE LIKE IT'S ALIVE.

A PUPPET IS ALL.

ERIS? THE WITCH?

THAT'D MAKE THE MOST SENSE. I'M THINKING SHE USED GLAREN'S BODY TO LEAD US HERE.

OR MAYBE AWAY FROM SOMEWHERES ELSE...OR BOTH.

IF IT'S TO HERE, WHY? WHAT IS THIS PLACE?

YOU THINK I GOT EVERY INCH OF THIS DESERT MEMORIZED?

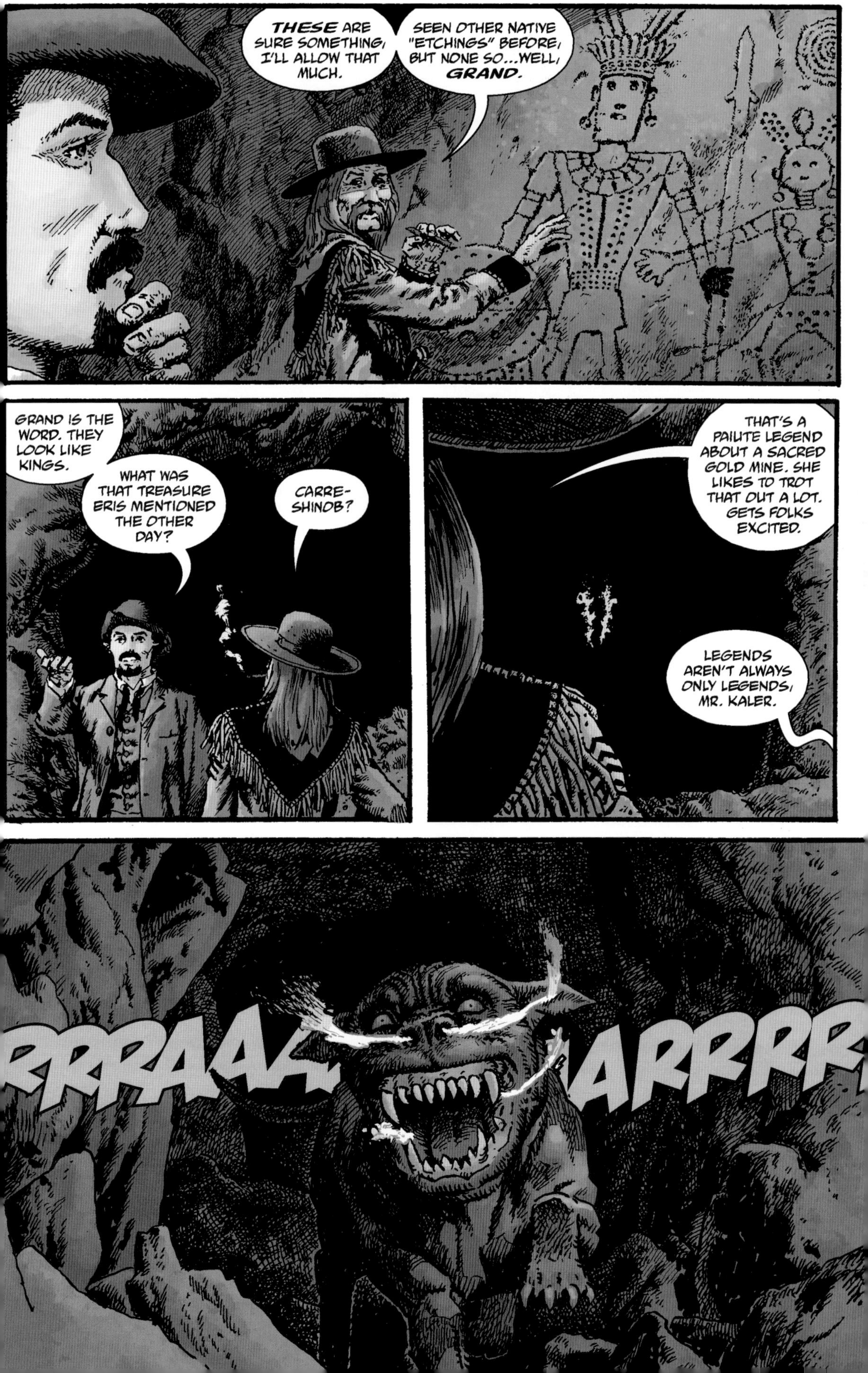

THESE ARE SURE SOMETHING, I'LL ALLOW THAT MUCH.
SEEN OTHER NATIVE "ETCHINGS" BEFORE, BUT NONE SO...WELL, GRAND.
GRAND IS THE WORD. THEY LOOK LIKE KINGS.
WHAT WAS THAT TREASURE ERIS MENTIONED THE OTHER DAY?
CARRE-SHINOB?
THAT'S A PAIUTE LEGEND ABOUT A SACRED GOLD MINE. SHE LIKES TO TROT THAT OUT A LOT. GETS FOLKS EXCITED.
LEGENDS AREN'T ALWAYS ONLY LEGENDS, MR. KALER.
RRRAAA ARRRR

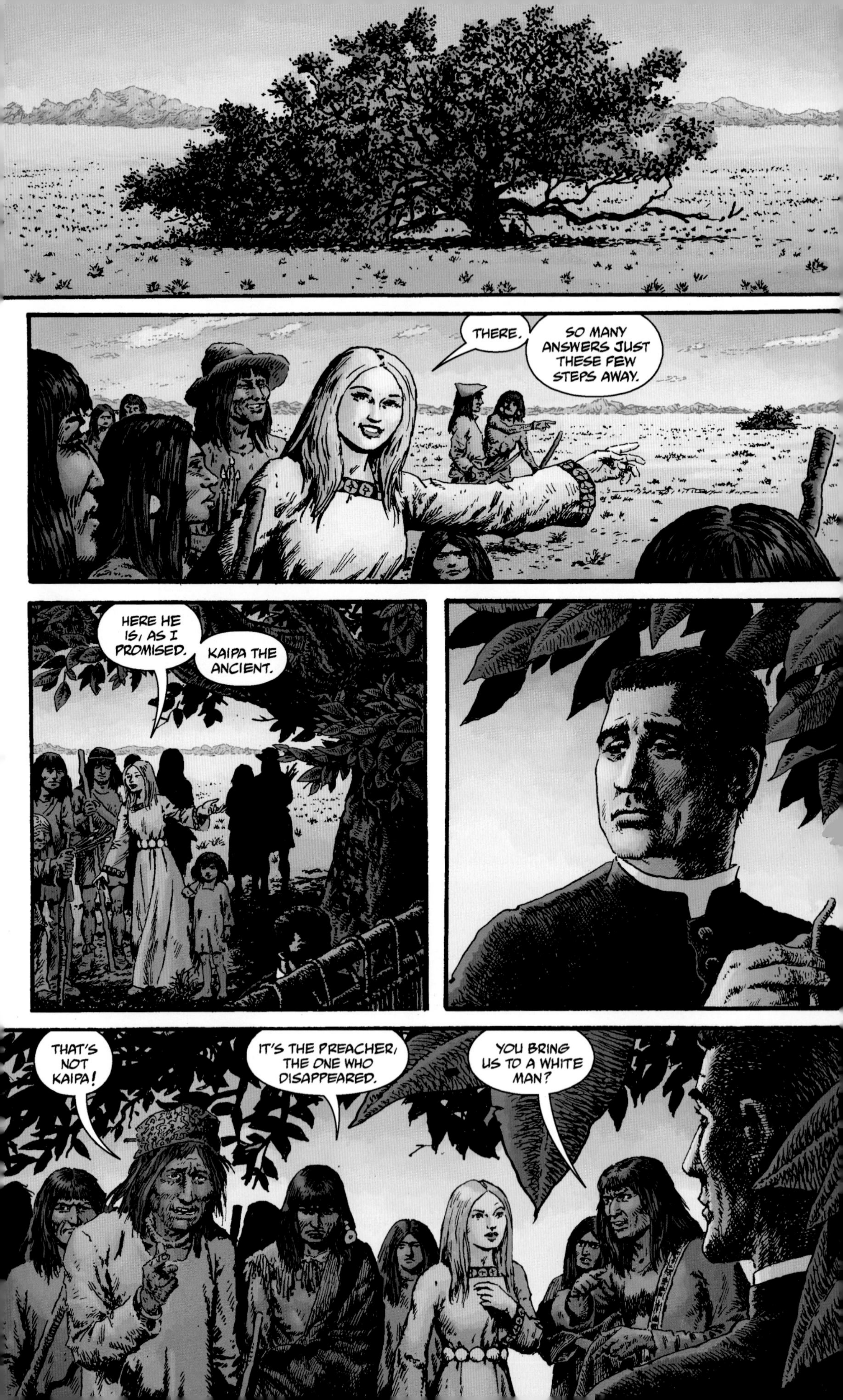
THERE.
SO MANY ANSWERS JUST THESE FEW STEPS AWAY.
HERE HE IS, AS I PROMISED.
KAIPA THE ANCIENT.
THAT'S NOT KAIPA!
IT'S THE PREACHER, THE ONE WHO DISAPPEARED.
YOU BRING US TO A WHITE MAN?

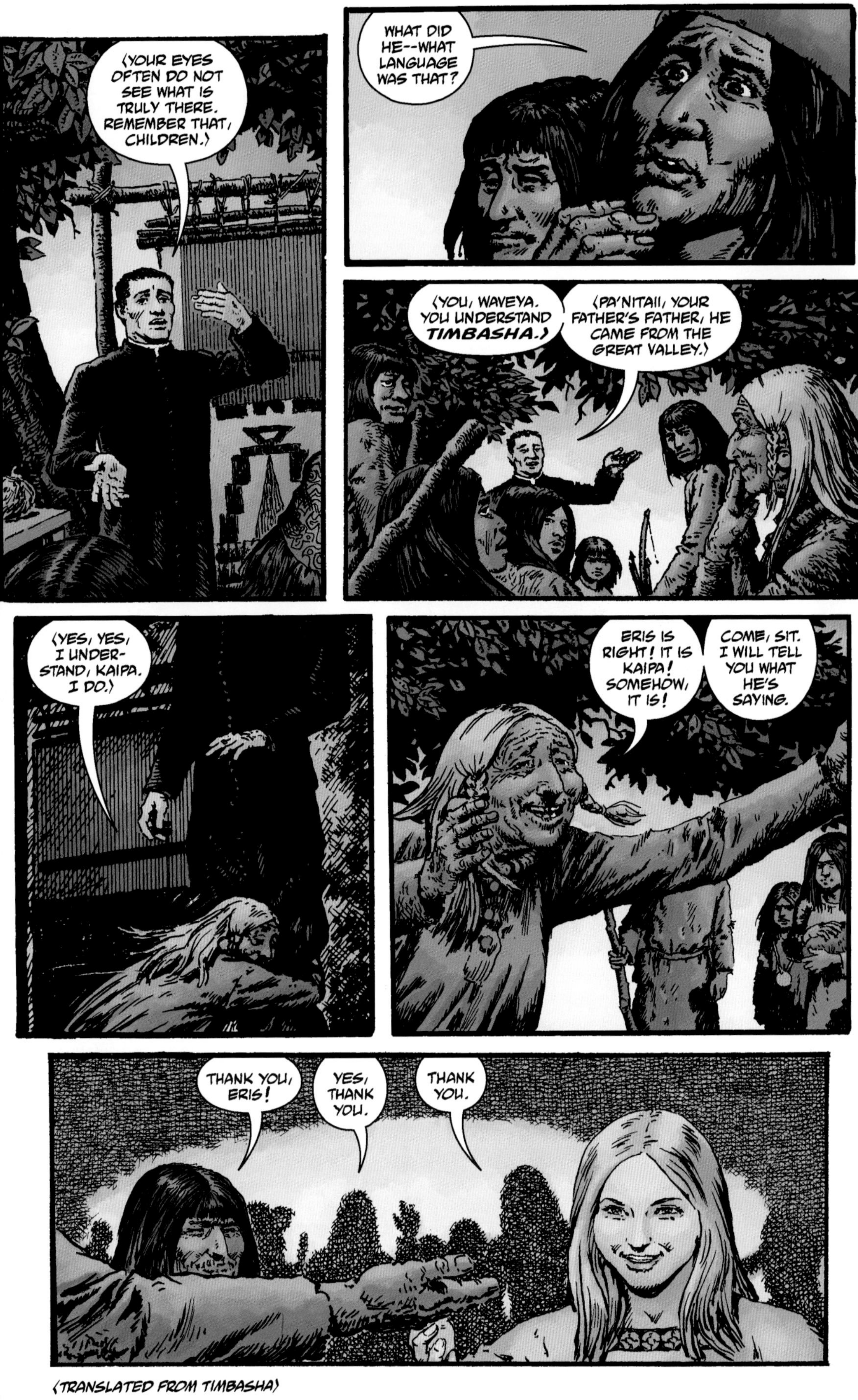
⟨YOUR EYES OFTEN DO NOT SEE WHAT IS TRULY THERE. REMEMBER THAT, CHILDREN.⟩
WHAT DID HE--WHAT LANGUAGE WAS THAT?
⟨YOU, WAVEYA. YOU UNDERSTAND *TIMBASHA.*⟩
⟨PA'NITAII, YOUR FATHER'S FATHER, HE CAME FROM THE GREAT VALLEY.⟩
⟨YES, YES, I UNDER-STAND, KAIPA. I DO.⟩
ERIS IS RIGHT! IT IS KAIPA! SOMEHOW, IT IS!
COME, SIT. I WILL TELL YOU WHAT HE'S SAYING.
THANK YOU, ERIS!
YES, THANK YOU.
THANK YOU.

⟨TRANSLATED FROM TIMBASHA⟩

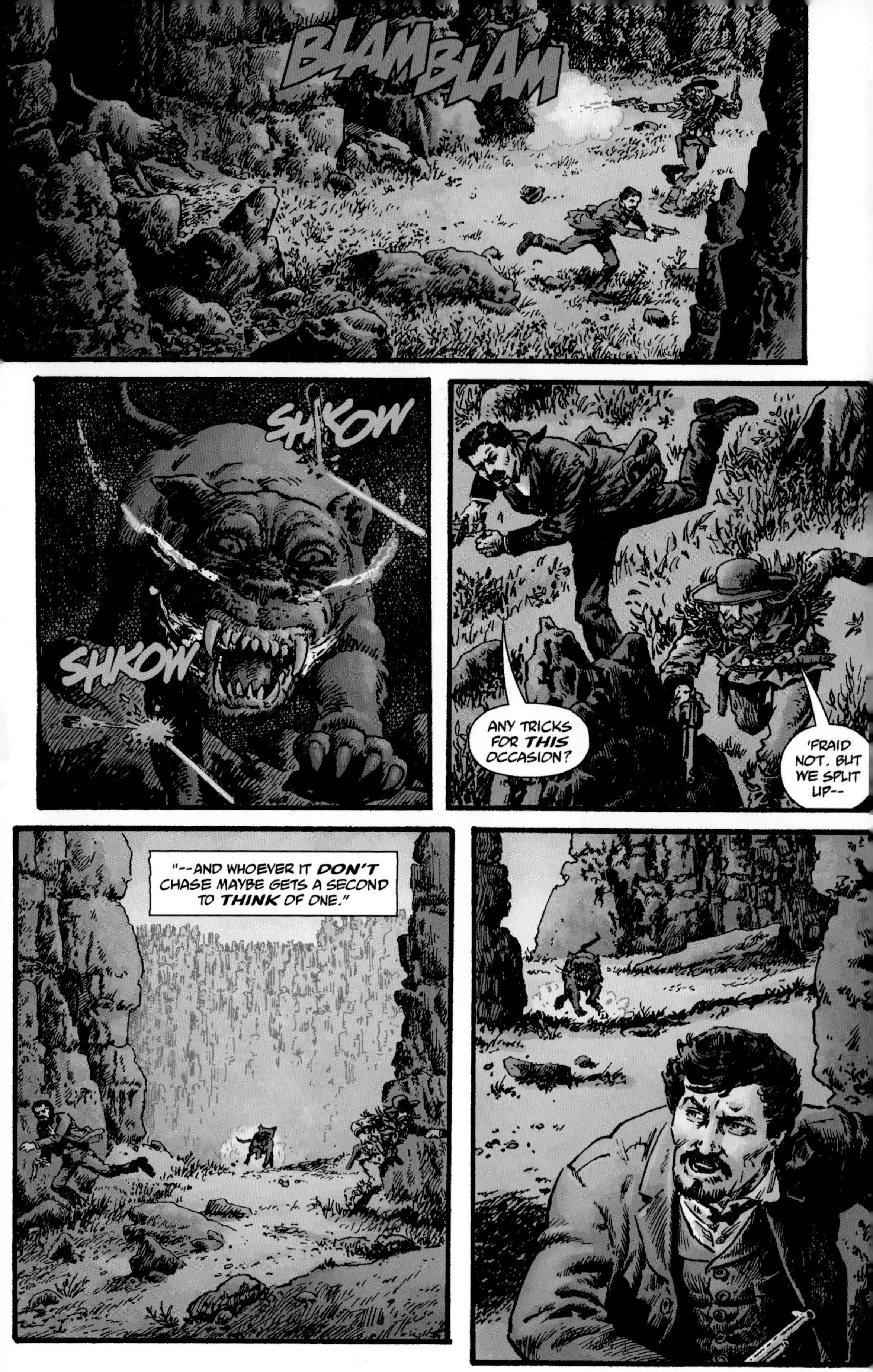
BLAMBLAM
SHKOW
SHKOW
ANY TRICKS FOR THIS OCCASION?
'FRAID NOT. BUT WE SPLIT UP--
"--AND WHOEVER IT DON'T CHASE MAYBE GETS A SECOND TO THINK OF ONE."

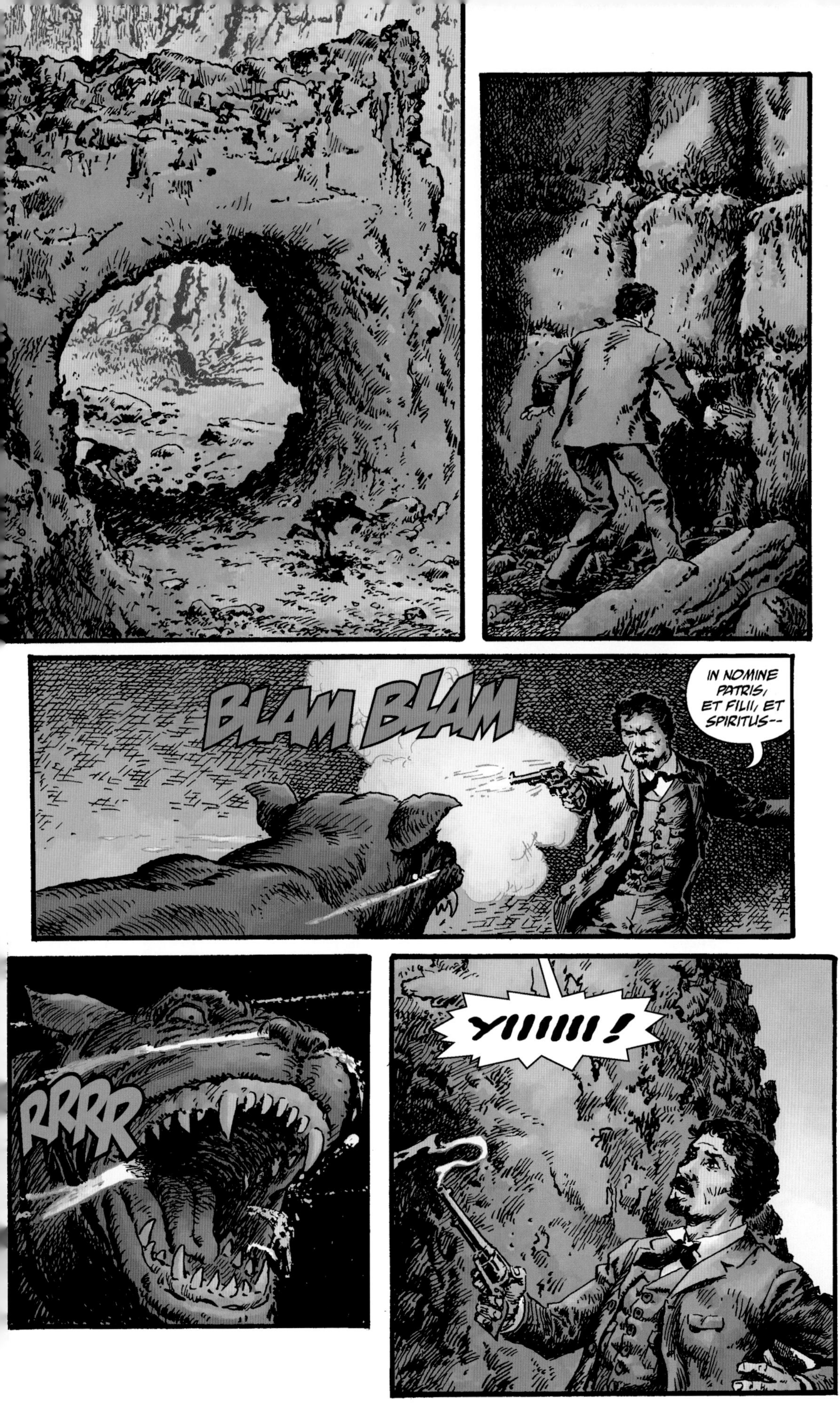
BLAM BLAM
IN NOMINE PATRIS, ET FILII, ET SPIRITUS--
RRRR
YIIIIII!

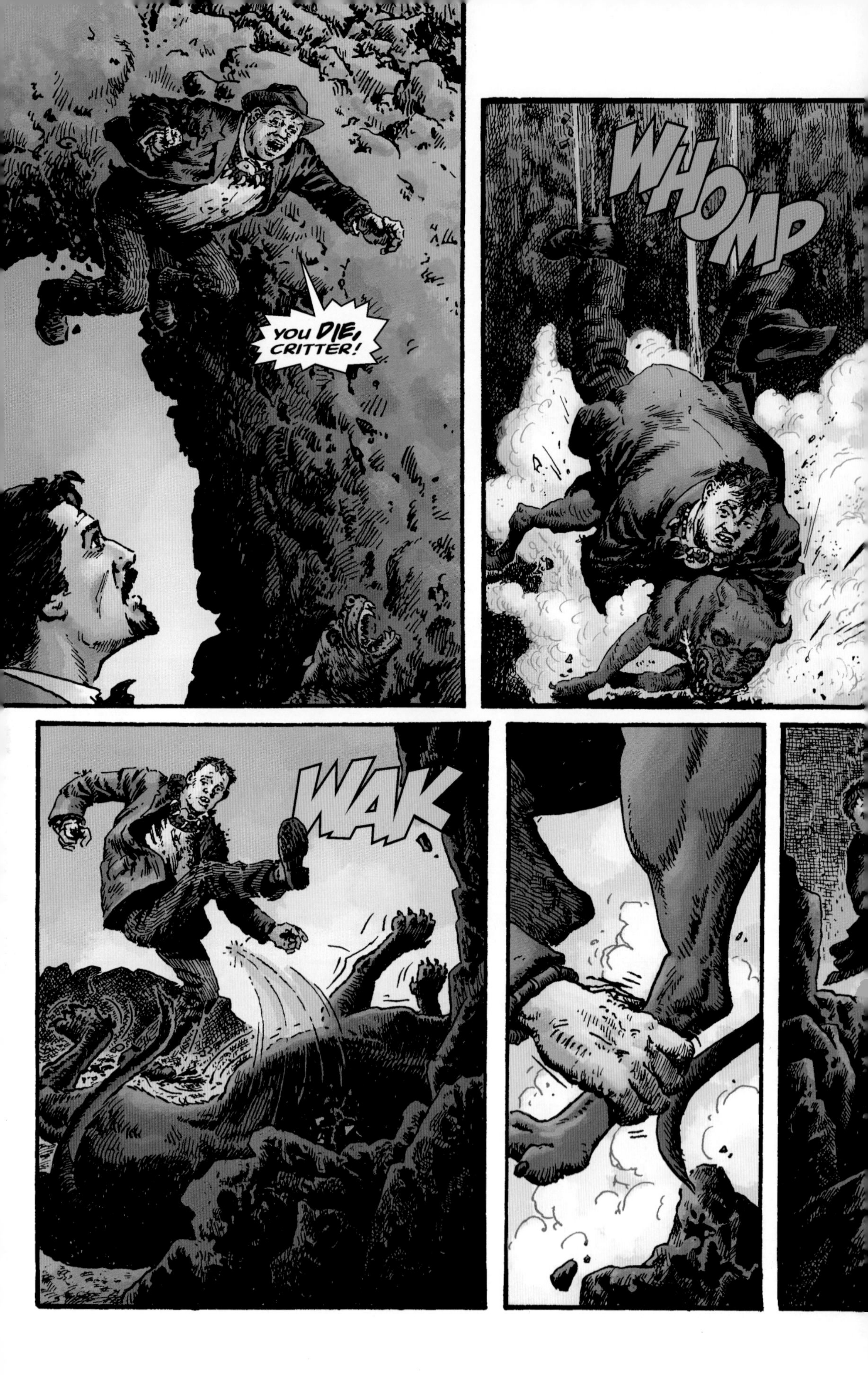
YOU DIE, CRITTER!
WHOMP
WAK

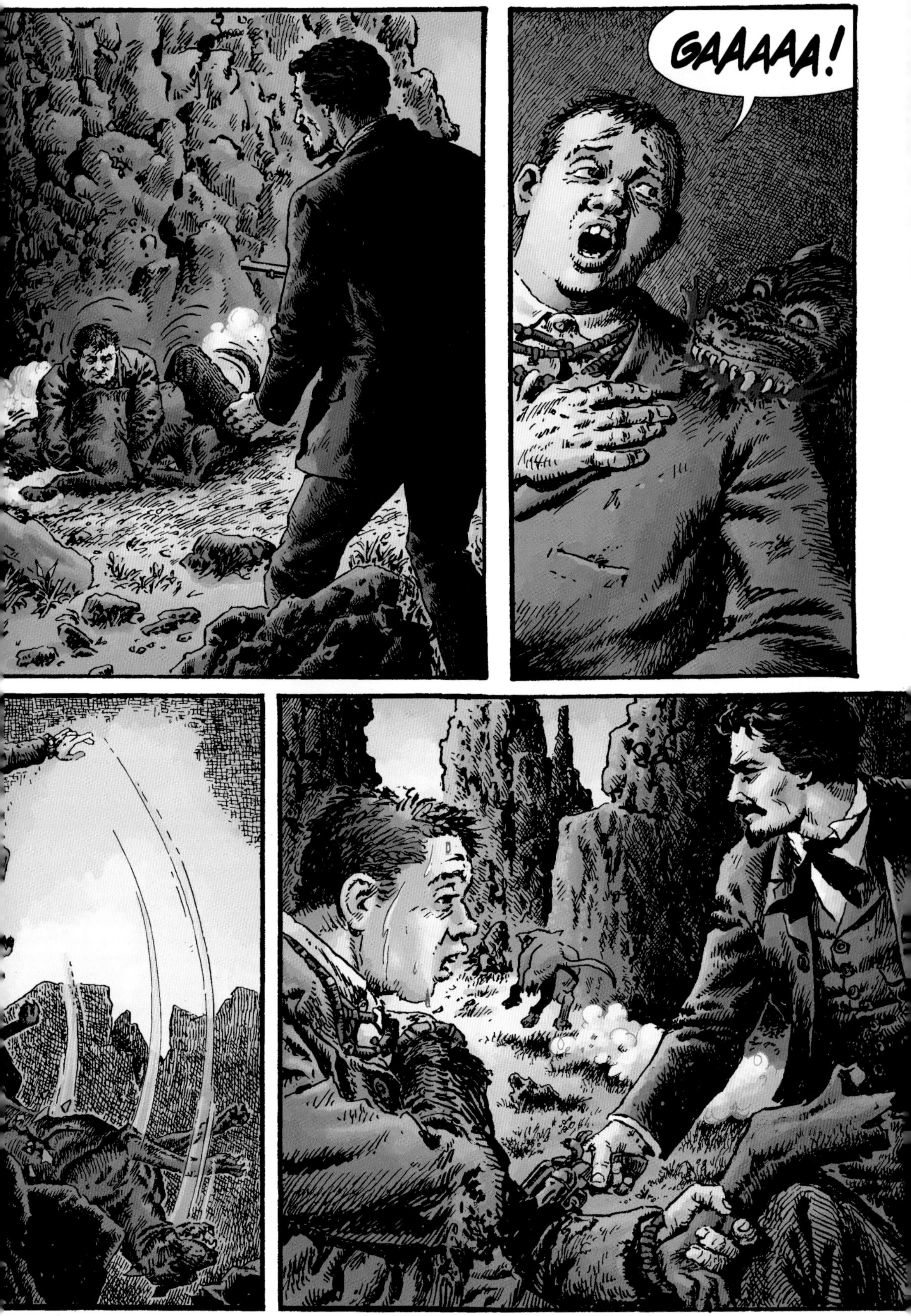
GAAAAA!

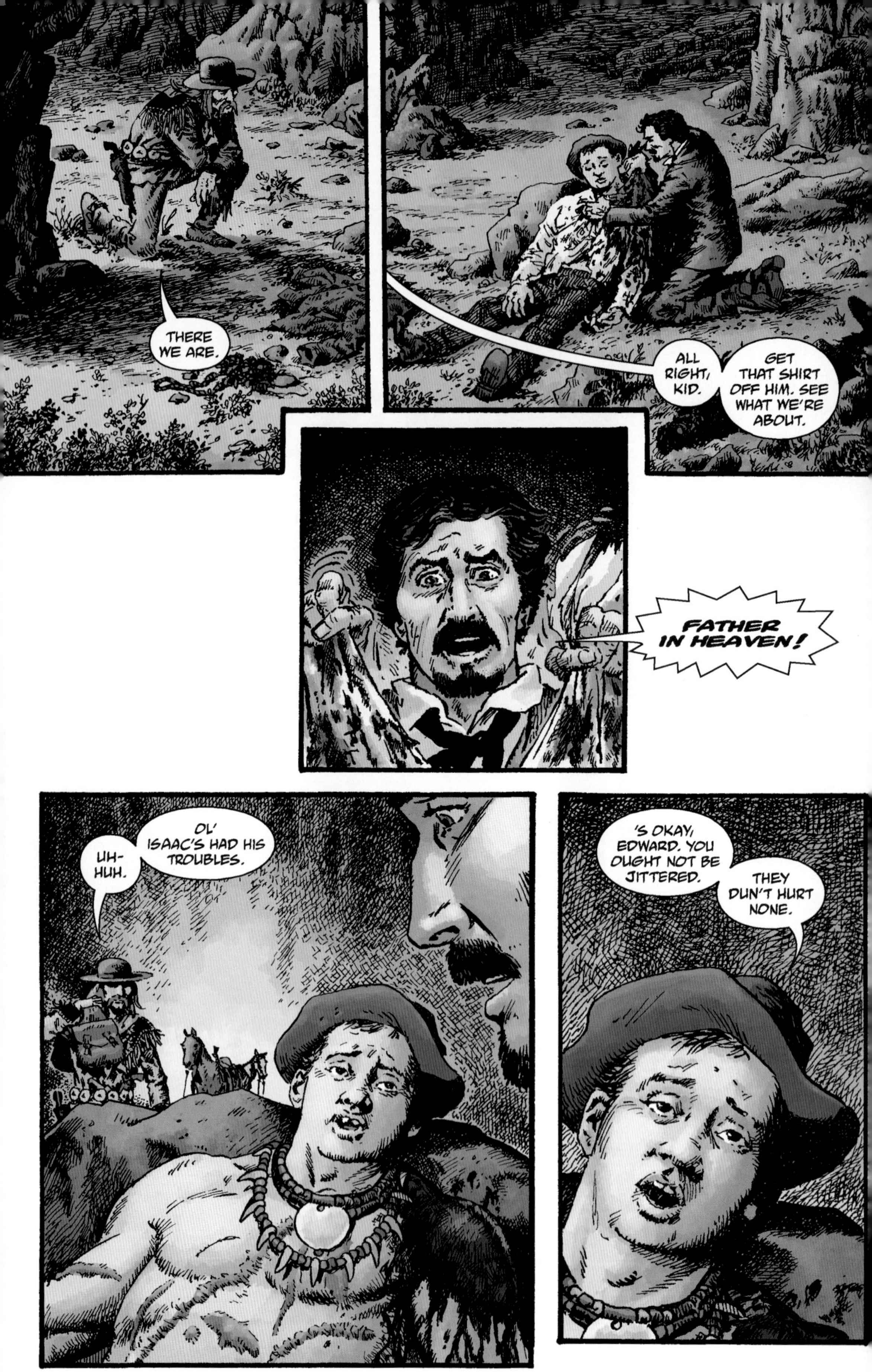
THERE WE ARE.
ALL RIGHT, KID.
GET THAT SHIRT OFF HIM. SEE WHAT WE'RE ABOUT.
FATHER IN HEAVEN!
UH-HUH.
OL' ISAAC'S HAD HIS TROUBLES.
'S OKAY, EDWARD. YOU OUGHT NOT BE JITTERED.
THEY DUN'T HURT NONE.

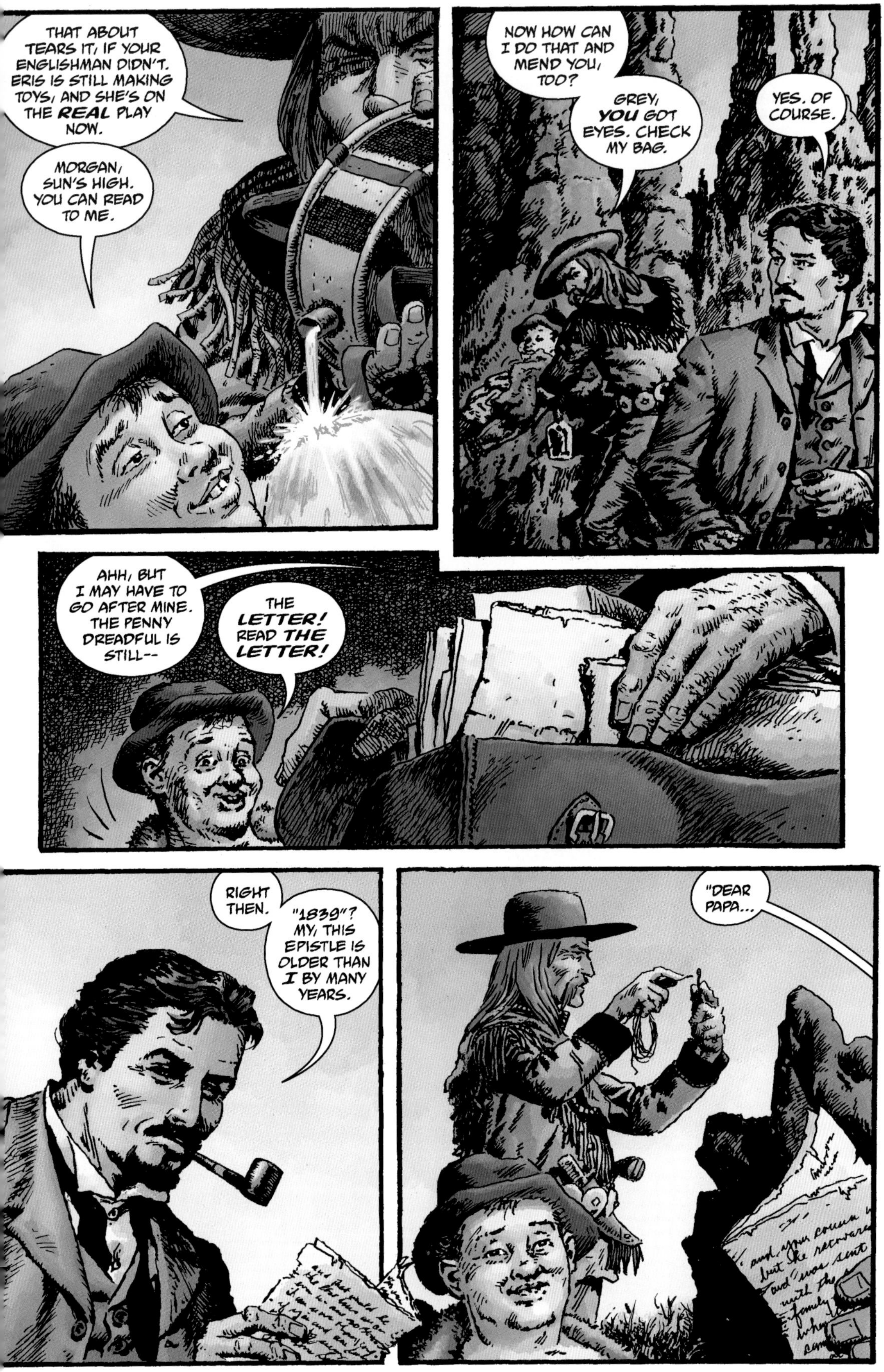
THAT ABOUT TEARS IT, IF YOUR ENGLISHMAN DIDN'T. ERIS IS STILL MAKING TOYS, AND SHE'S ON THE REAL PLAY NOW.
MORGAN, SUN'S HIGH. YOU CAN READ TO ME.
NOW HOW CAN I DO THAT AND MEND YOU, TOO?
GREY, YOU GOT EYES. CHECK MY BAG.
YES. OF COURSE.
AHH, BUT I MAY HAVE TO GO AFTER MINE. THE PENNY DREADFUL IS STILL--
THE LETTER! READ THE LETTER!
RIGHT THEN.
"1839"? MY, THIS EPISTLE IS OLDER THAN I BY MANY YEARS.
"DEAR PAPA...

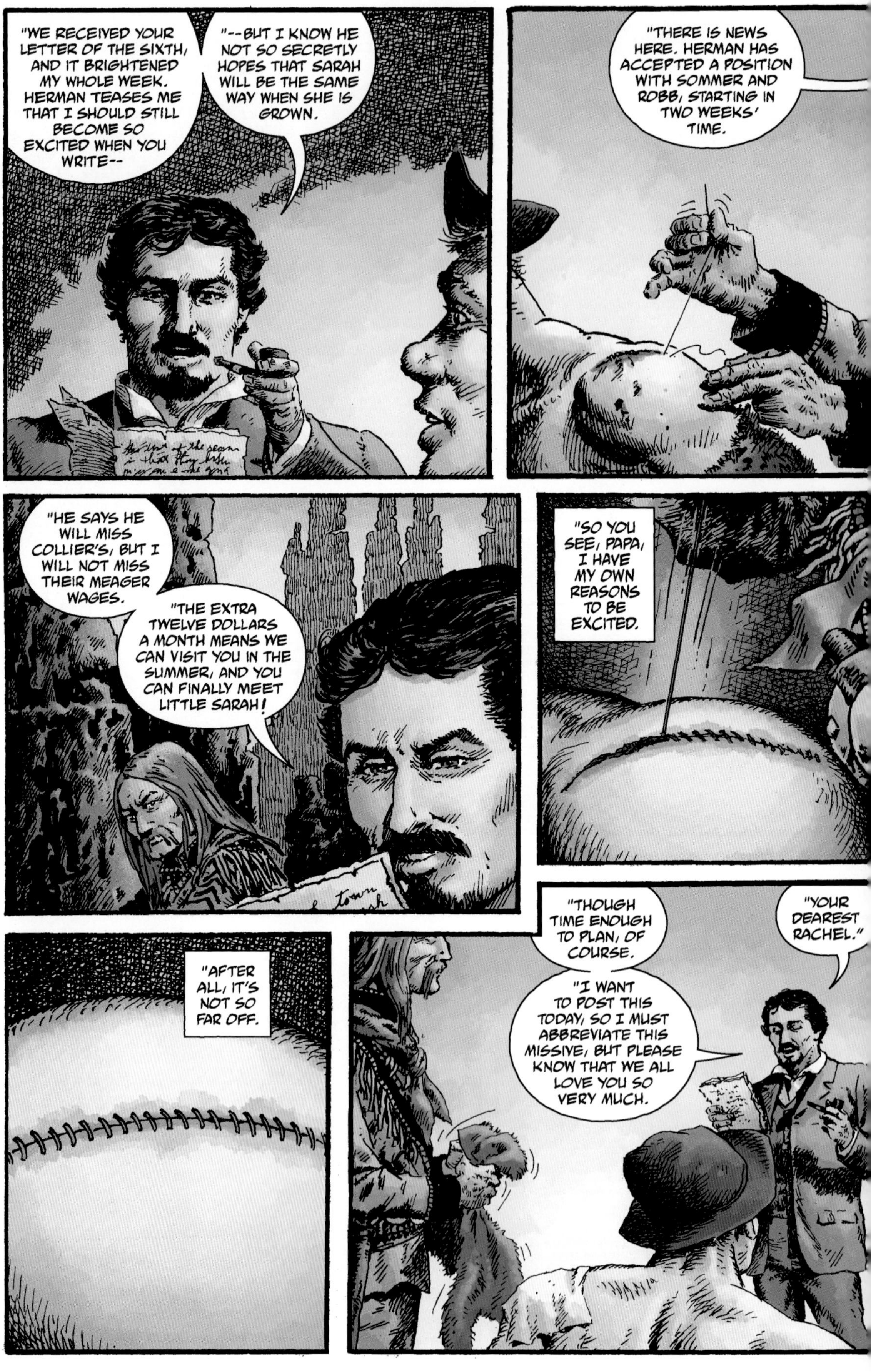
"WE RECEIVED YOUR LETTER OF THE SIXTH, AND IT BRIGHTENED MY WHOLE WEEK. HERMAN TEASES ME THAT I SHOULD STILL BECOME SO EXCITED WHEN YOU WRITE--
"--BUT I KNOW HE NOT SO SECRETLY HOPES THAT SARAH WILL BE THE SAME WAY WHEN SHE IS GROWN.
"THERE IS NEWS HERE. HERMAN HAS ACCEPTED A POSITION WITH SOMMER AND ROBB, STARTING IN TWO WEEKS' TIME.
"HE SAYS HE WILL MISS COLLIER'S, BUT I WILL NOT MISS THEIR MEAGER WAGES.
"THE EXTRA TWELVE DOLLARS A MONTH MEANS WE CAN VISIT YOU IN THE SUMMER, AND YOU CAN FINALLY MEET LITTLE SARAH!
"SO YOU SEE, PAPA, I HAVE MY OWN REASONS TO BE EXCITED.
"AFTER ALL, IT'S NOT SO FAR OFF.
"THOUGH TIME ENOUGH TO PLAN, OF COURSE.
"I WANT TO POST THIS TODAY, SO I MUST ABBREVIATE THIS MISSIVE, BUT PLEASE KNOW THAT WE ALL LOVE YOU SO VERY MUCH.
"YOUR DEAREST RACHEL."

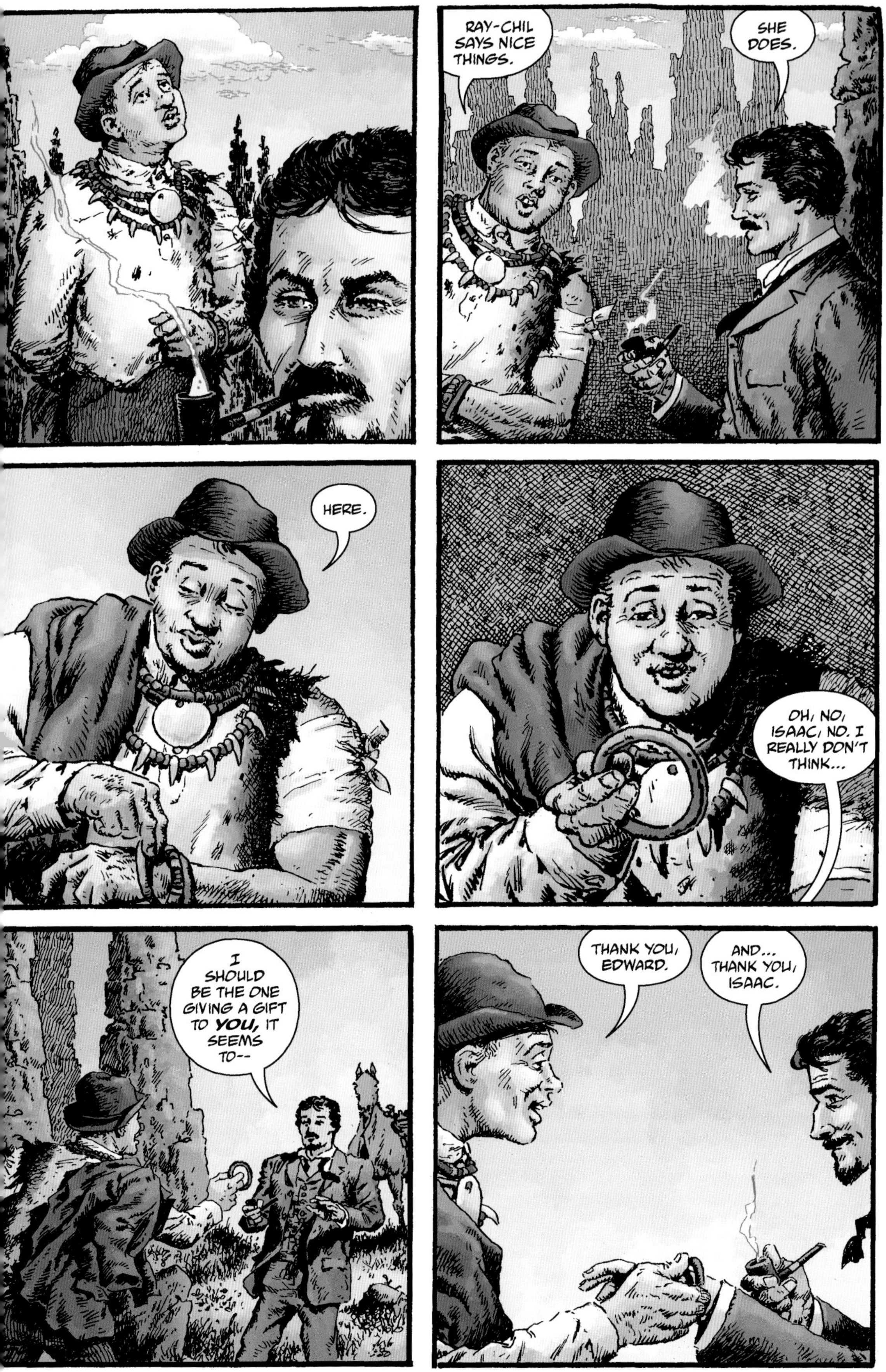

RAY-CHIL SAYS NICE THINGS.
SHE DOES.
HERE.
OH, NO, ISAAC, NO. I REALLY DON'T THINK...
I SHOULD BE THE ONE GIVING A GIFT TO **YOU,** IT SEEMS TO--
THANK YOU, EDWARD.
AND... THANK YOU, ISAAC.

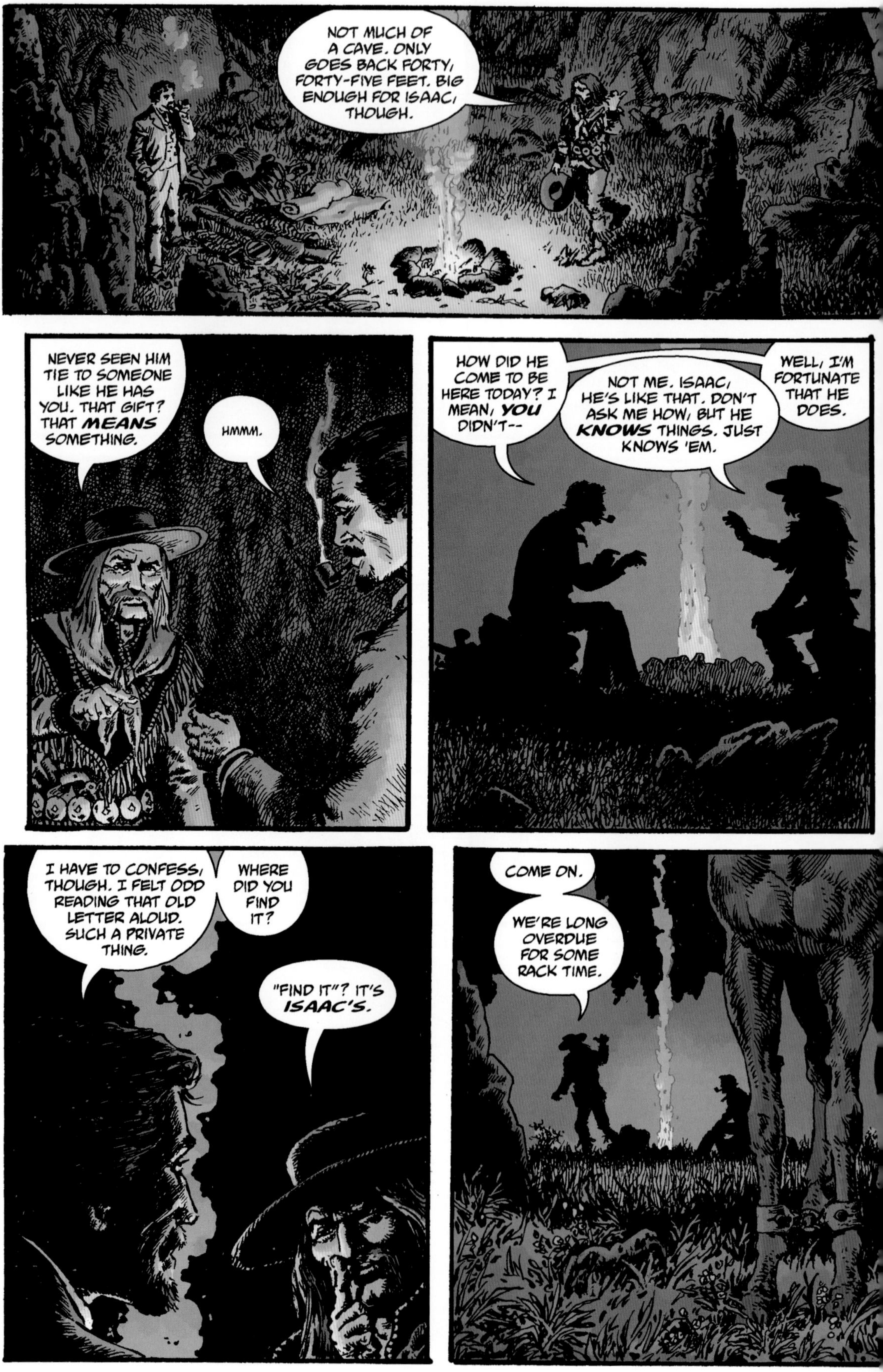
NOT MUCH OF A CAVE. ONLY GOES BACK FORTY, FORTY-FIVE FEET. BIG ENOUGH FOR ISAAC, THOUGH.
NEVER SEEN HIM TIE TO SOMEONE LIKE HE HAS YOU. THAT GIFT? THAT MEANS SOMETHING.
HMMM.
HOW DID HE COME TO BE HERE TODAY? I MEAN, YOU DIDN'T--
NOT ME. ISAAC, HE'S LIKE THAT. DON'T ASK ME HOW, BUT HE KNOWS THINGS. JUST KNOWS 'EM.
WELL, I'M FORTUNATE THAT HE DOES.
I HAVE TO CONFESS, THOUGH. I FELT ODD READING THAT OLD LETTER ALOUD. SUCH A PRIVATE THING.
WHERE DID YOU FIND IT?
"FIND IT"? IT'S ISAAC'S.
COME ON.
WE'RE LONG OVERDUE FOR SOME RACK TIME.

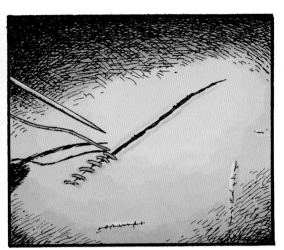

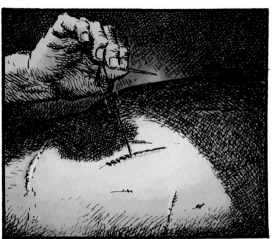

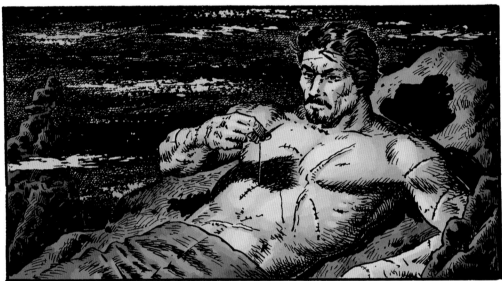

EDWARD GREY.

?

MARY!

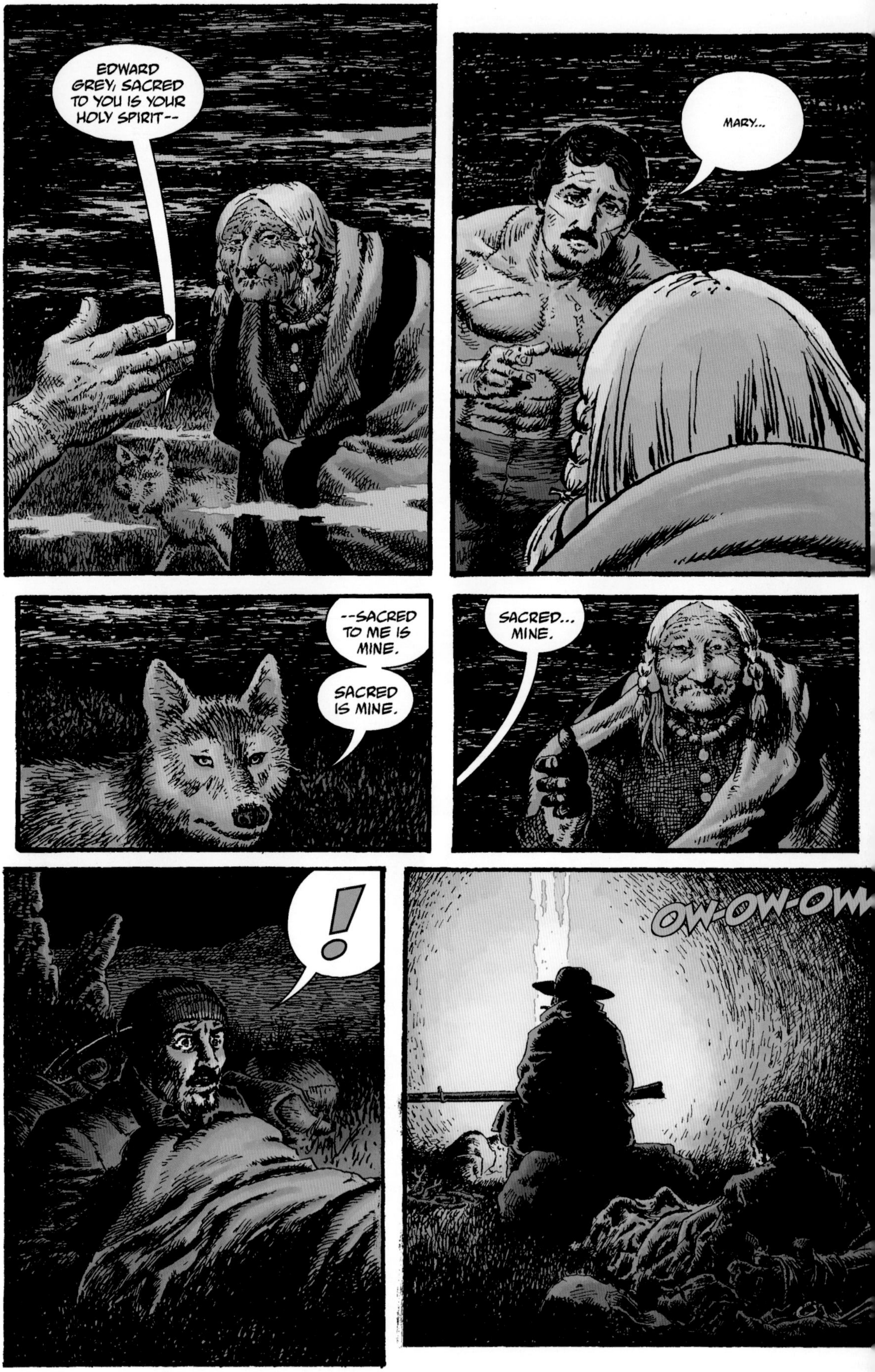
EDWARD GREY, SACRED TO YOU IS YOUR HOLY SPIRIT--
MARY...
--SACRED TO ME IS MINE.
SACRED IS MINE.
SACRED... MINE.
!
OW-OW-OW

CHAPTER FOUR

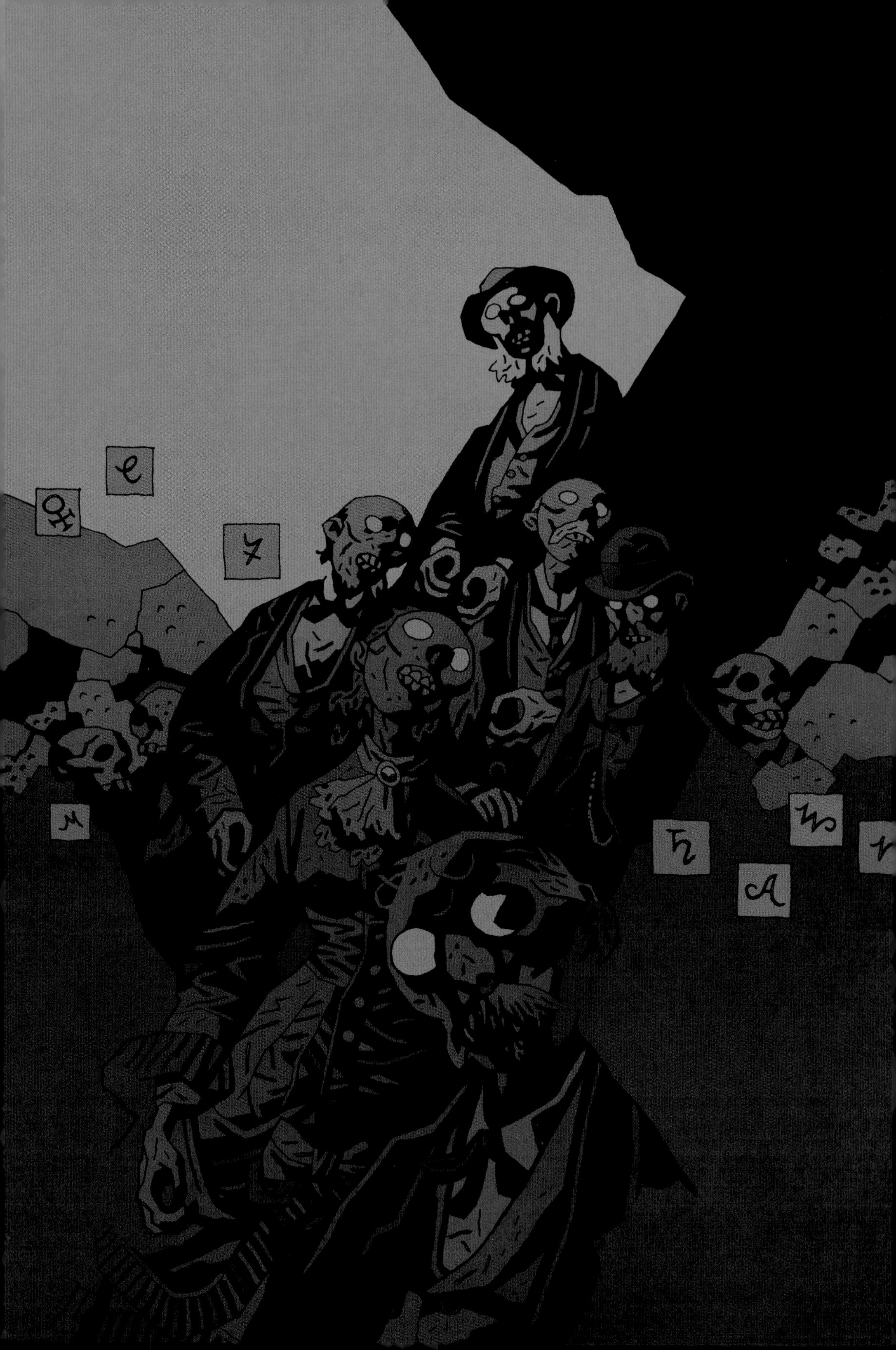

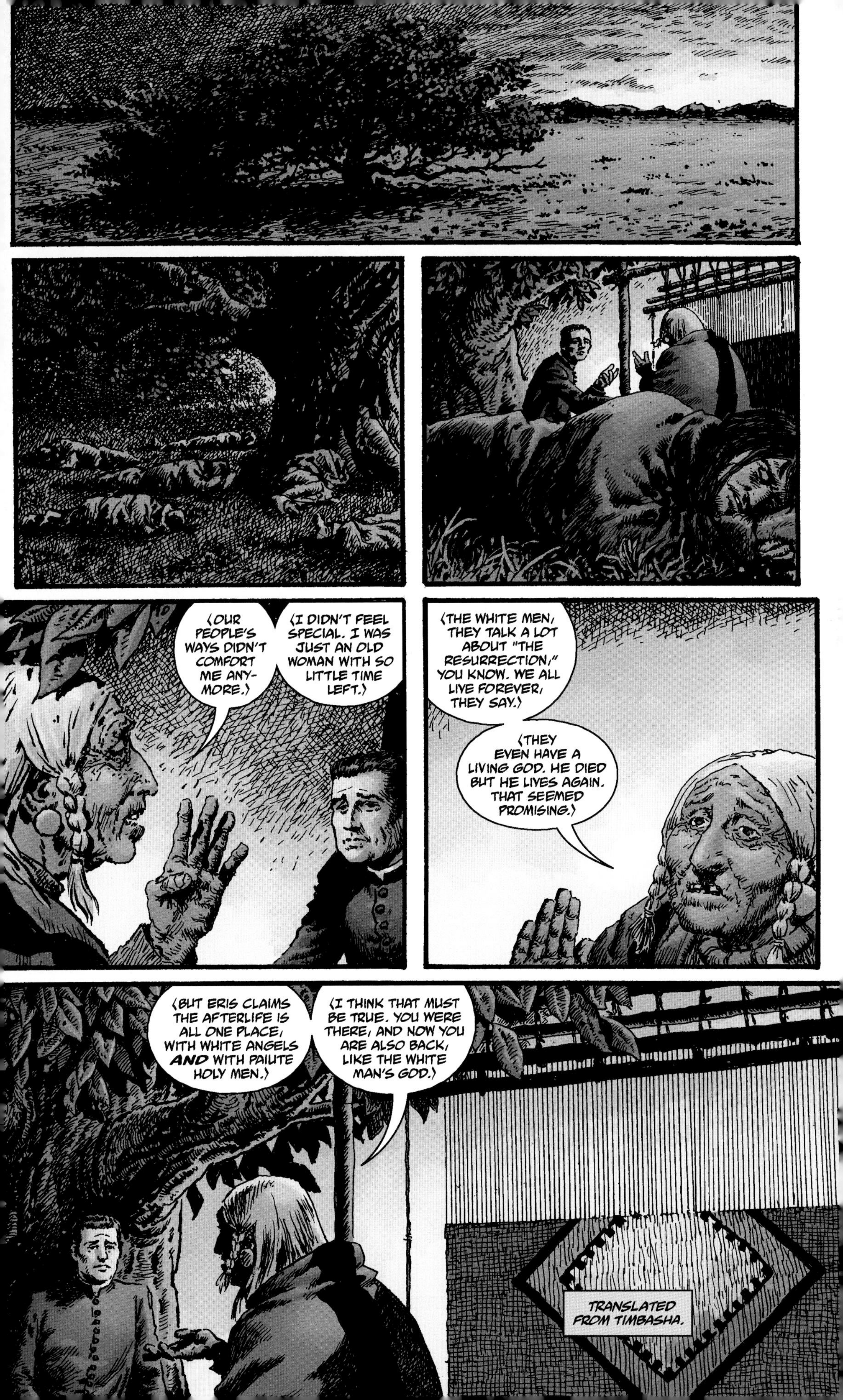

⟨OUR PEOPLE'S WAYS DIDN'T COMFORT ME ANY-MORE.⟩
⟨I DIDN'T FEEL SPECIAL. I WAS JUST AN OLD WOMAN WITH SO LITTLE TIME LEFT.⟩
⟨THE WHITE MEN, THEY TALK A LOT ABOUT "THE RESURRECTION," YOU KNOW. WE ALL LIVE FOREVER, THEY SAY.⟩
⟨THEY EVEN HAVE A LIVING GOD. HE DIED BUT HE LIVES AGAIN. THAT SEEMED PROMISING.⟩
⟨BUT ERIS CLAIMS THE AFTERLIFE IS ALL ONE PLACE, WITH WHITE ANGELS **AND** WITH PAIUTE HOLY MEN.⟩
⟨I THINK THAT MUST BE TRUE. YOU WERE THERE, AND NOW YOU ARE ALSO BACK, LIKE THE WHITE MAN'S GOD.⟩
TRANSLATED FROM TIMBASHA.

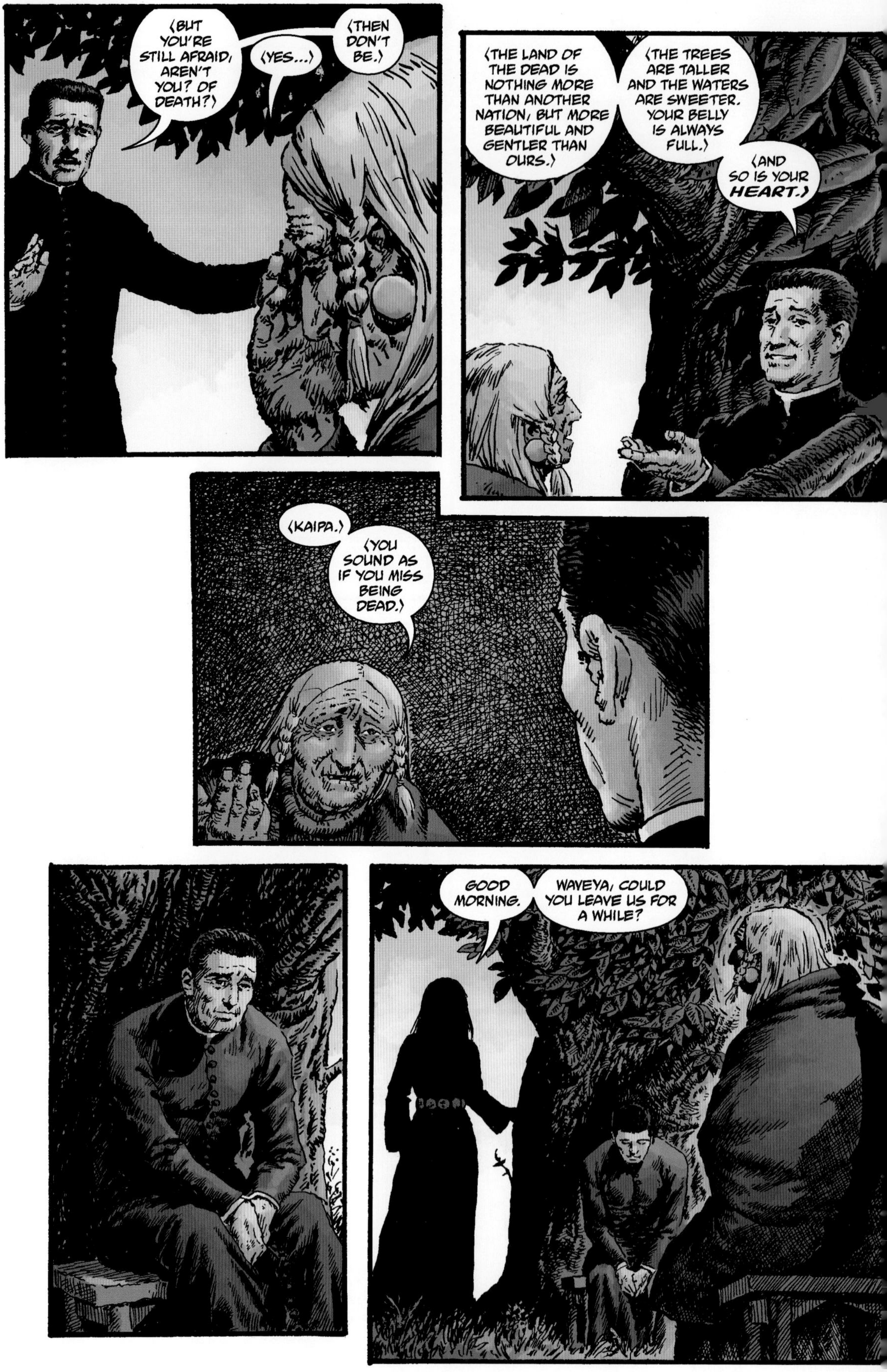
‹BUT YOU'RE STILL AFRAID, AREN'T YOU? OF DEATH?›
‹YES...›
‹THEN DON'T BE.›
‹THE LAND OF THE DEAD IS NOTHING MORE THAN ANOTHER NATION, BUT MORE BEAUTIFUL AND GENTLER THAN OURS.›
‹THE TREES ARE TALLER AND THE WATERS ARE SWEETER. YOUR BELLY IS ALWAYS FULL.›
‹AND SO IS YOUR HEART.›
‹KAIPA.›
‹YOU SOUND AS IF YOU MISS BEING DEAD.›
GOOD MORNING.
WAVEYA, COULD YOU LEAVE US FOR A WHILE?

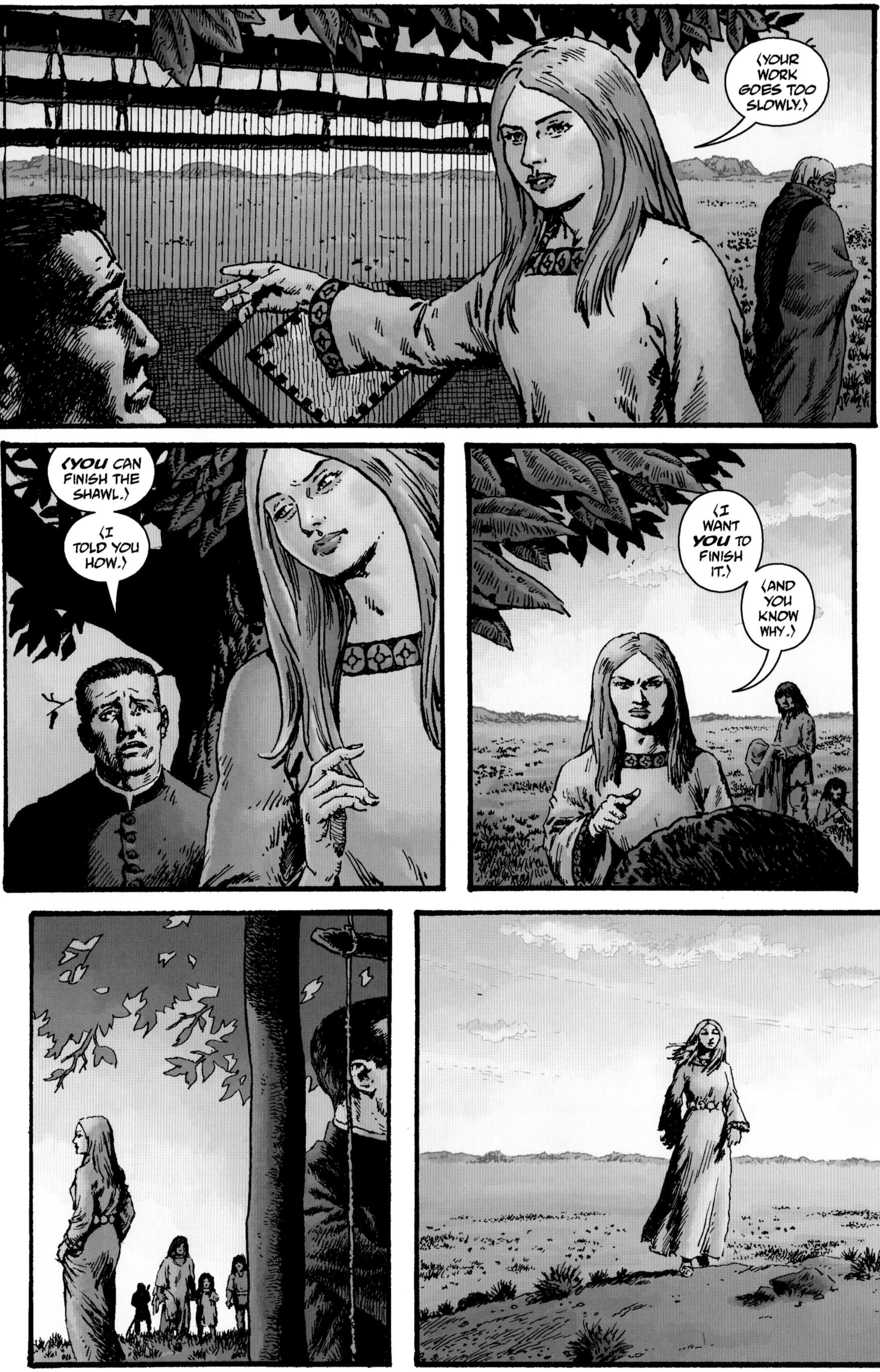
‹YOUR WORK GOES TOO SLOWLY.›
‹YOU CAN FINISH THE SHAWL.›
‹I TOLD YOU HOW.›
‹I WANT YOU TO FINISH IT.›
‹AND YOU KNOW WHY.›

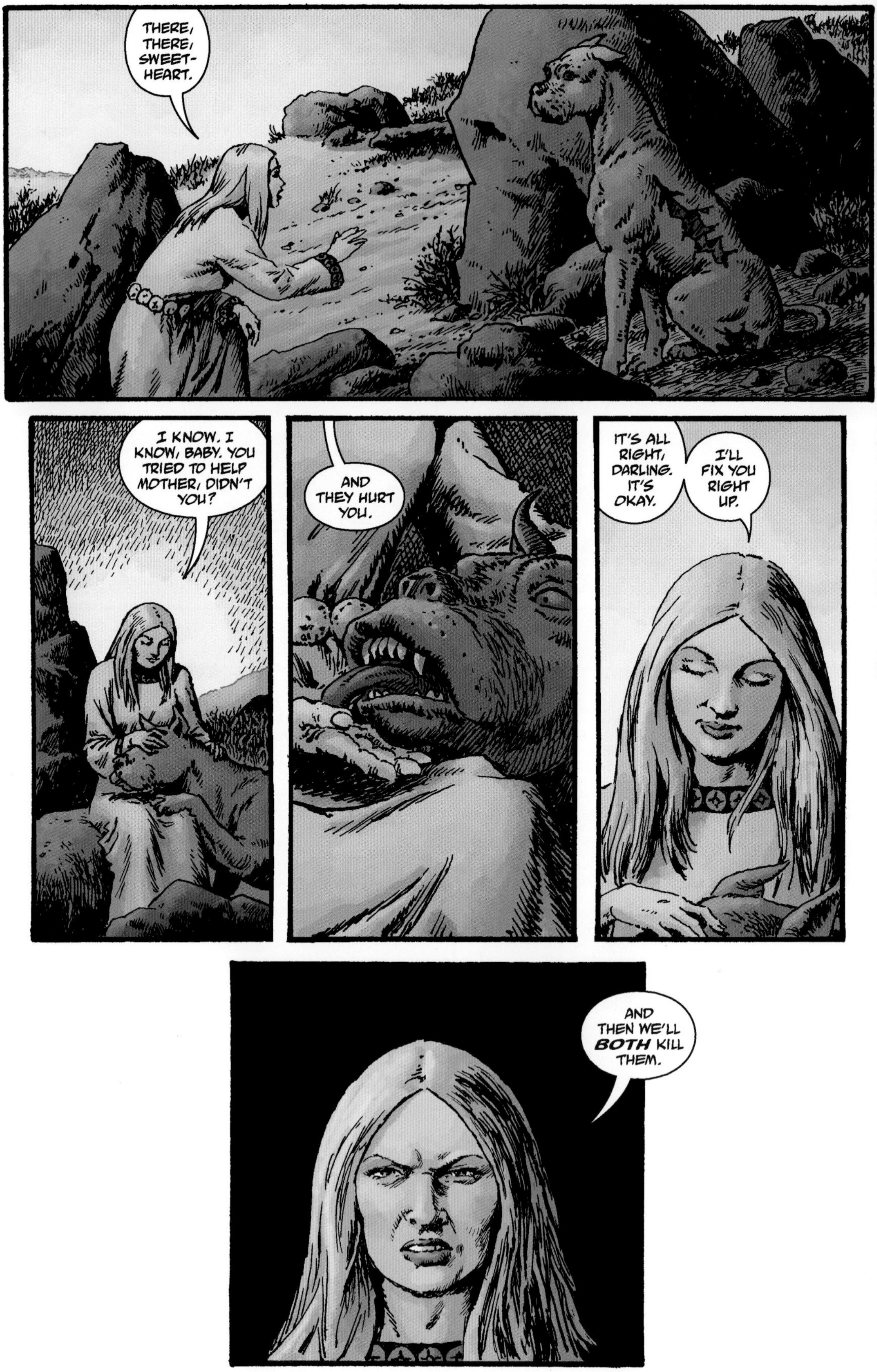

THERE, THERE, SWEET-HEART.
I KNOW. I KNOW, BABY. YOU TRIED TO HELP MOTHER, DIDN'T YOU?
AND THEY HURT YOU.
IT'S ALL RIGHT, DARLING. IT'S OKAY.
I'LL FIX YOU RIGHT UP.
AND THEN WE'LL BOTH KILL THEM.

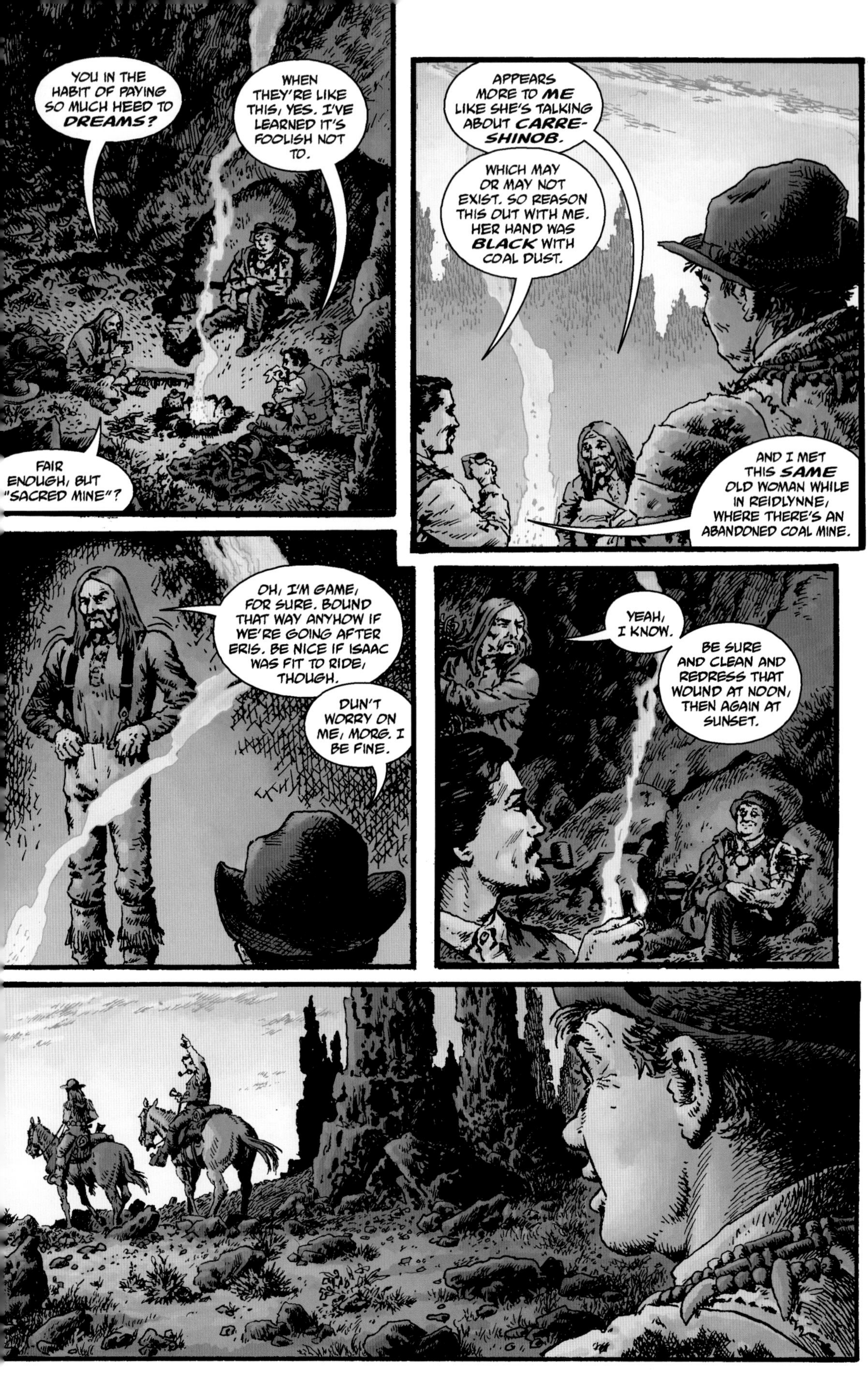
YOU IN THE HABIT OF PAYING SO MUCH HEED TO DREAMS?
WHEN THEY'RE LIKE THIS, YES. I'VE LEARNED IT'S FOOLISH NOT TO.
FAIR ENOUGH, BUT "SACRED MINE"?
APPEARS MORE TO ME LIKE SHE'S TALKING ABOUT CARRE-SHINOB.
WHICH MAY OR MAY NOT EXIST. SO REASON THIS OUT WITH ME. HER HAND WAS BLACK WITH COAL DUST.
AND I MET THIS SAME OLD WOMAN WHILE IN REIDLYNNE, WHERE THERE'S AN ABANDONED COAL MINE.
OH, I'M GAME, FOR SURE. BOUND THAT WAY ANYHOW IF WE'RE GOING AFTER ERIS. BE NICE IF ISAAC WAS FIT TO RIDE, THOUGH.
DUN'T WORRY ON ME, MORG. I BE FINE.
YEAH, I KNOW.
BE SURE AND CLEAN AND REDRESS THAT WOUND AT NOON, THEN AGAIN AT SUNSET.

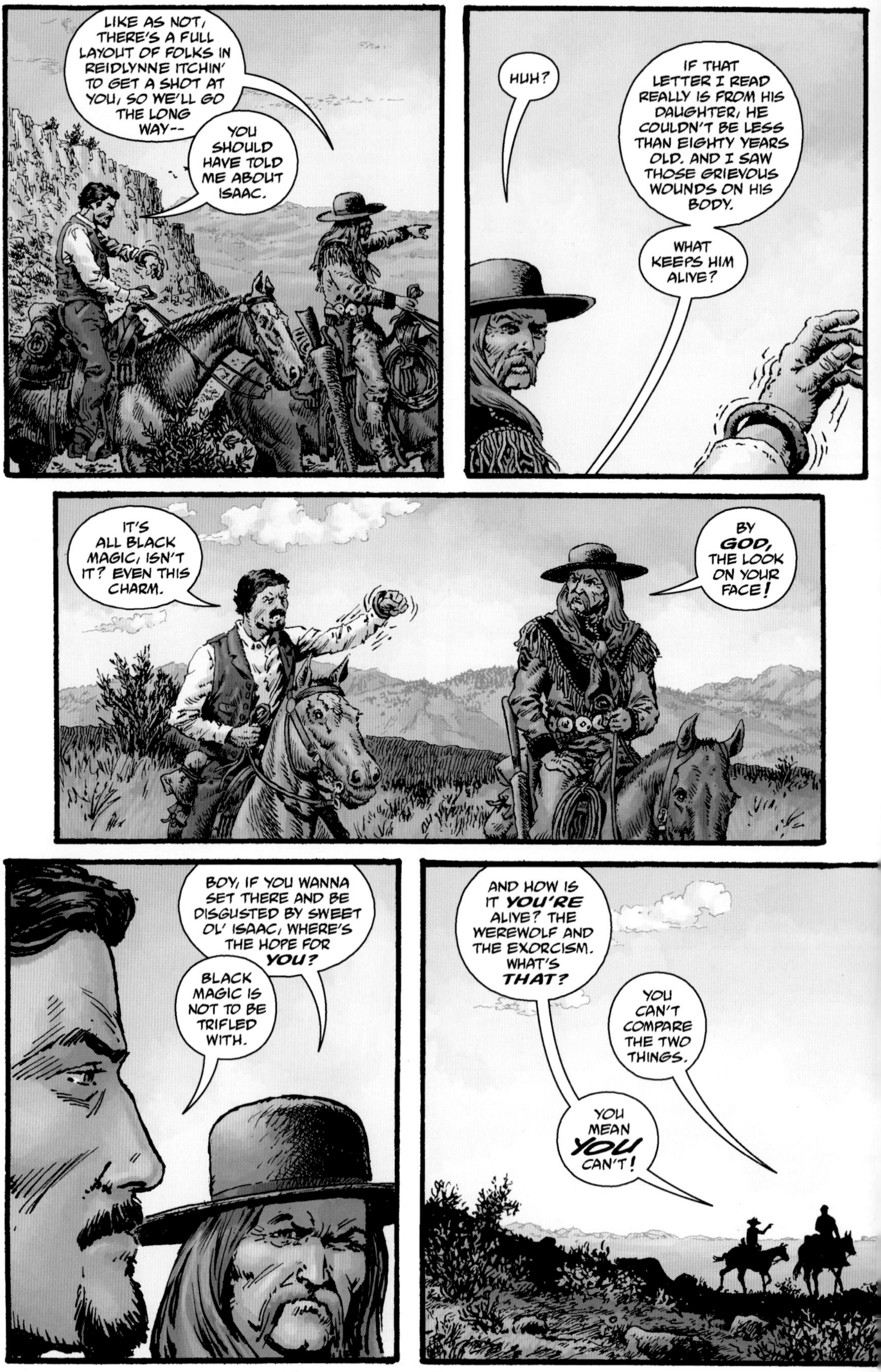

LIKE AS NOT, THERE'S A FULL LAYOUT OF FOLKS IN REIDLYNNE ITCHIN' TO GET A SHOT AT YOU, SO WE'LL GO THE LONG WAY--
YOU SHOULD HAVE TOLD ME ABOUT ISAAC.
HUH?
IF THAT LETTER I READ REALLY IS FROM HIS DAUGHTER, HE COULDN'T BE LESS THAN EIGHTY YEARS OLD. AND I SAW THOSE GRIEVOUS WOUNDS ON HIS BODY.
WHAT KEEPS HIM ALIVE?
IT'S ALL BLACK MAGIC, ISN'T IT? EVEN THIS CHARM.
BY GOD, THE LOOK ON YOUR FACE!
BOY, IF YOU WANNA SET THERE AND BE DISGUSTED BY SWEET OL' ISAAC, WHERE'S THE HOPE FOR YOU?
BLACK MAGIC IS NOT TO BE TRIFLED WITH.
AND HOW IS IT YOU'RE ALIVE? THE WEREWOLF AND THE EXORCISM. WHAT'S THAT?
YOU CAN'T COMPARE THE TWO THINGS.
YOU MEAN YOU CAN'T!

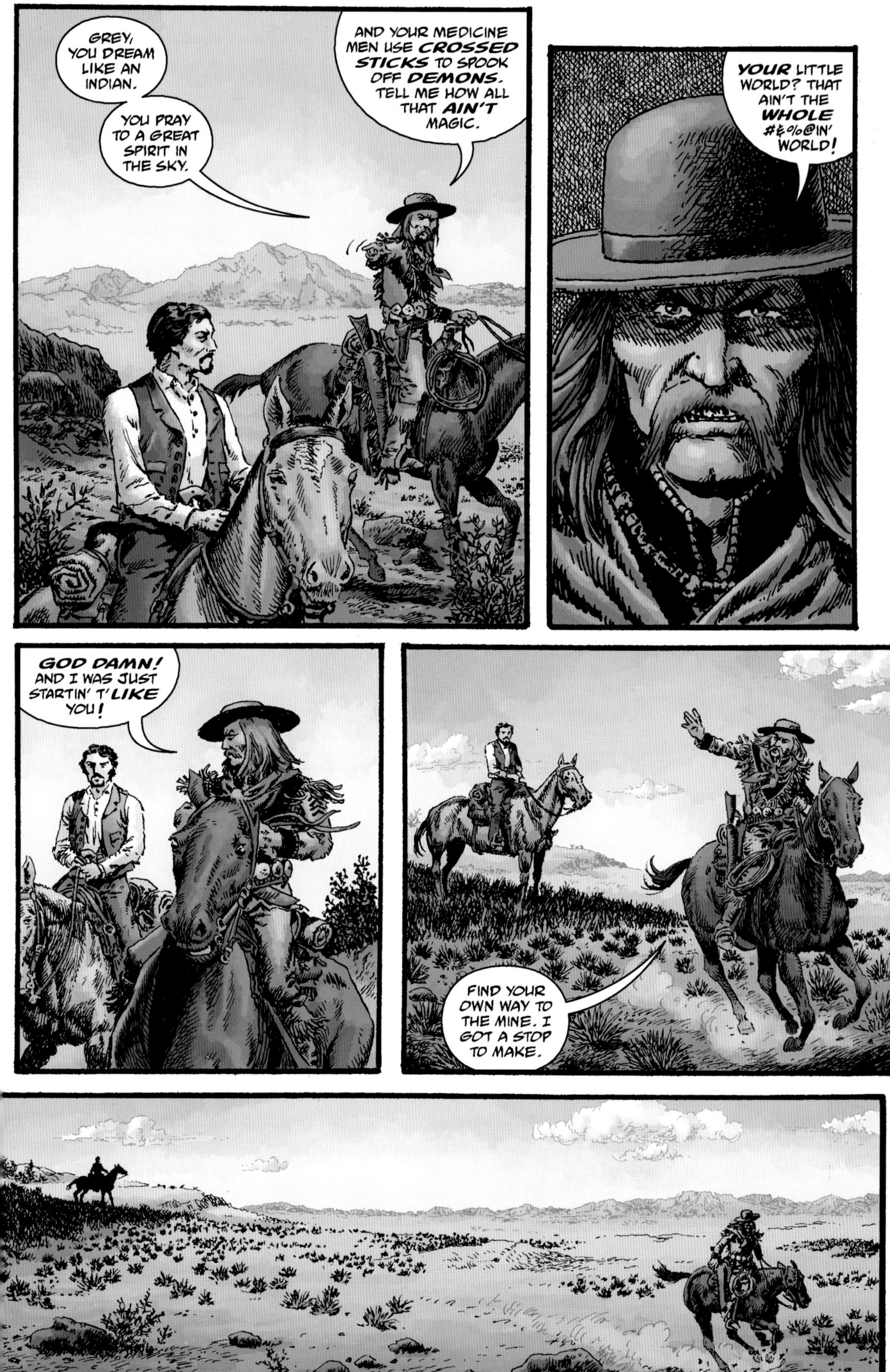
GREY, YOU DREAM LIKE AN INDIAN.
YOU PRAY TO A GREAT SPIRIT IN THE SKY.
AND YOUR MEDICINE MEN USE CROSSED STICKS TO SPOOK OFF DEMONS. TELL ME HOW ALL THAT AIN'T MAGIC.
YOUR LITTLE WORLD? THAT AIN'T THE WHOLE #&%@IN' WORLD!
GOD DAMN! AND I WAS JUST STARTIN' T'LIKE YOU!
FIND YOUR OWN WAY TO THE MINE. I GOT A STOP TO MAKE.

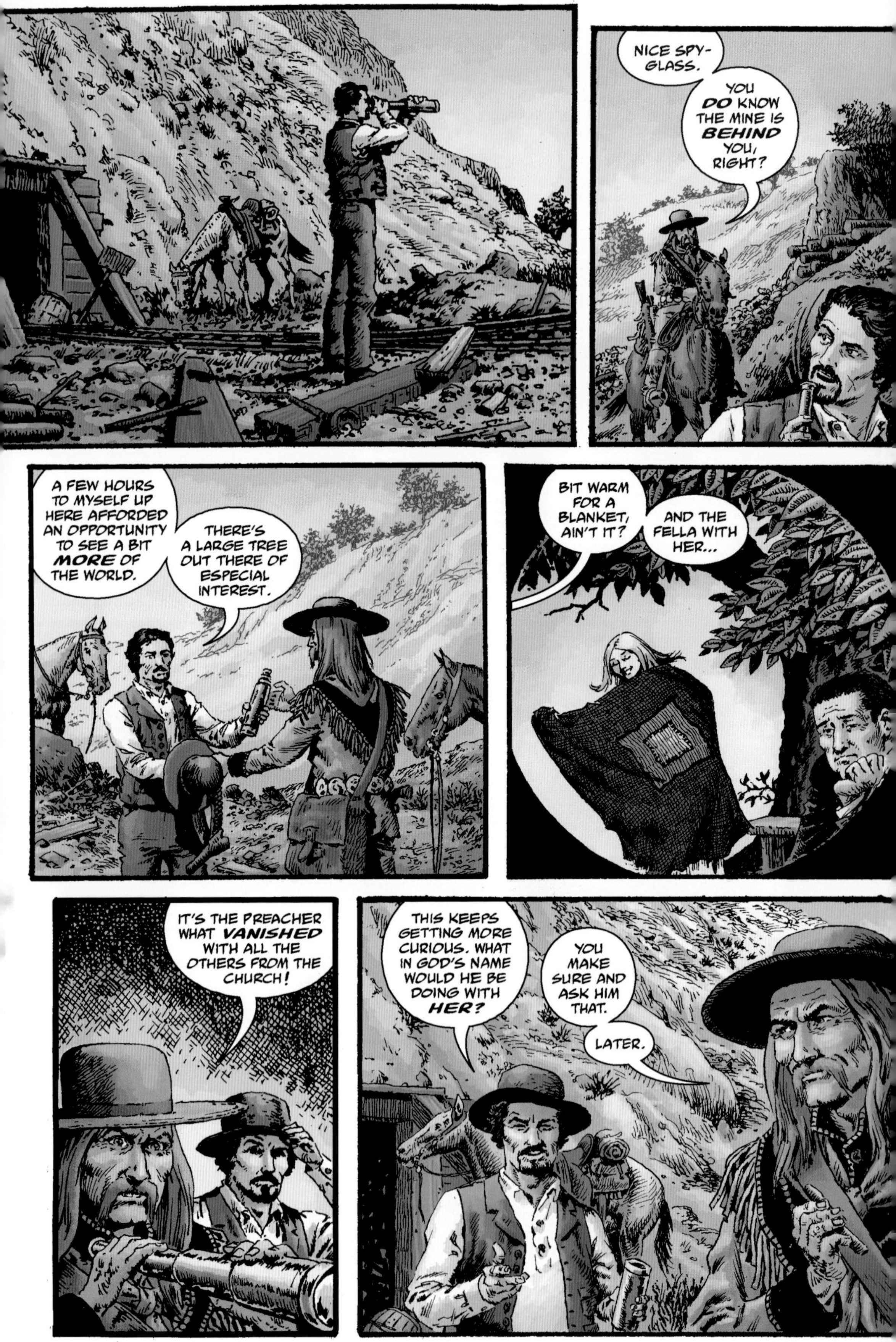

NICE SPY-GLASS.
YOU DO KNOW THE MINE IS BEHIND YOU, RIGHT?
A FEW HOURS TO MYSELF UP HERE AFFORDED AN OPPORTUNITY TO SEE A BIT MORE OF THE WORLD.
THERE'S A LARGE TREE OUT THERE OF ESPECIAL INTEREST.
BIT WARM FOR A BLANKET, AIN'T IT?
AND THE FELLA WITH HER...
IT'S THE PREACHER WHAT VANISHED WITH ALL THE OTHERS FROM THE CHURCH!
THIS KEEPS GETTING MORE CURIOUS. WHAT IN GOD'S NAME WOULD HE BE DOING WITH HER?
YOU MAKE SURE AND ASK HIM THAT.
LATER.

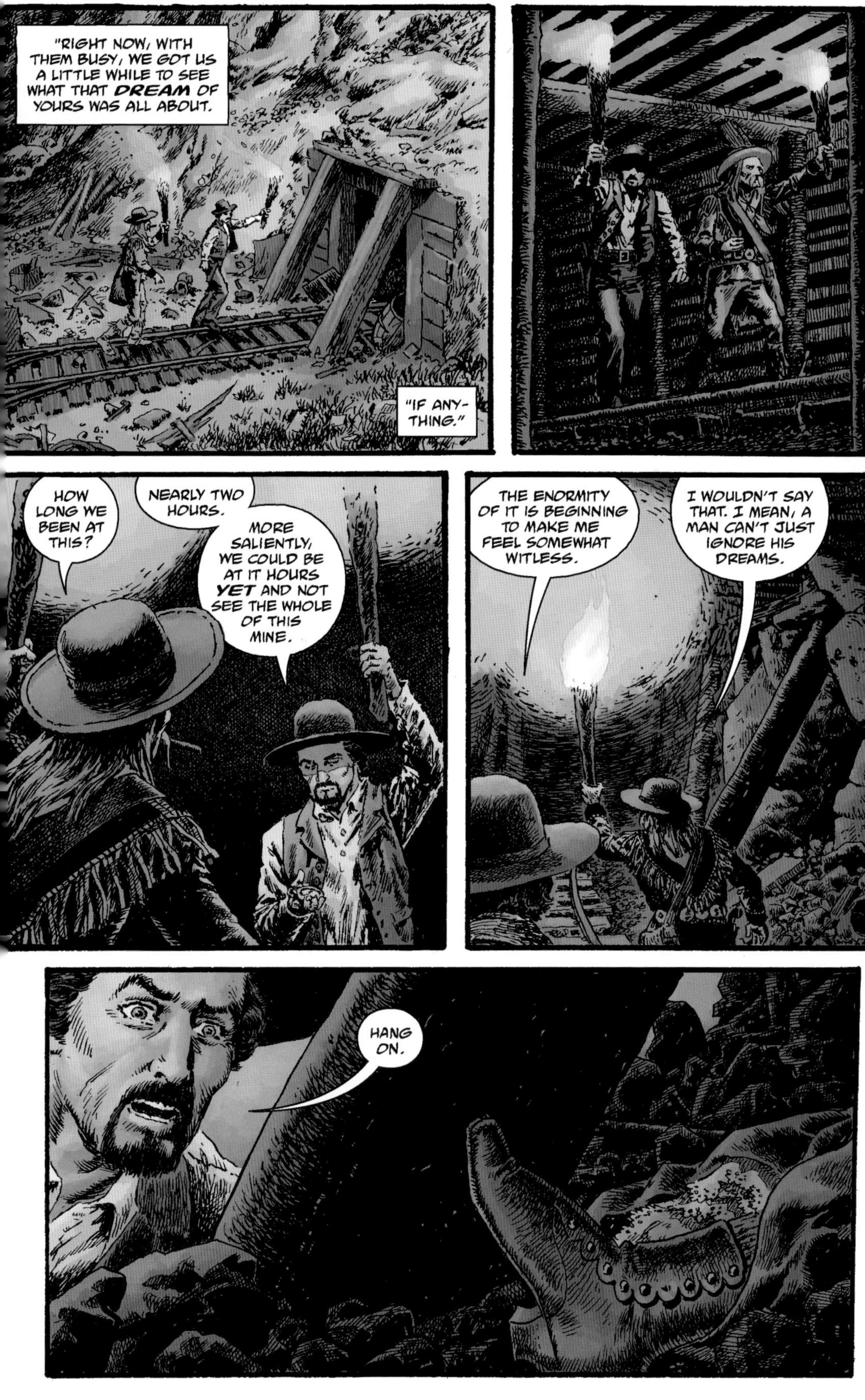
"RIGHT NOW, WITH THEM BUSY, WE GOT US A LITTLE WHILE TO SEE WHAT THAT DREAM OF YOURS WAS ALL ABOUT.
"IF ANY-THING."
HOW LONG WE BEEN AT THIS?
NEARLY TWO HOURS.
MORE SALIENTLY, WE COULD BE AT IT HOURS YET AND NOT SEE THE WHOLE OF THIS MINE.
THE ENORMITY OF IT IS BEGINNING TO MAKE ME FEEL SOMEWHAT WITLESS.
I WOULDN'T SAY THAT. I MEAN, A MAN CAN'T JUST IGNORE HIS DREAMS.
HANG ON.

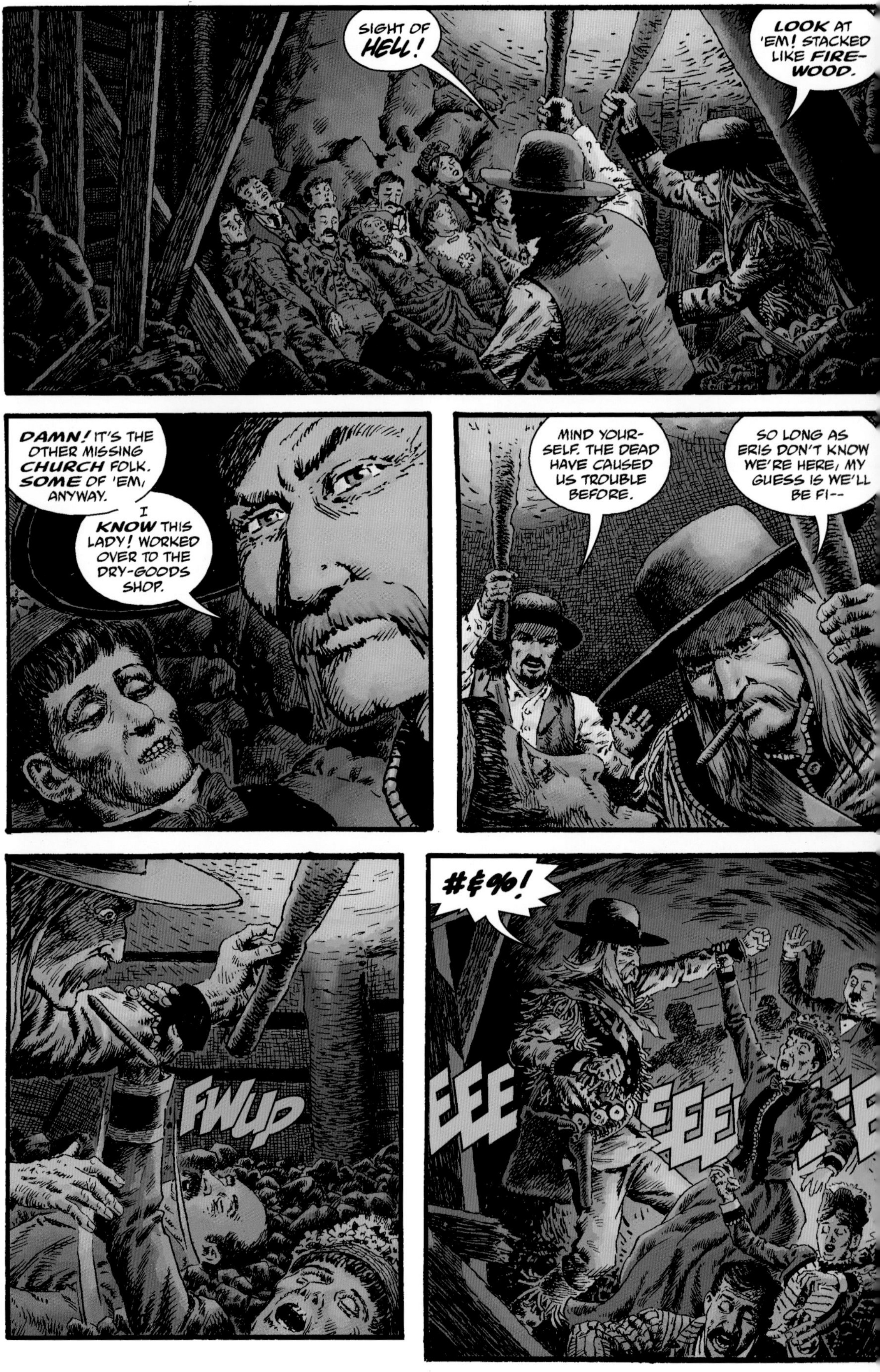
SIGHT OF HELL!
LOOK AT 'EM! STACKED LIKE FIRE-WOOD.
DAMN! IT'S THE OTHER MISSING CHURCH FOLK. SOME OF 'EM, ANYWAY.
I KNOW THIS LADY! WORKED OVER TO THE DRY-GOODS SHOP.
MIND YOUR-SELF. THE DEAD HAVE CAUSED US TROUBLE BEFORE.
SO LONG AS ERIS DON'T KNOW WE'RE HERE, MY GUESS IS WE'LL BE FI--
FWUP
#&%!
EEE
EEE

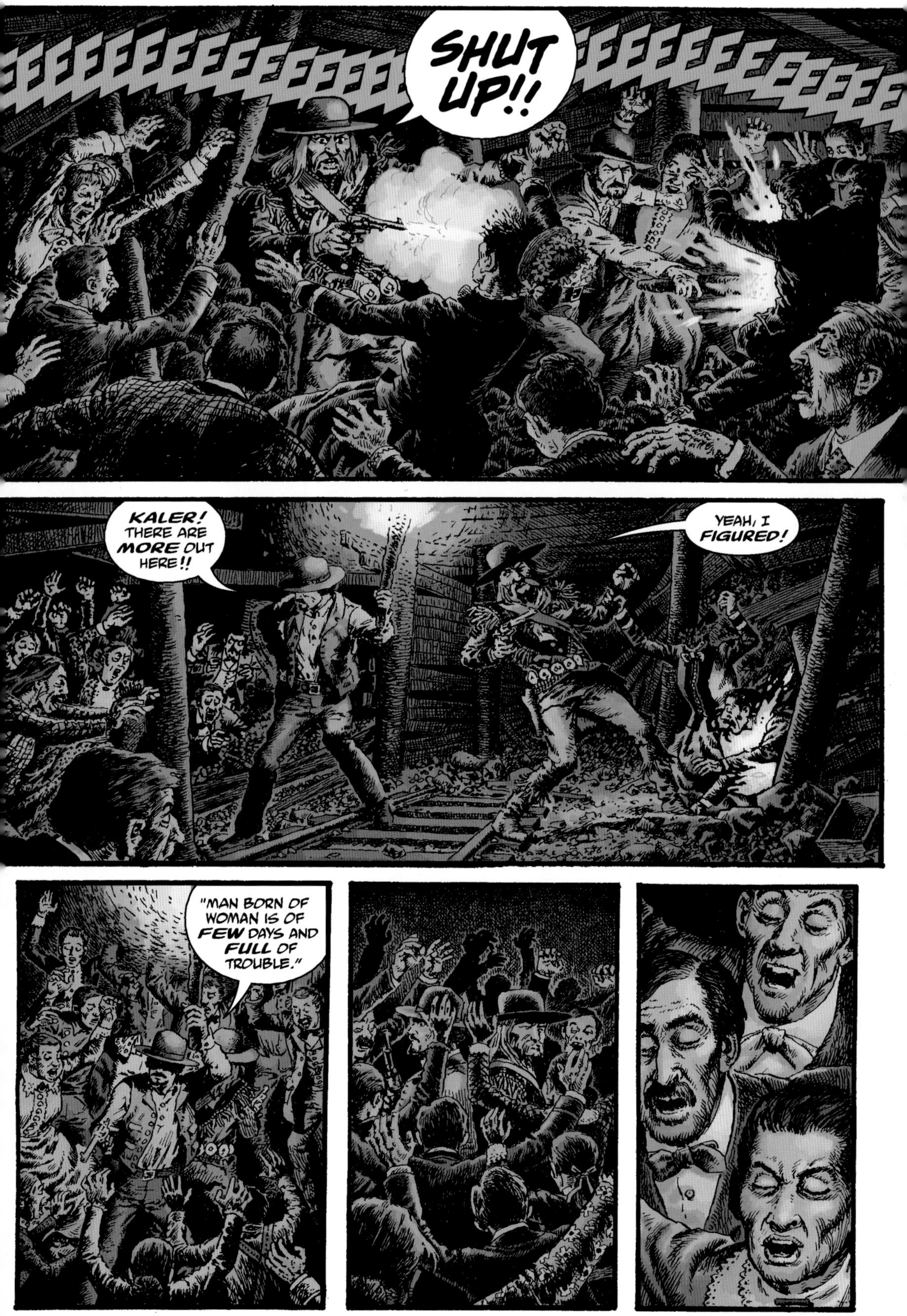
EEEEEEEEEEEEEEEEEEEEEEEEEEEEEE
SHUT UP!!
KALER! THERE ARE MORE OUT HERE!!
YEAH, I FIGURED!
"MAN BORN OF WOMAN IS OF FEW DAYS AND FULL OF TROUBLE."

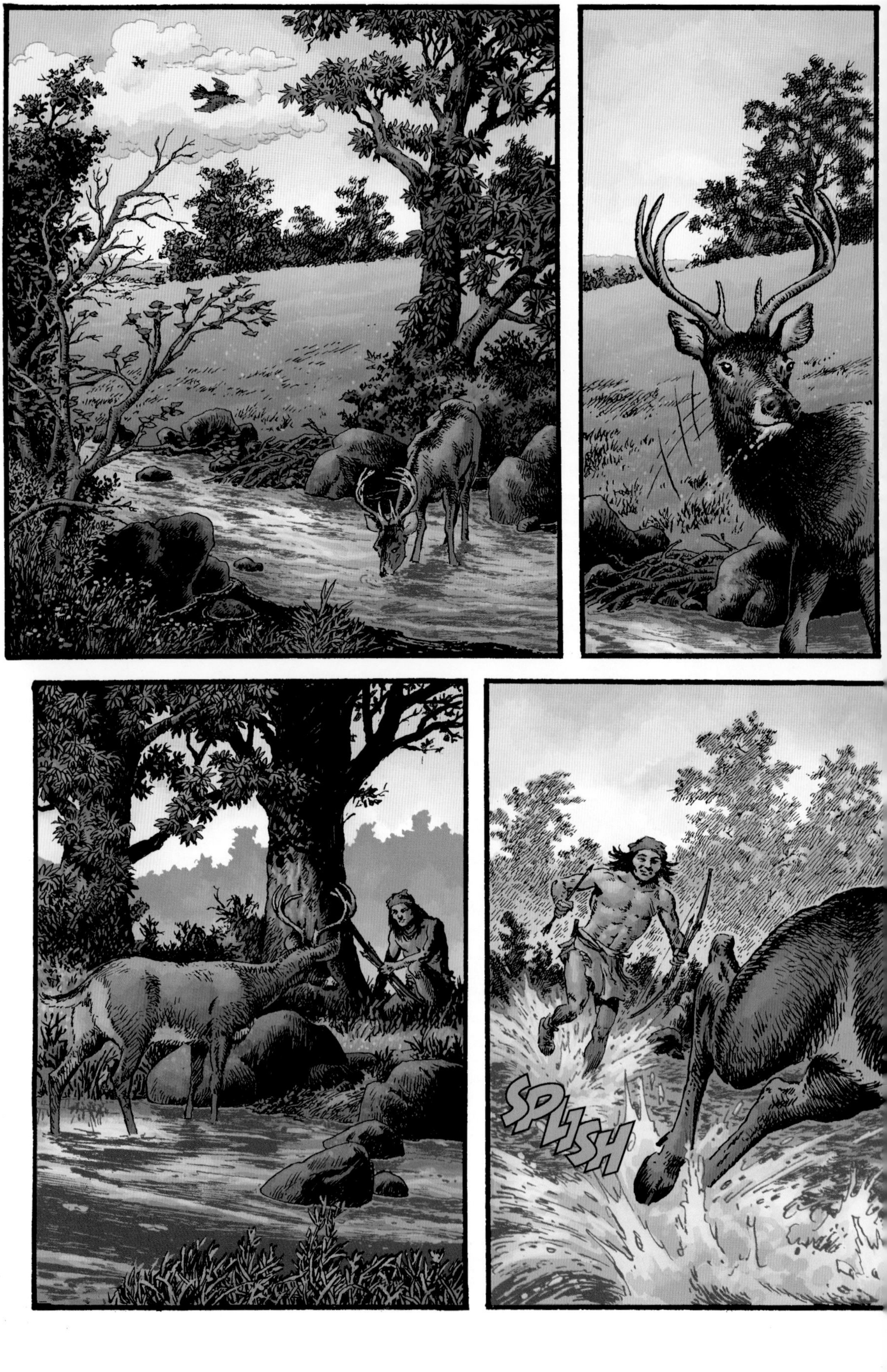
SPLISH

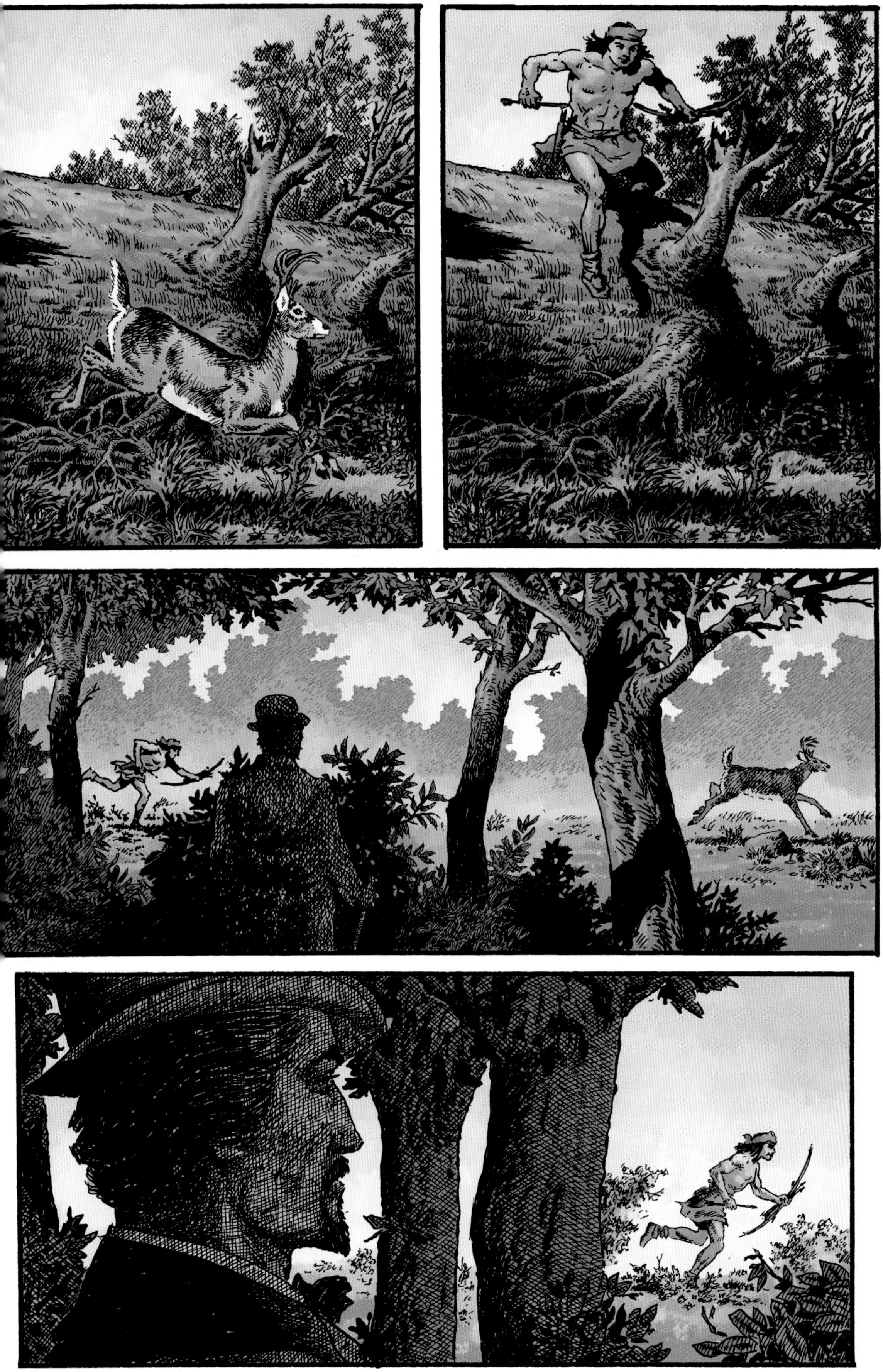

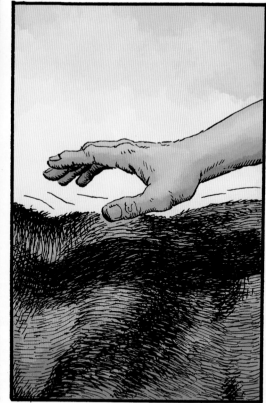
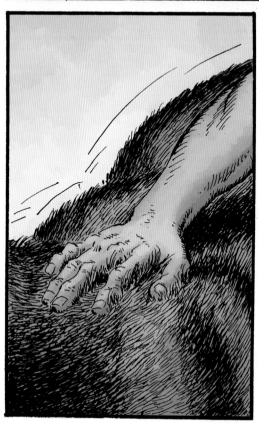

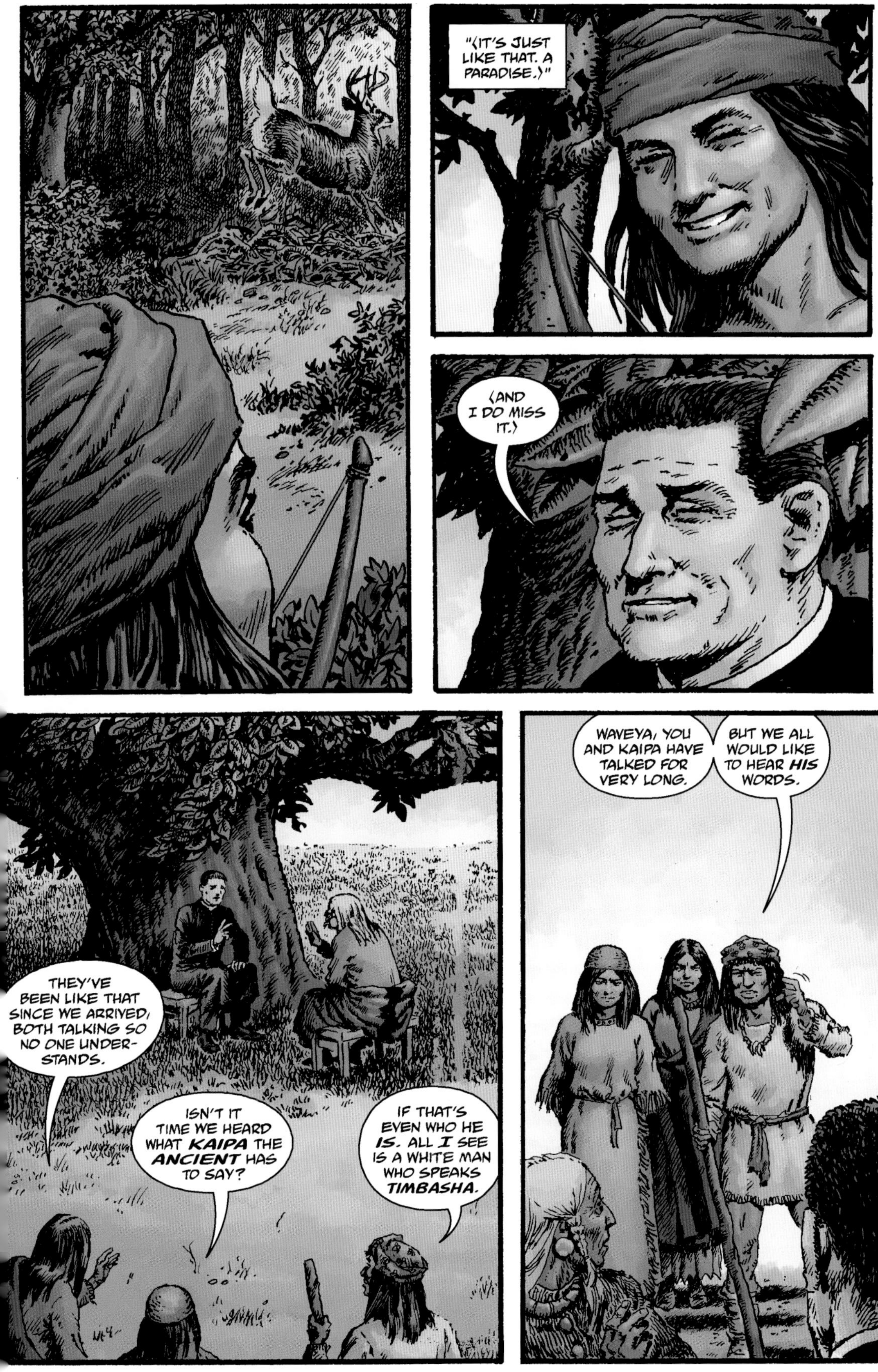
"⟨IT'S JUST LIKE THAT. A PARADISE.⟩"
⟨AND I DO MISS IT.⟩
THEY'VE BEEN LIKE THAT SINCE WE ARRIVED, BOTH TALKING SO NO ONE UNDERSTANDS.
ISN'T IT TIME WE HEARD WHAT KAIPA THE ANCIENT HAS TO SAY?
IF THAT'S EVEN WHO HE IS. ALL I SEE IS A WHITE MAN WHO SPEAKS TIMBASHA.
WAVEYA, YOU AND KAIPA HAVE TALKED FOR VERY LONG.
BUT WE ALL WOULD LIKE TO HEAR HIS WORDS.

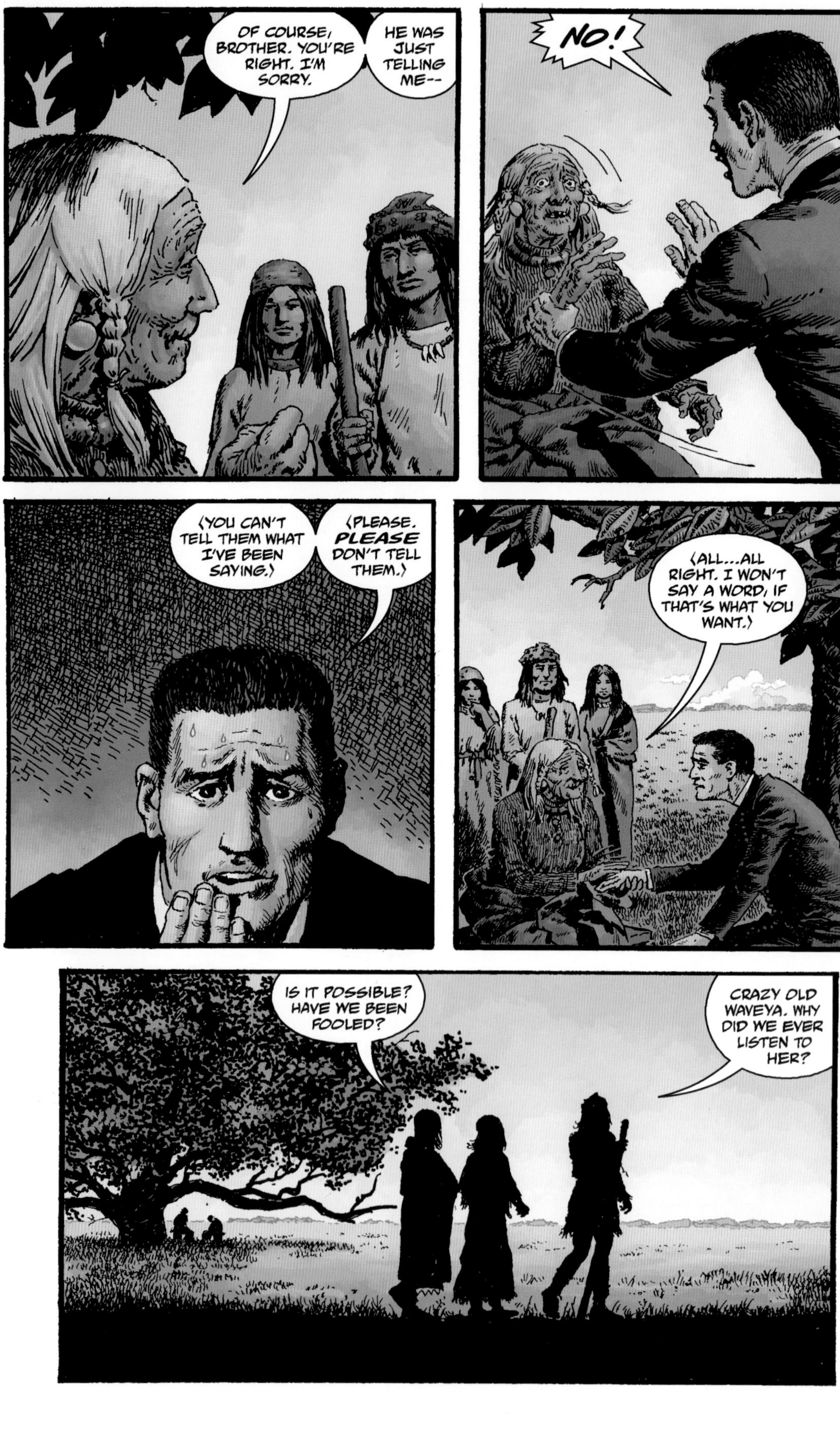
OF COURSE, BROTHER. YOU'RE RIGHT. I'M SORRY.
HE WAS JUST TELLING ME--
NO!
‹YOU CAN'T TELL THEM WHAT I'VE BEEN SAYING.›
‹PLEASE. **PLEASE** DON'T TELL THEM.›
‹ALL...ALL RIGHT. I WON'T SAY A WORD, IF THAT'S WHAT YOU WANT.›
IS IT POSSIBLE? HAVE WE BEEN FOOLED?
CRAZY OLD WAVEYA. WHY DID WE EVER LISTEN TO HER?

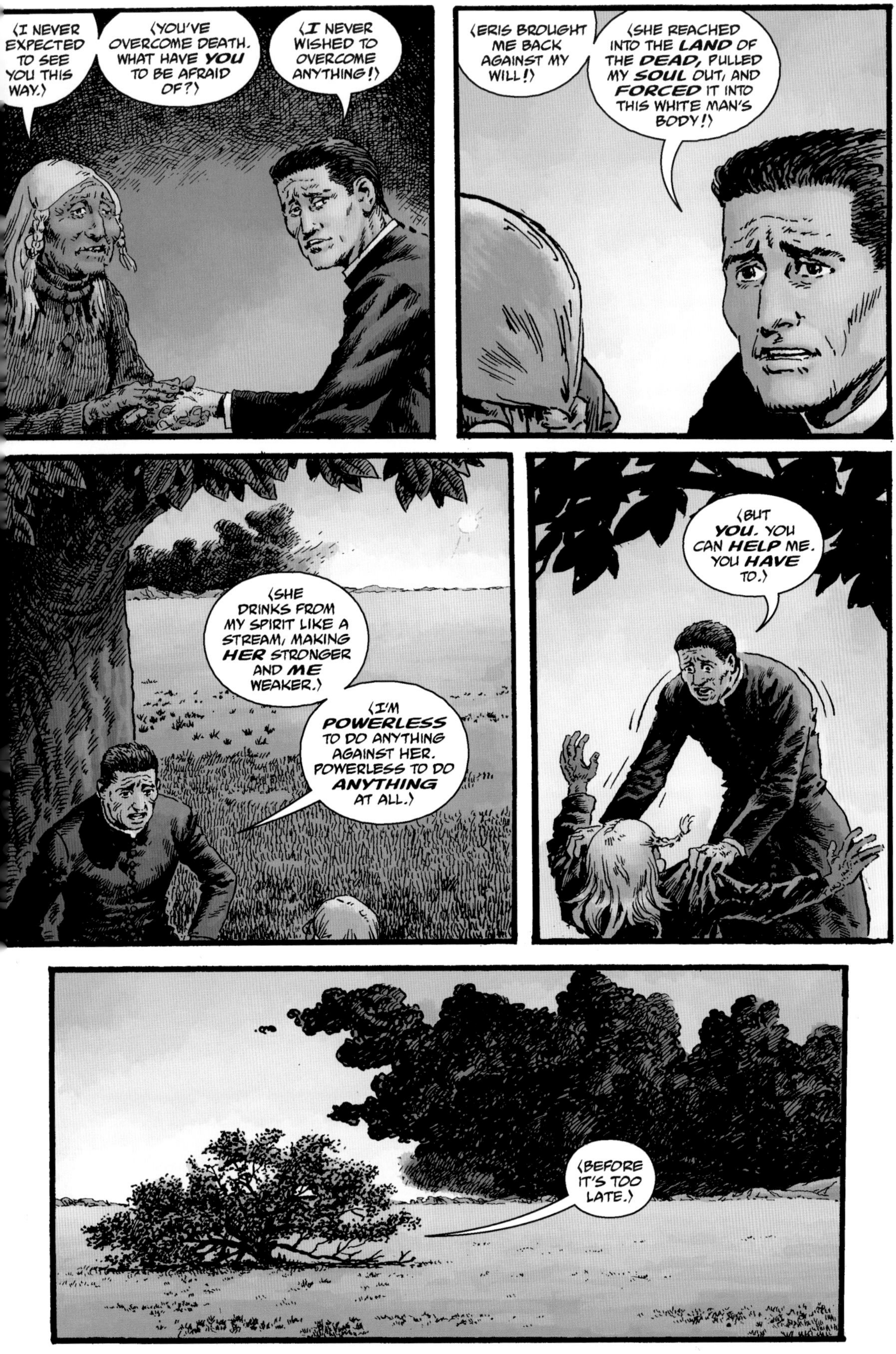
⟨I NEVER EXPECTED TO SEE YOU THIS WAY.⟩
⟨YOU'VE OVERCOME DEATH. WHAT HAVE **YOU** TO BE AFRAID OF?⟩
⟨**I** NEVER WISHED TO OVERCOME ANYTHING**!**⟩
⟨ERIS BROUGHT ME BACK AGAINST MY WILL**!**⟩
⟨SHE REACHED INTO THE **LAND** OF THE **DEAD,** PULLED MY **SOUL** OUT, AND **FORCED** IT INTO THIS WHITE MAN'S BODY**!**⟩
⟨SHE DRINKS FROM MY SPIRIT LIKE A STREAM, MAKING **HER** STRONGER AND **ME** WEAKER.⟩
⟨I'M **POWERLESS** TO DO ANYTHING AGAINST HER. POWERLESS TO DO **ANYTHING** AT ALL.⟩
⟨BUT **YOU.** YOU CAN **HELP** ME. YOU **HAVE** TO.⟩
⟨BEFORE IT'S TOO LATE.⟩

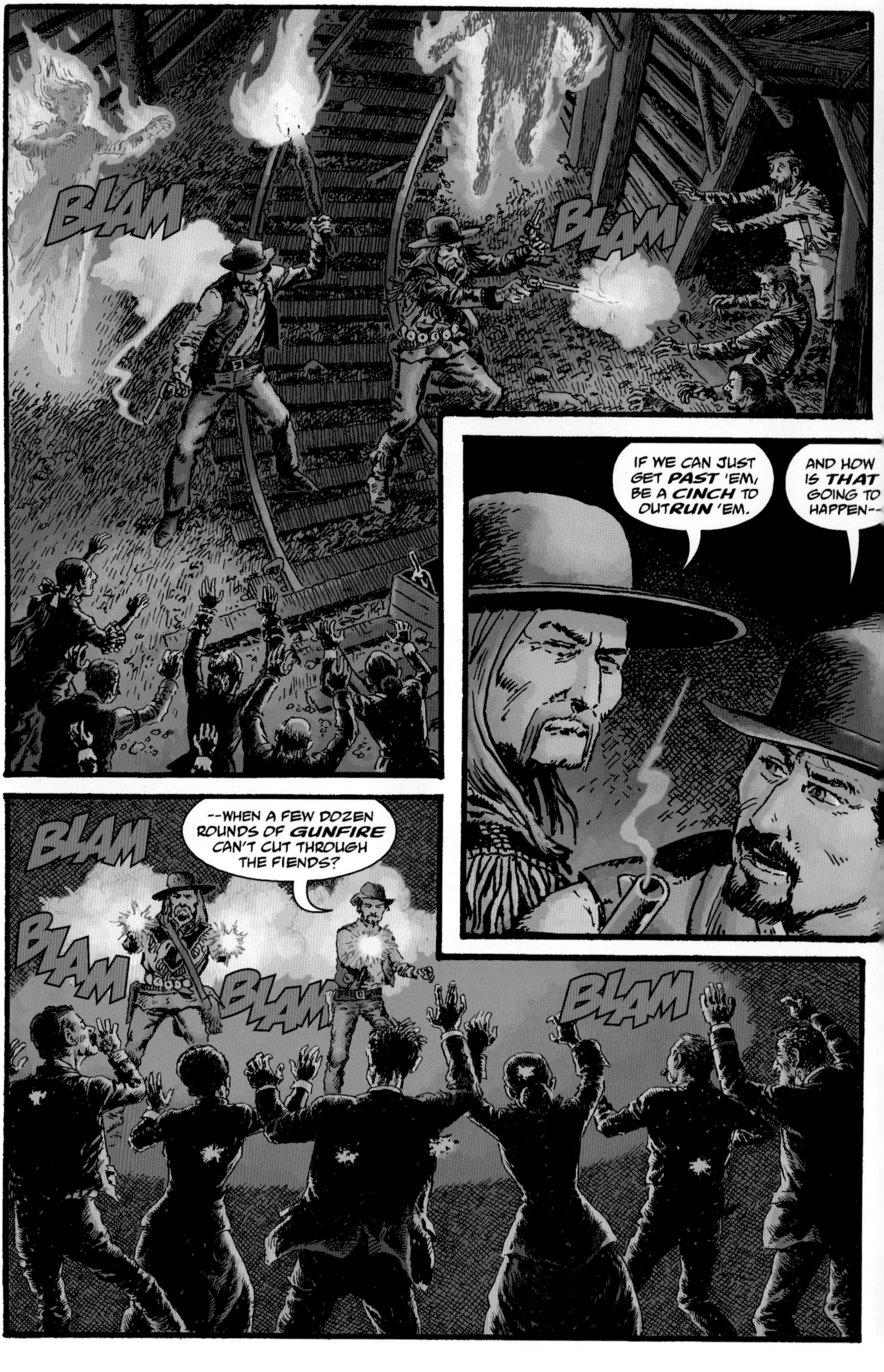
BLAM
BLAM
IF WE CAN JUST GET PAST 'EM, BE A CINCH TO OUTRUN 'EM.
AND HOW IS THAT GOING TO HAPPEN--
--WHEN A FEW DOZEN ROUNDS OF GUNFIRE CAN'T CUT THROUGH THE FIENDS?
BLAM
BLAM
BLAM
BLAM

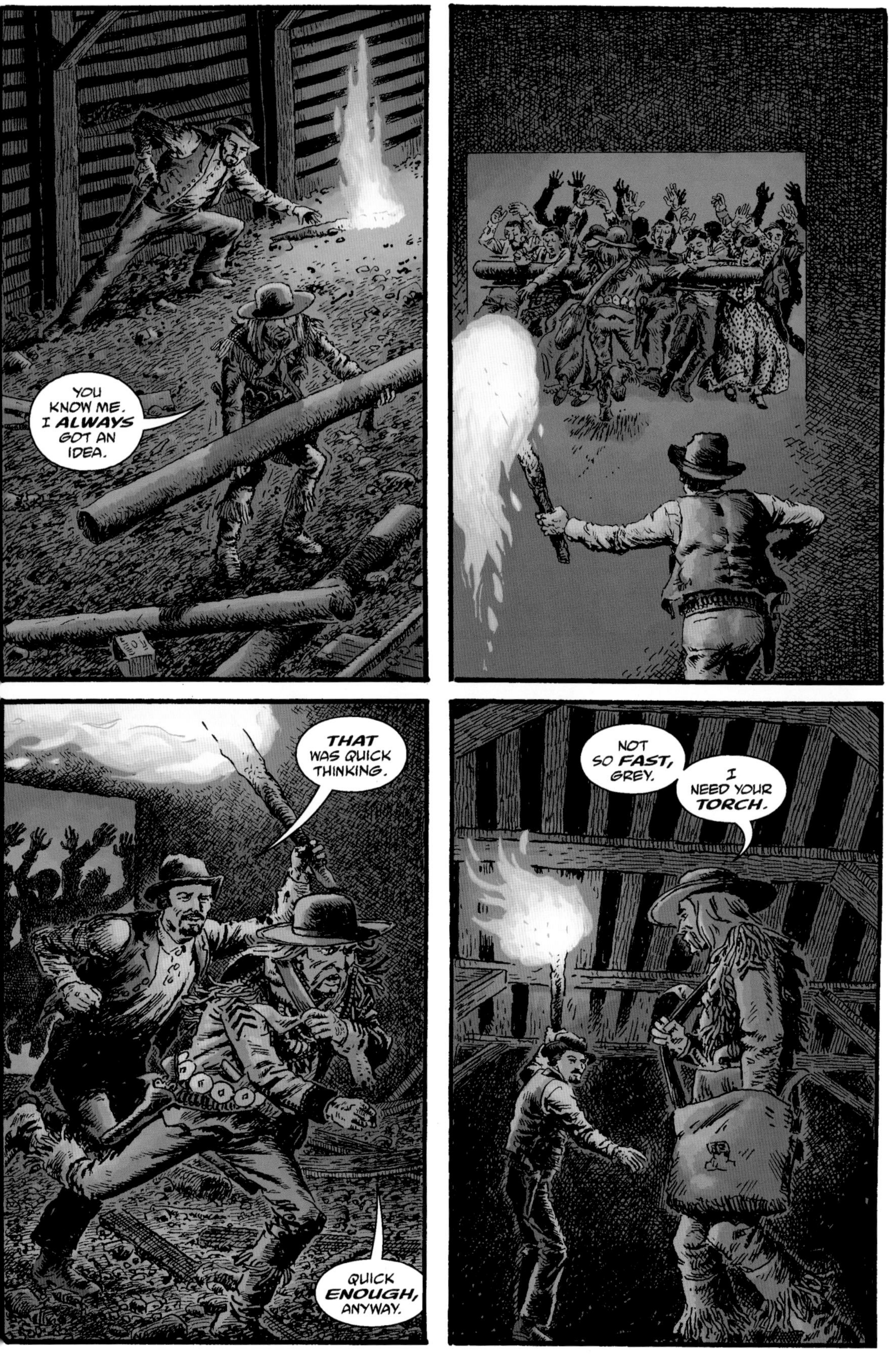
YOU KNOW ME. I ALWAYS GOT AN IDEA.
THAT WAS QUICK THINKING.
QUICK ENOUGH, ANYWAY.
NOT SO FAST, GREY.
I NEED YOUR TORCH.

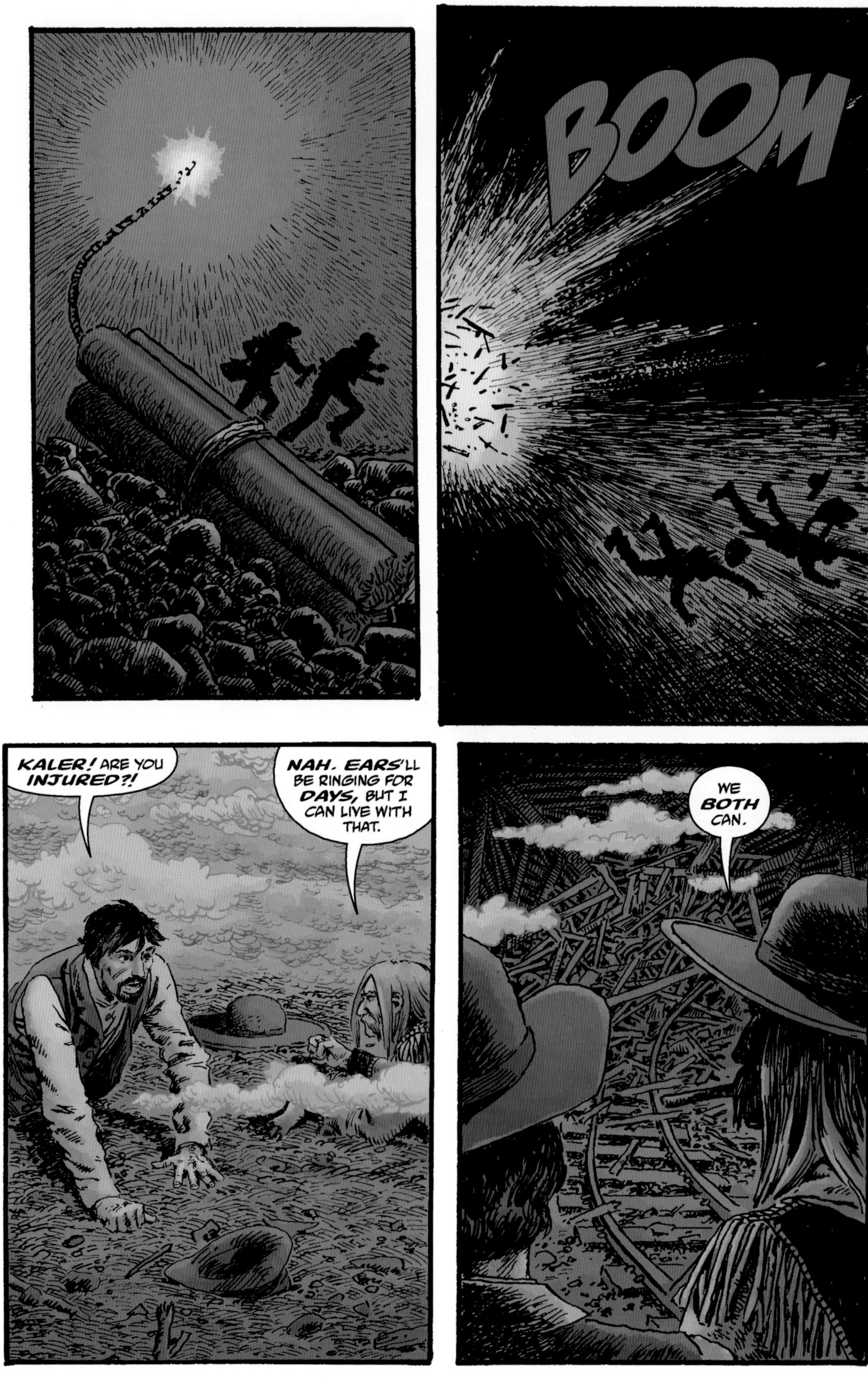
BOOM
KALER! ARE YOU INJURED?!
NAH. EARS'LL BE RINGING FOR DAYS, BUT I CAN LIVE WITH THAT.
WE BOTH CAN.

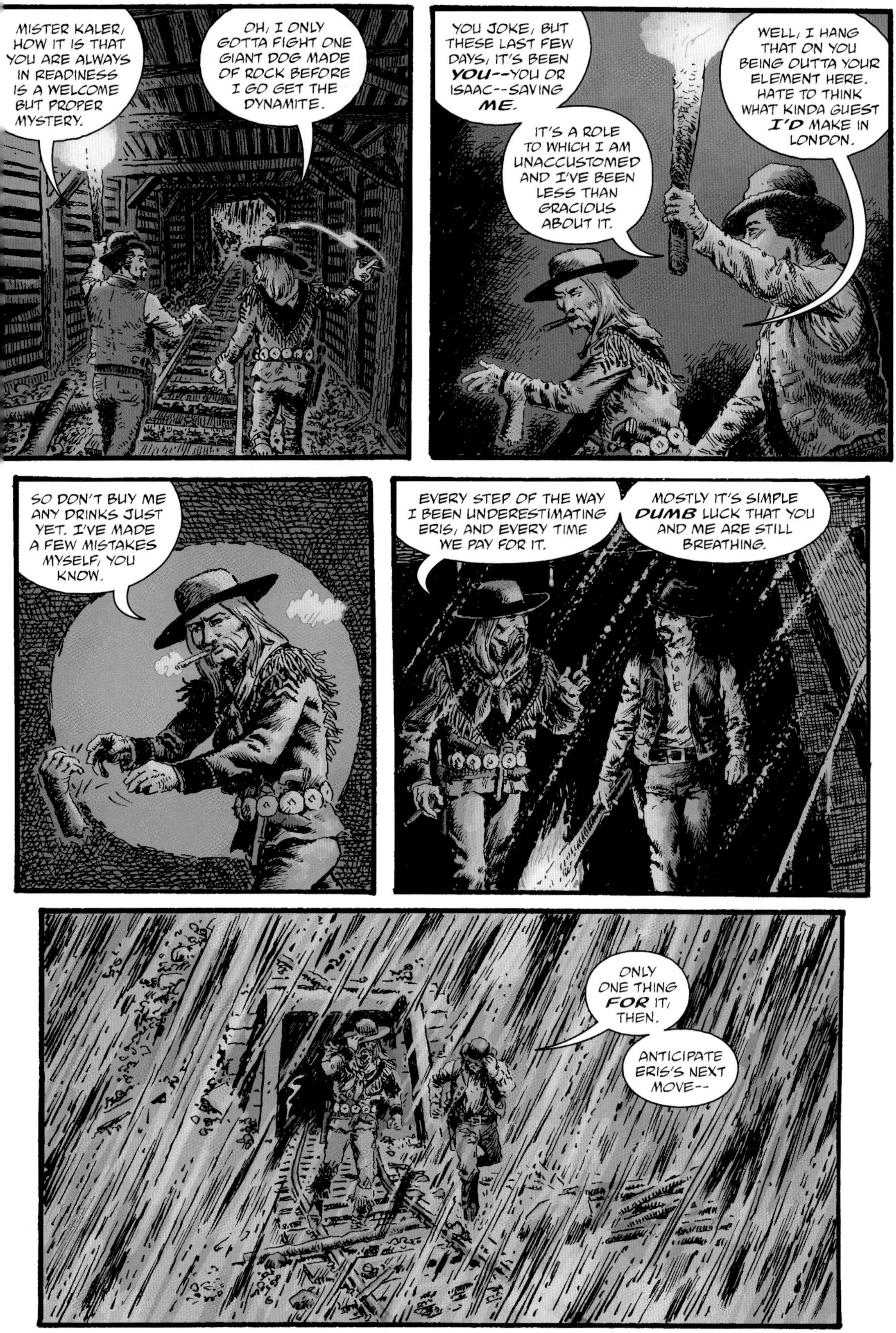
MISTER KALER, HOW IT IS THAT YOU ARE ALWAYS IN READINESS IS A WELCOME BUT PROPER MYSTERY.
OH, I ONLY GOTTA FIGHT ONE GIANT DOG MADE OF ROCK BEFORE I GO GET THE DYNAMITE.
YOU JOKE, BUT THESE LAST FEW DAYS, IT'S BEEN YOU--YOU OR ISAAC--SAVING ME.
IT'S A ROLE TO WHICH I AM UNACCUSTOMED AND I'VE BEEN LESS THAN GRACIOUS ABOUT IT.
WELL, I HANG THAT ON YOU BEING OUTTA YOUR ELEMENT HERE. HATE TO THINK WHAT KINDA GUEST I'D MAKE IN LONDON.
SO DON'T BUY ME ANY DRINKS JUST YET. I'VE MADE A FEW MISTAKES MYSELF, YOU KNOW.
EVERY STEP OF THE WAY I BEEN UNDERESTIMATING ERIS, AND EVERY TIME WE PAY FOR IT.
MOSTLY IT'S SIMPLE DUMB LUCK THAT YOU AND ME ARE STILL BREATHING.
ONLY ONE THING FOR IT, THEN.
ANTICIPATE ERIS'S NEXT MOVE--

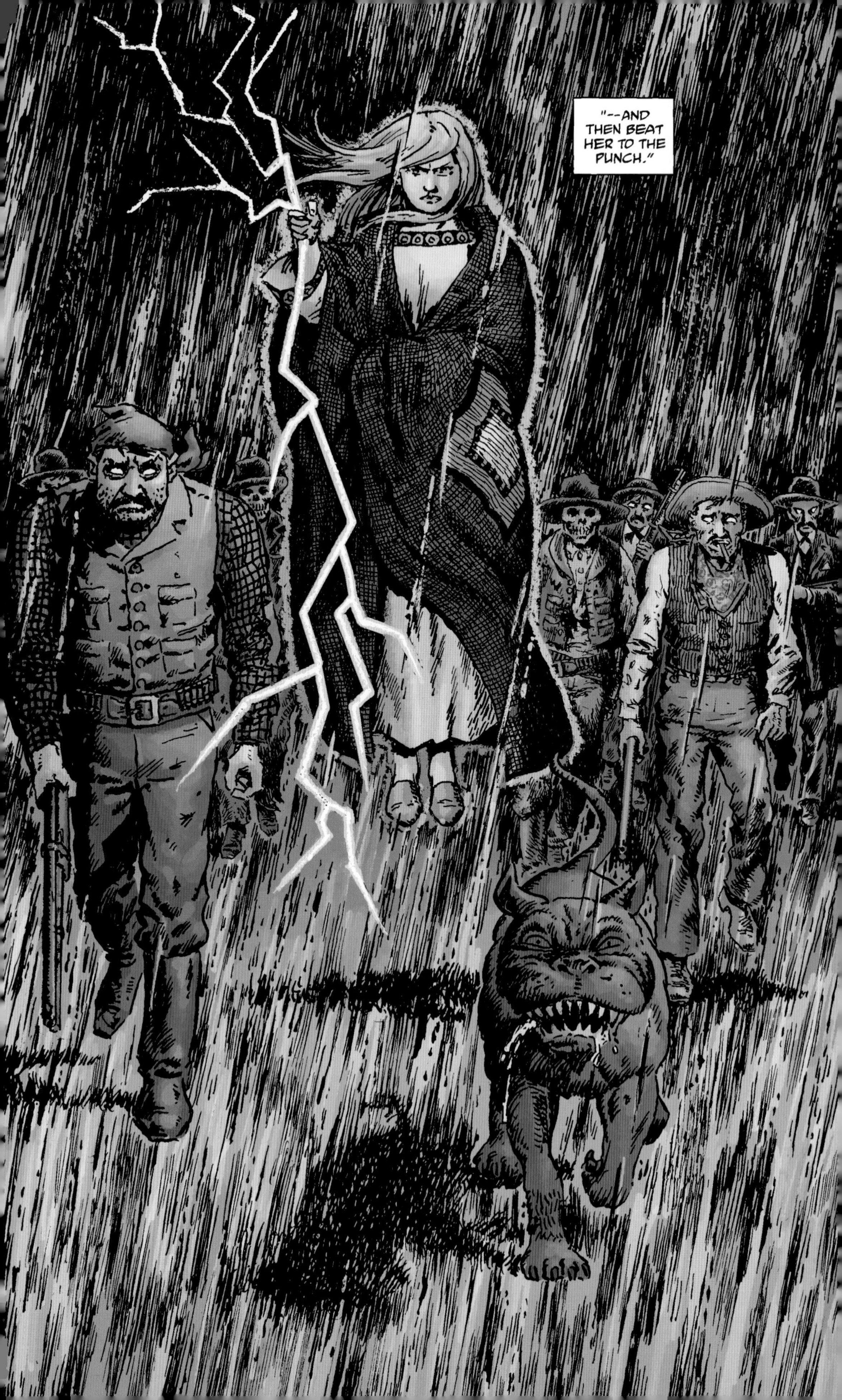
"--AND THEN BEAT HER TO THE PUNCH."

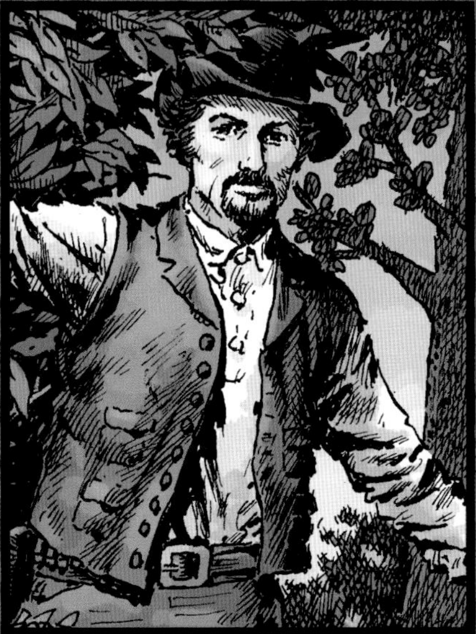

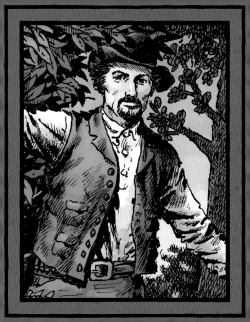

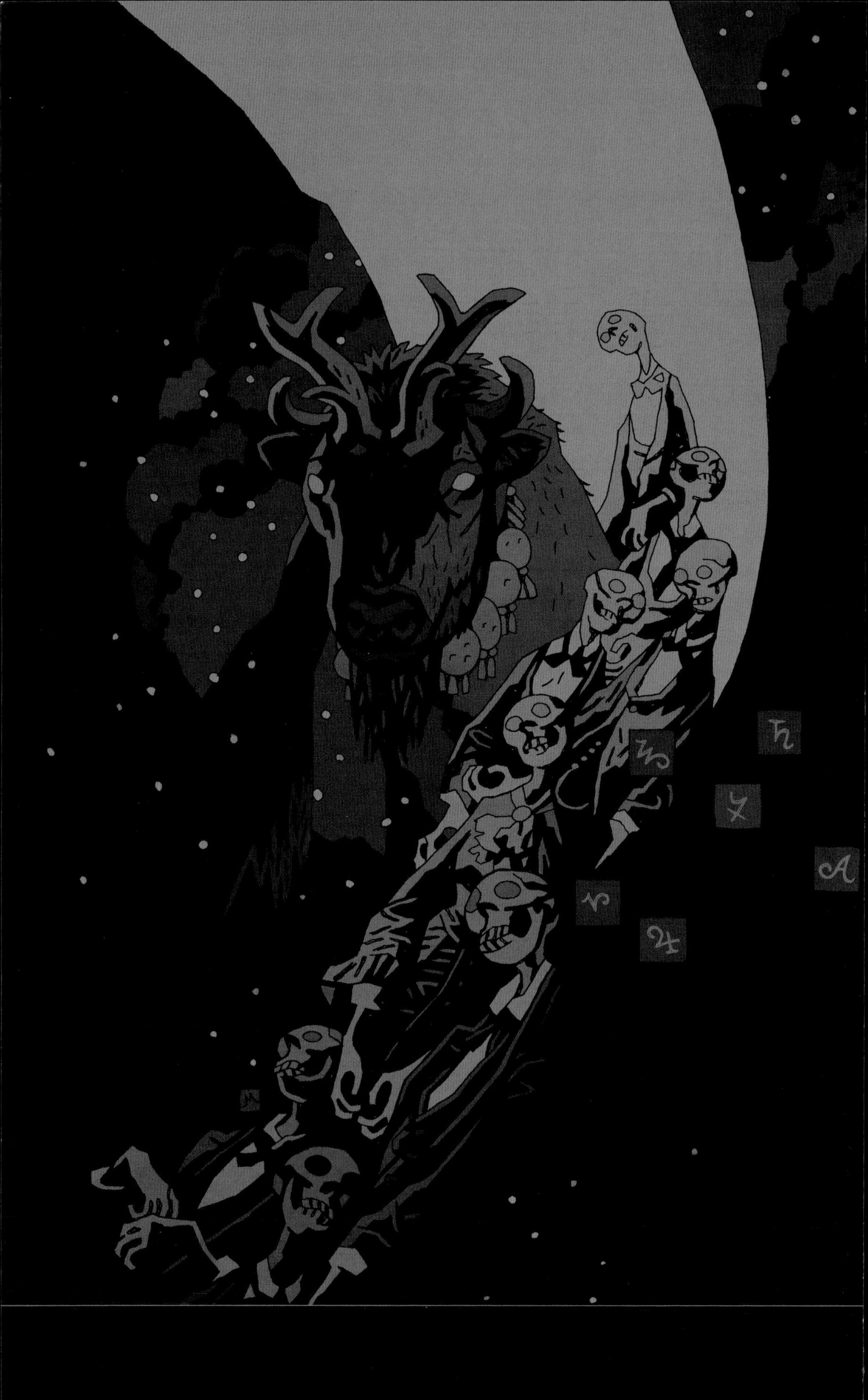

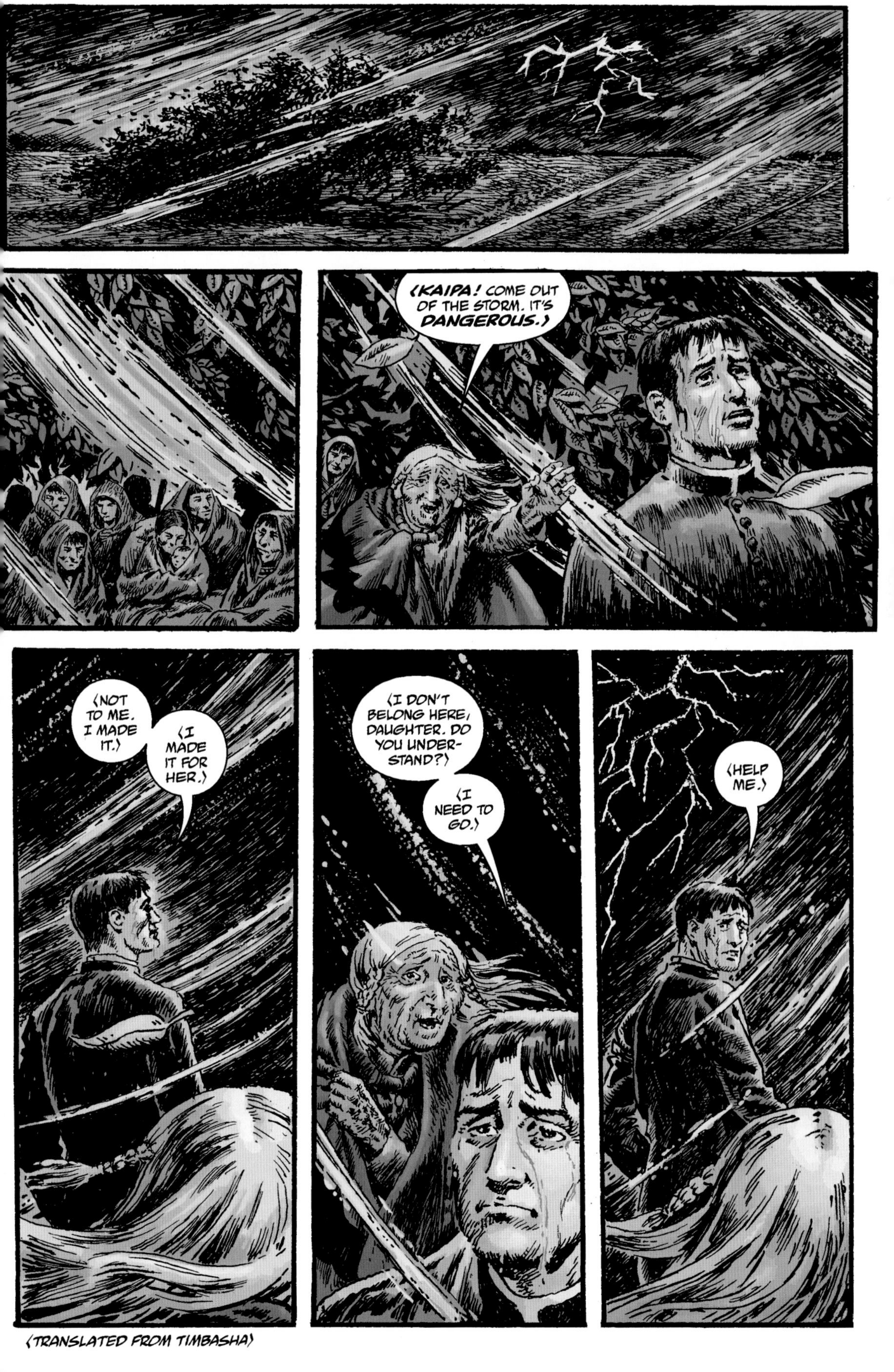
‹KAIPA! COME OUT OF THE STORM. IT'S DANGEROUS.›
‹NOT TO ME. I MADE IT.›
‹I MADE IT FOR HER.›
‹I DON'T BELONG HERE, DAUGHTER. DO YOU UNDER-STAND?›
‹I NEED TO GO.›
‹HELP ME.›

‹TRANSLATED FROM TIMBASHA›

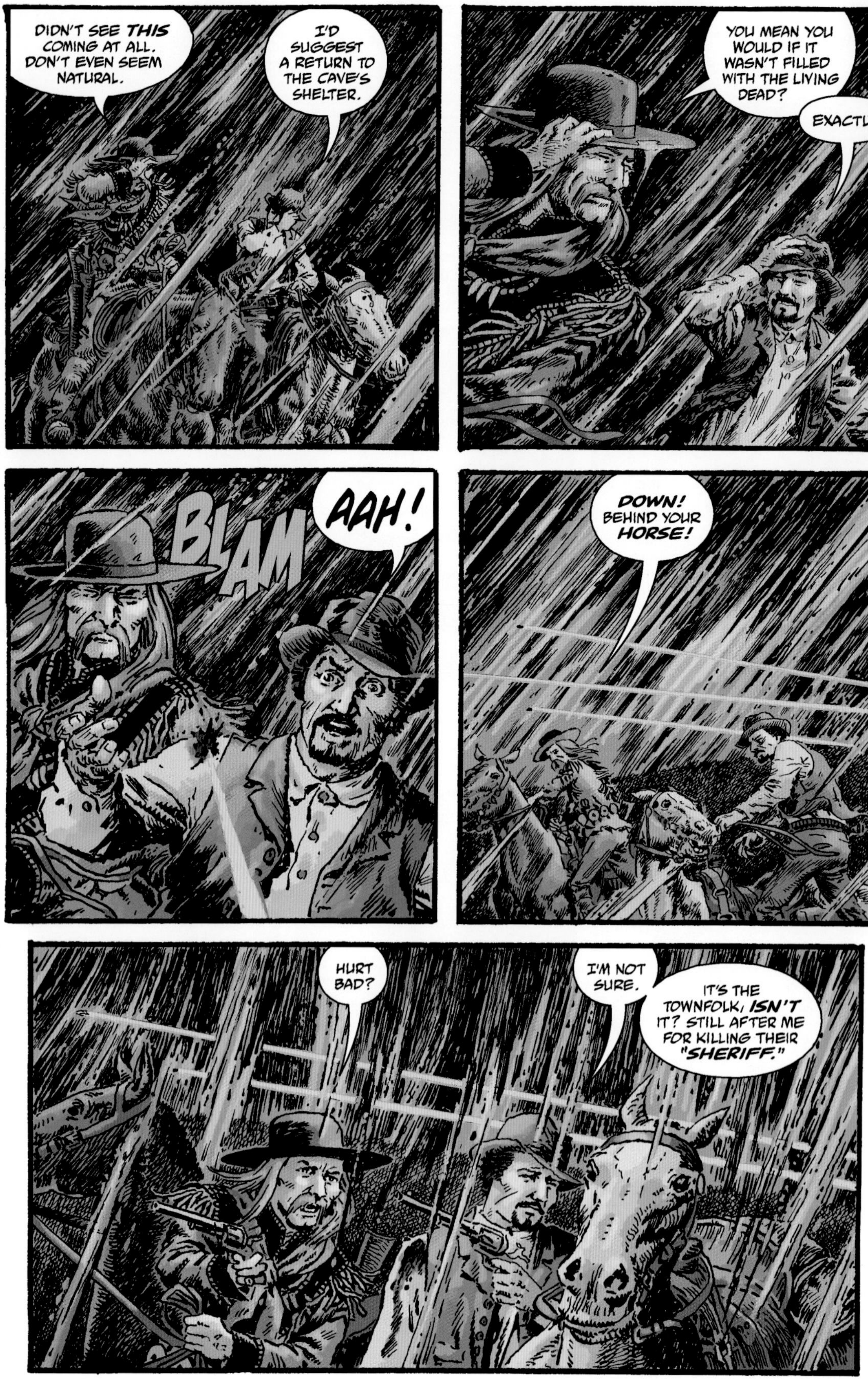
DIDN'T SEE THIS COMING AT ALL. DON'T EVEN SEEM NATURAL.
I'D SUGGEST A RETURN TO THE CAVE'S SHELTER.
YOU MEAN YOU WOULD IF IT WASN'T FILLED WITH THE LIVING DEAD?
EXACTLY.
BLAM
AAH!
DOWN! BEHIND YOUR HORSE!
HURT BAD?
I'M NOT SURE.
IT'S THE TOWNFOLK, ISN'T IT? STILL AFTER ME FOR KILLING THEIR "SHERIFF."

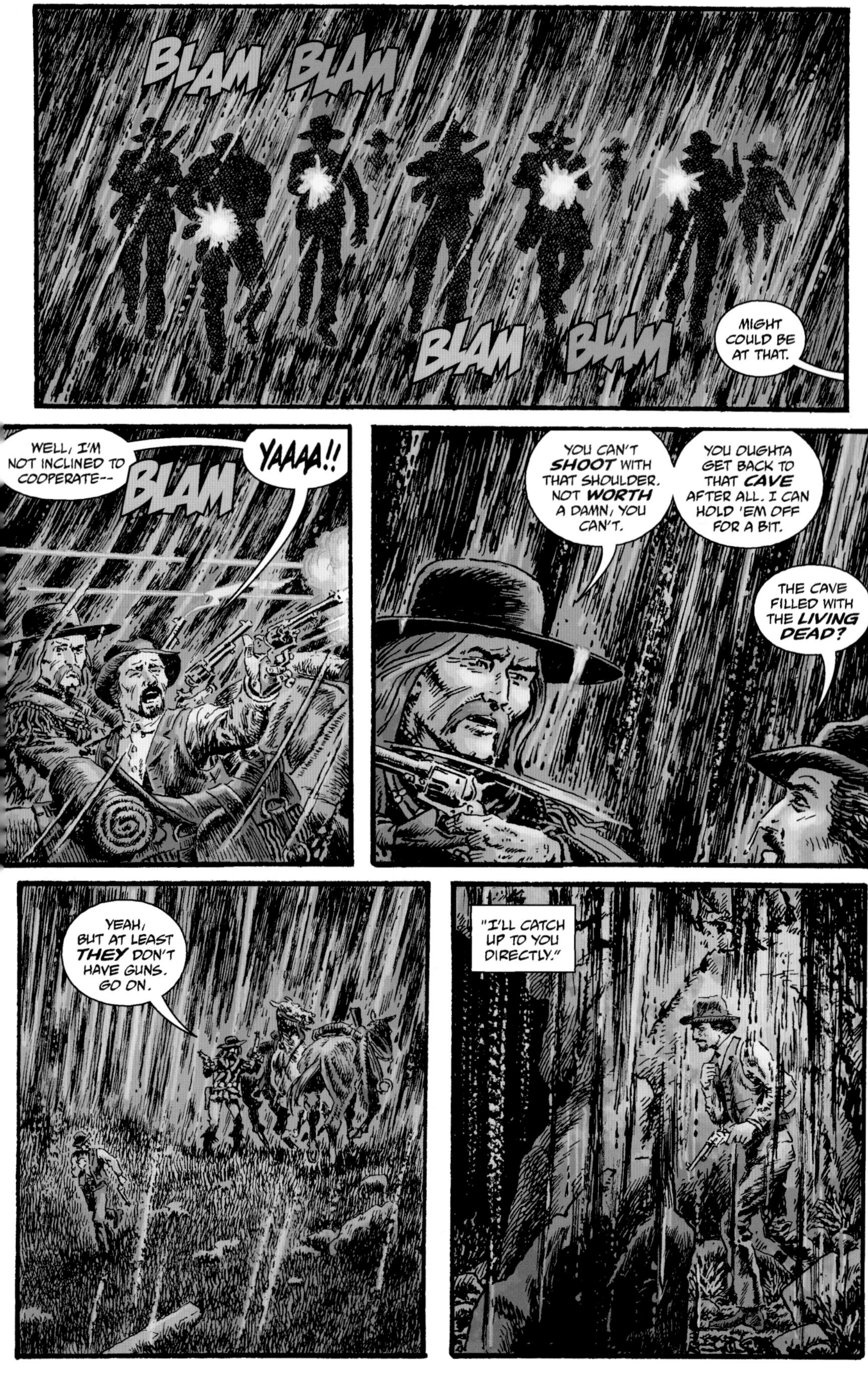
BLAM BLAM
BLAM BLAM
MIGHT COULD BE AT THAT.
WELL, I'M NOT INCLINED TO COOPERATE--
BLAM
YAAAA!!
YOU CAN'T SHOOT WITH THAT SHOULDER. NOT WORTH A DAMN, YOU CAN'T.
YOU OUGHTA GET BACK TO THAT CAVE AFTER ALL. I CAN HOLD 'EM OFF FOR A BIT.
THE CAVE FILLED WITH THE LIVING DEAD?
YEAH, BUT AT LEAST THEY DON'T HAVE GUNS. GO ON.
"I'LL CATCH UP TO YOU DIRECTLY."

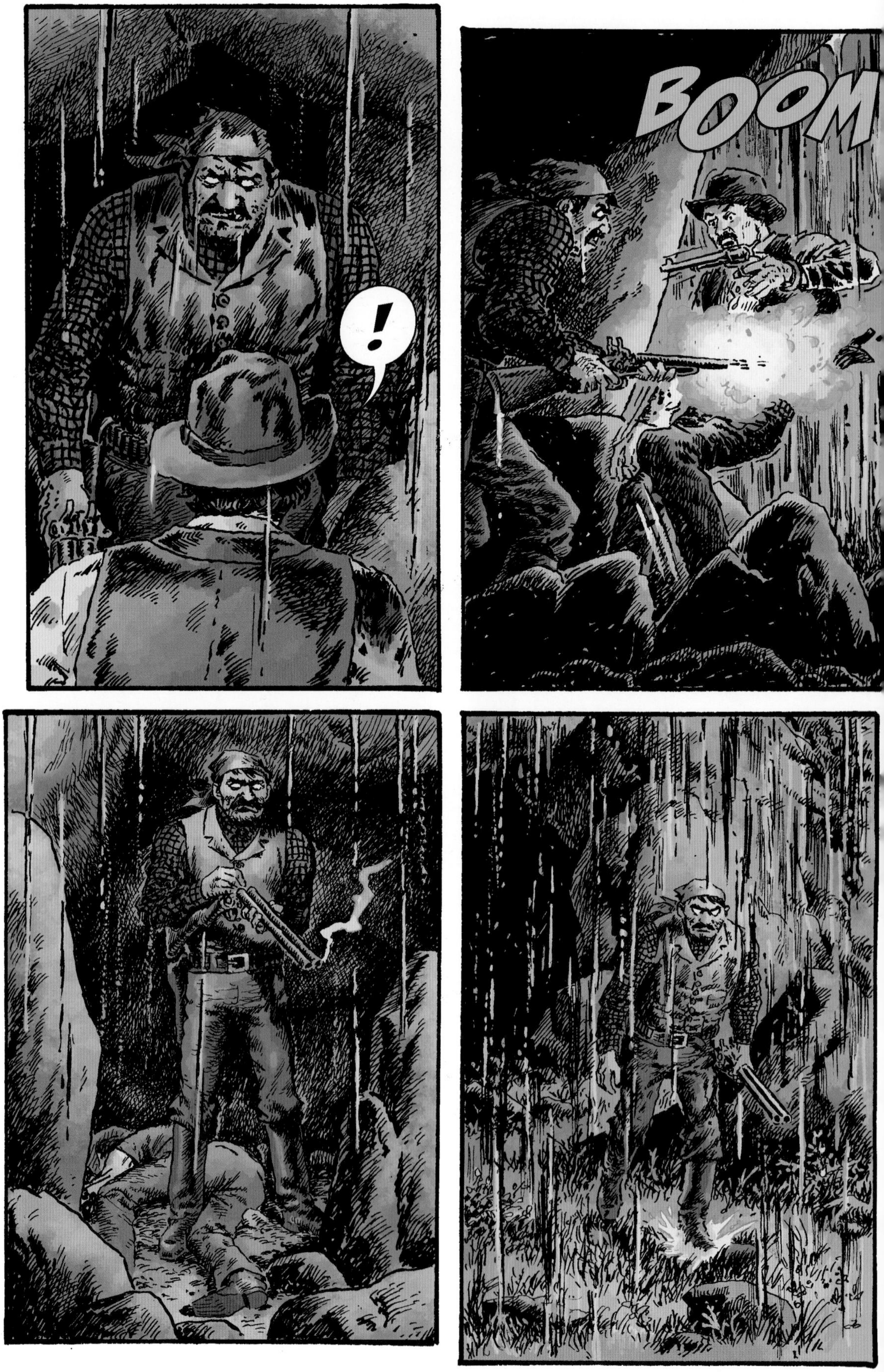
!
BOOM

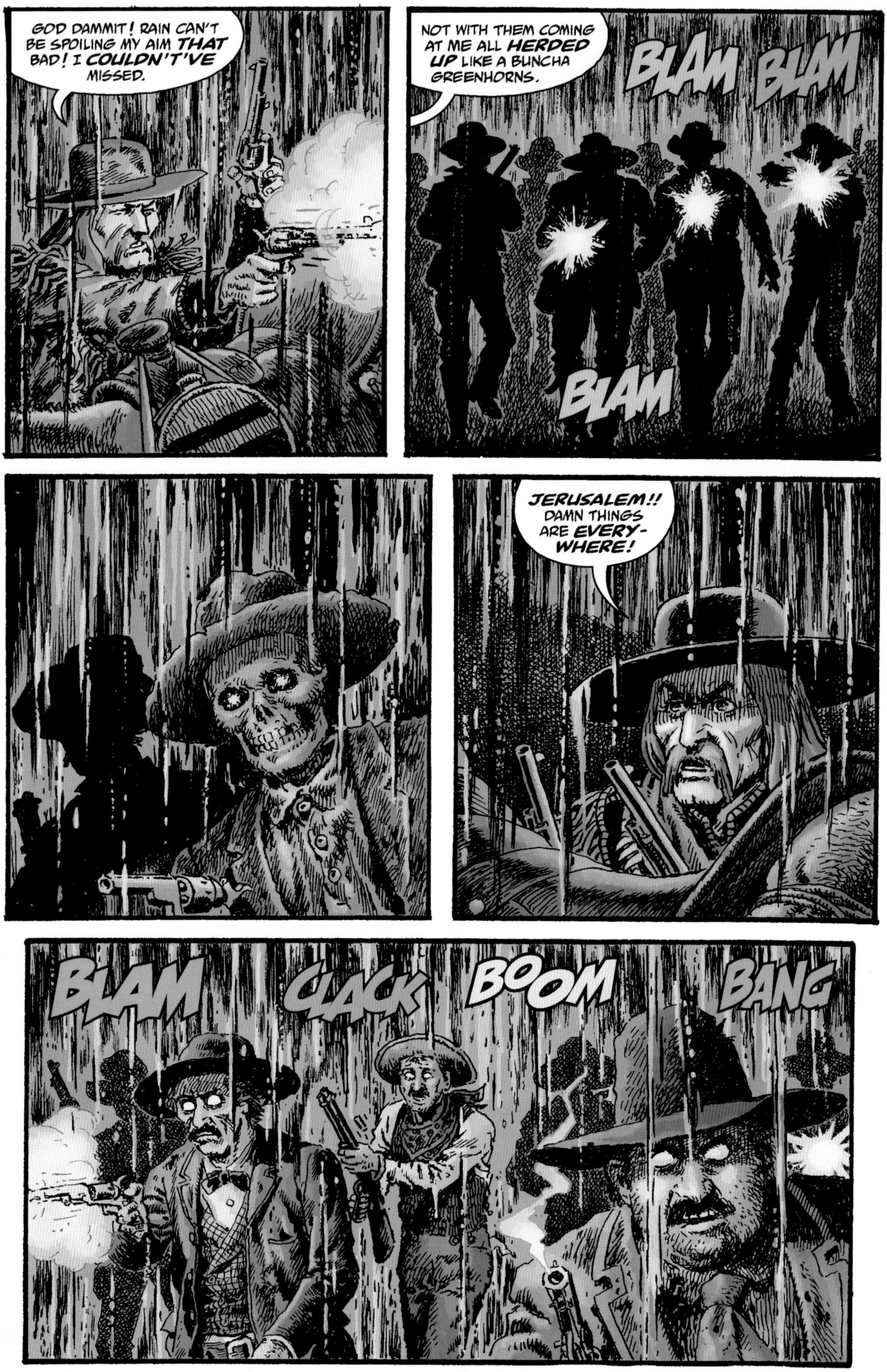
GOD DAMMIT! RAIN CAN'T BE SPOILING MY AIM THAT BAD! I COULDN'T'VE MISSED.
NOT WITH THEM COMING AT ME ALL HERDED UP LIKE A BUNCHA GREENHORNS.
BLAM BLAM
BLAM
JERUSALEM!! DAMN THINGS ARE EVERY-WHERE!
BLAM
CLACK
BOOM
BANG

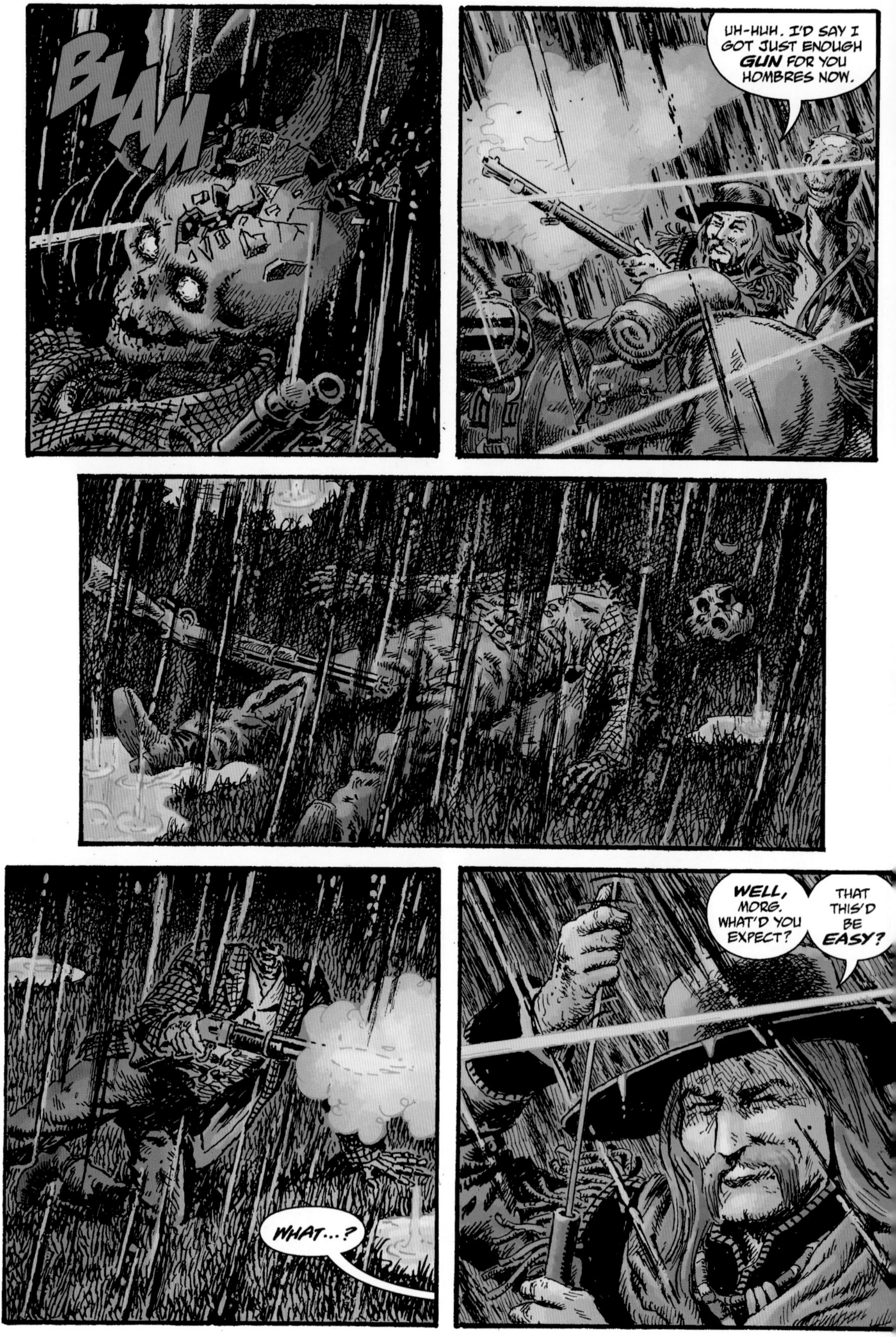
BLAM
UH-HUH. I'D SAY I GOT JUST ENOUGH GUN FOR YOU HOMBRES NOW.
WHAT...?
WELL, MORG. WHAT'D YOU EXPECT?
THAT THIS'D BE EASY?

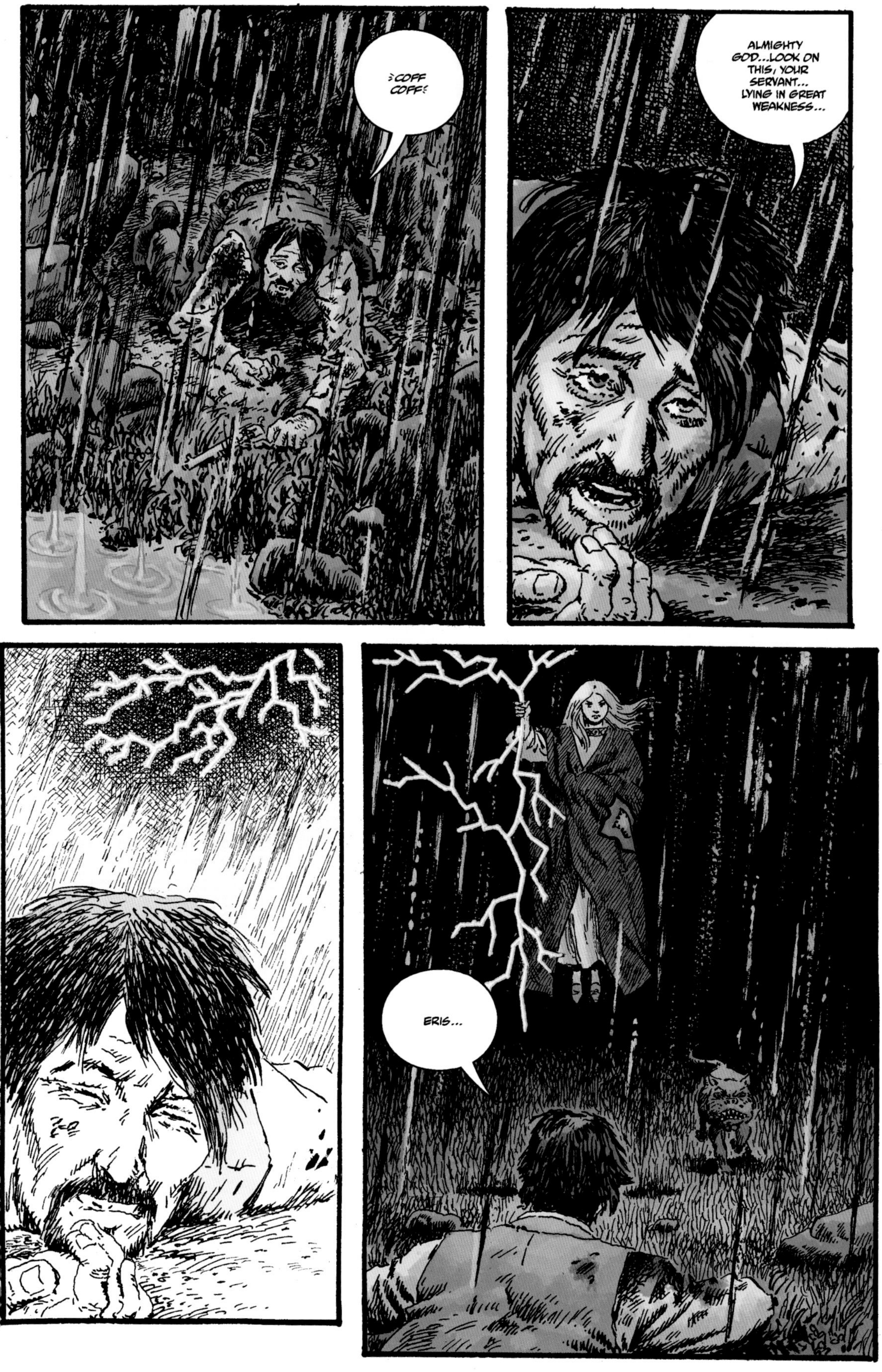

COFF COFF
ALMIGHTY GOD...LOOK ON THIS, YOUR SERVANT... LYING IN GREAT WEAKNESS...
ERIS...

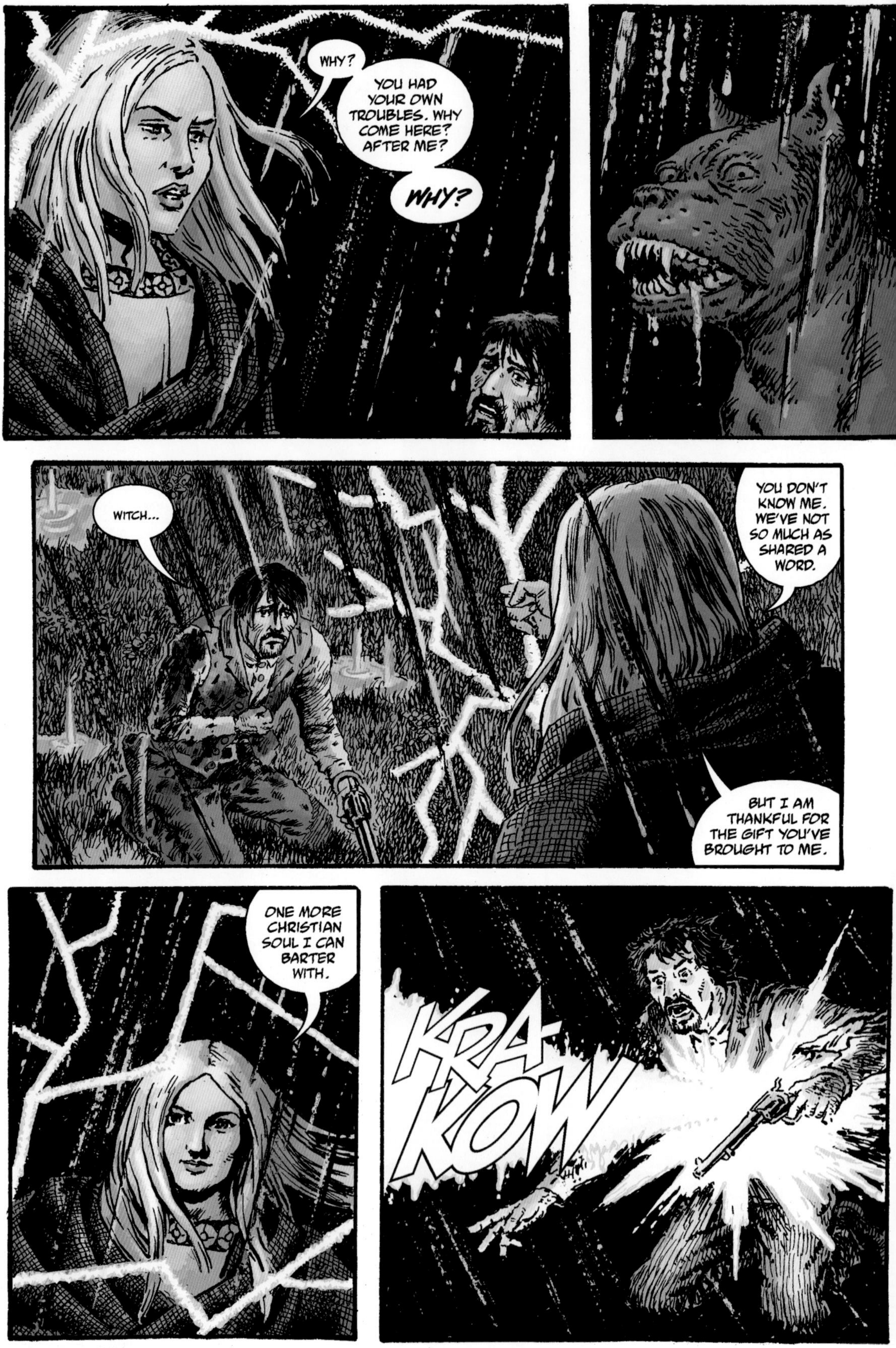
WHY?
YOU HAD YOUR OWN TROUBLES. WHY COME HERE? AFTER ME?
WHY?
WITCH...
YOU DON'T KNOW ME. WE'VE NOT SO MUCH AS SHARED A WORD.
BUT I AM THANKFUL FOR THE GIFT YOU'VE BROUGHT TO ME.
ONE MORE CHRISTIAN SOUL I CAN BARTER WITH.
KRA-KOW

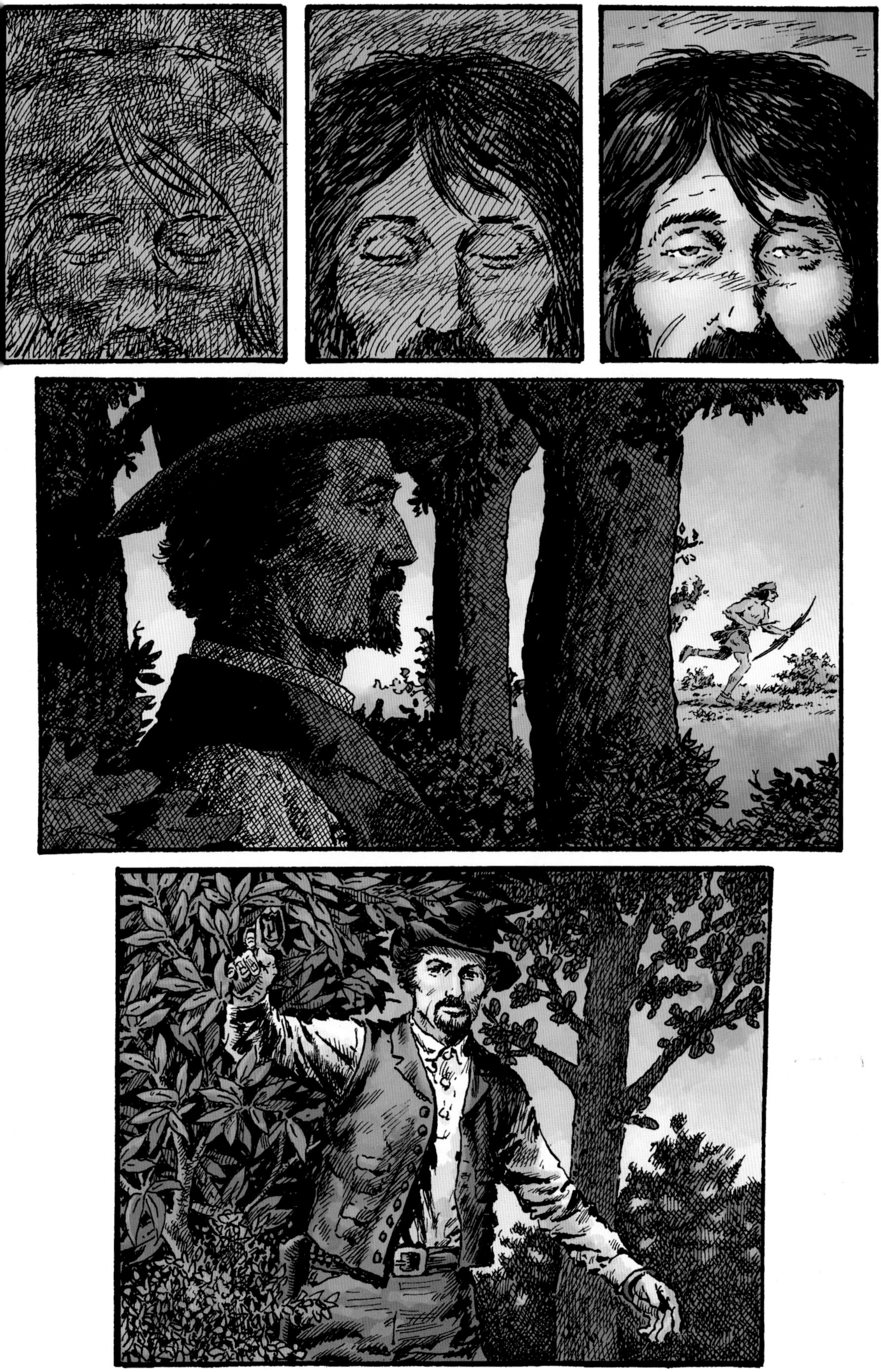

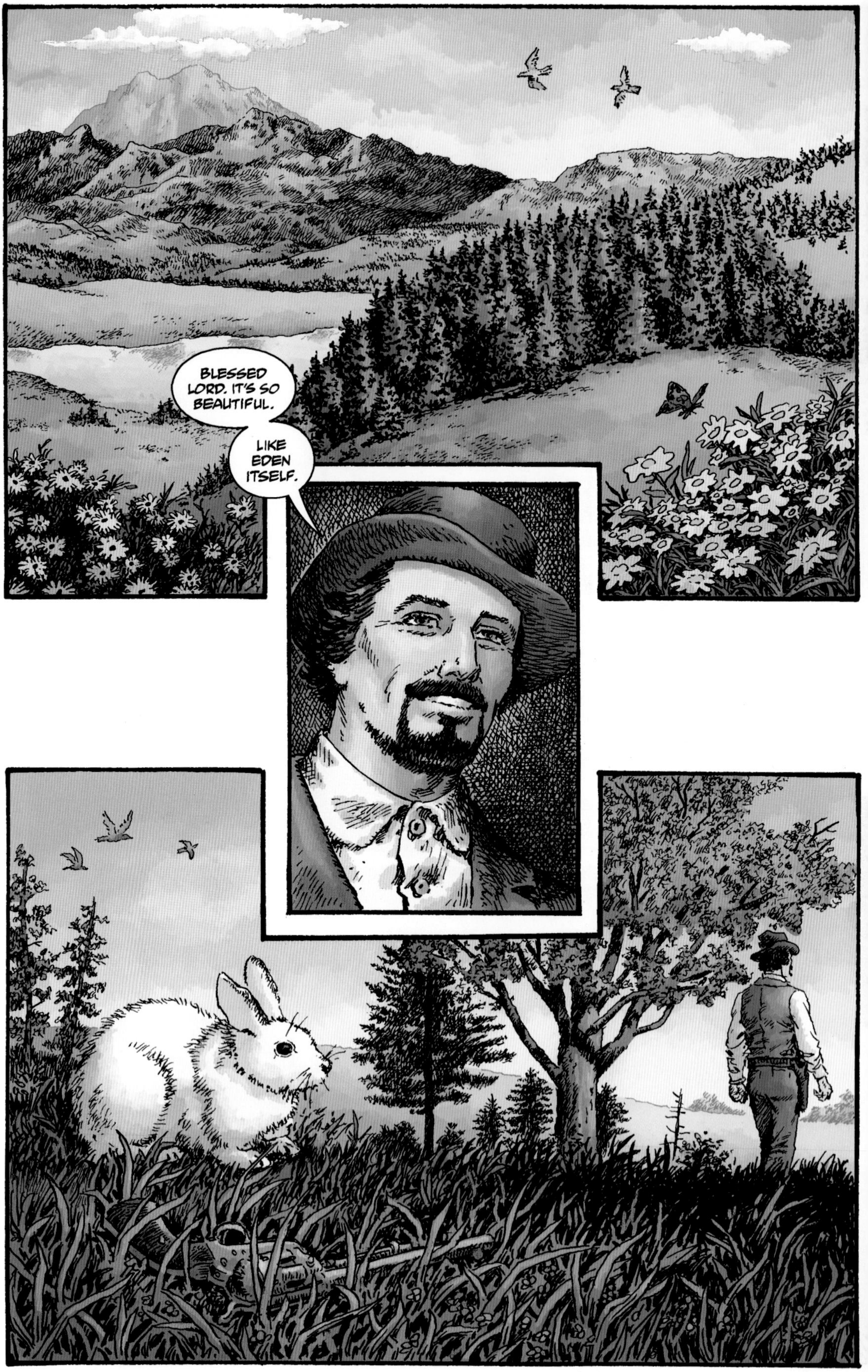
BLESSED LORD. IT'S SO BEAUTIFUL.
LIKE EDEN ITSELF.

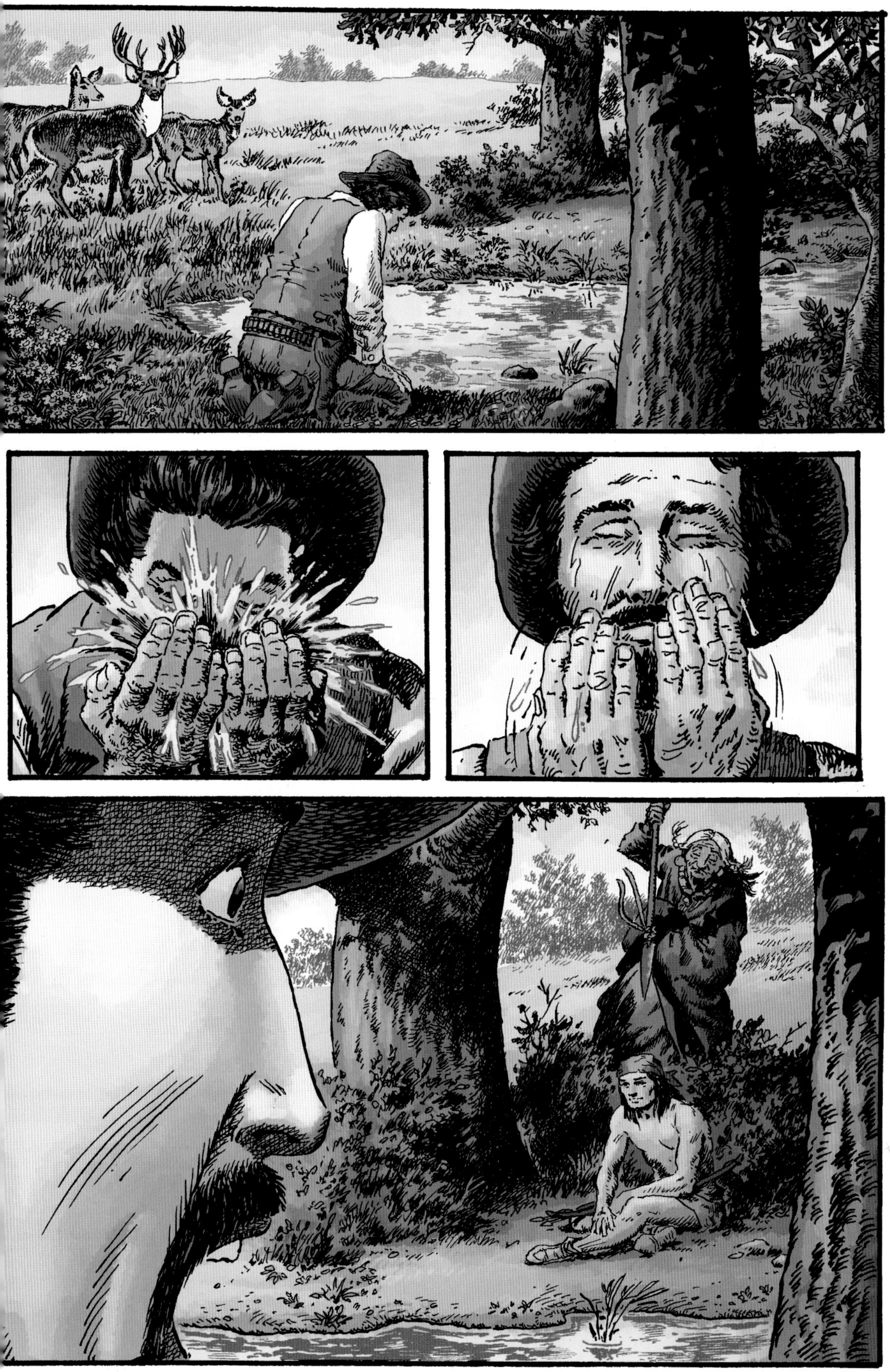

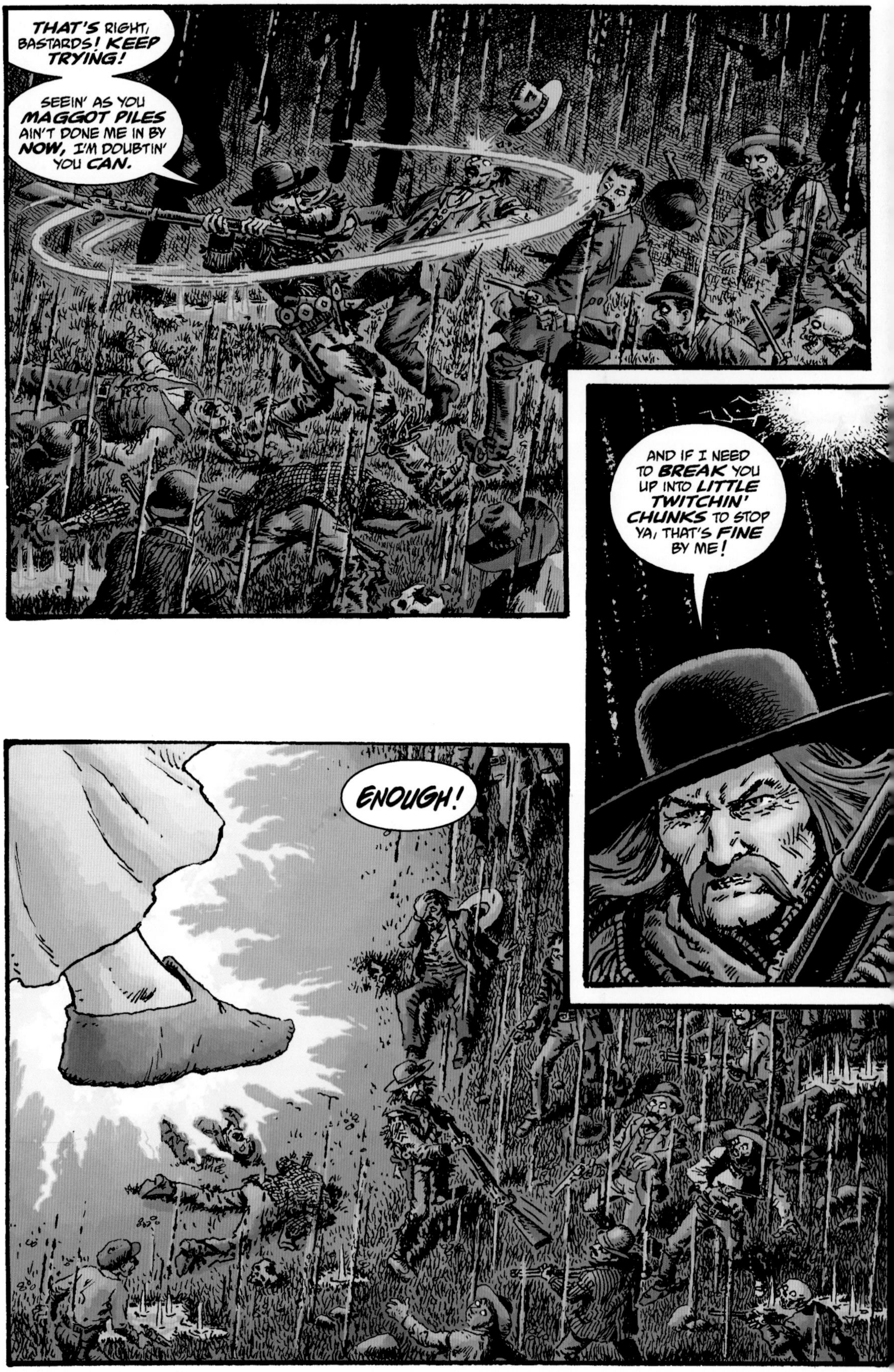
THAT'S RIGHT, BASTARDS! KEEP TRYING!
SEEIN' AS YOU MAGGOT PILES AIN'T DONE ME IN BY NOW, I'M DOUBTIN' YOU CAN.
AND IF I NEED TO BREAK YOU UP INTO LITTLE TWITCHIN' CHUNKS TO STOP YA, THAT'S FINE BY ME!
ENOUGH!

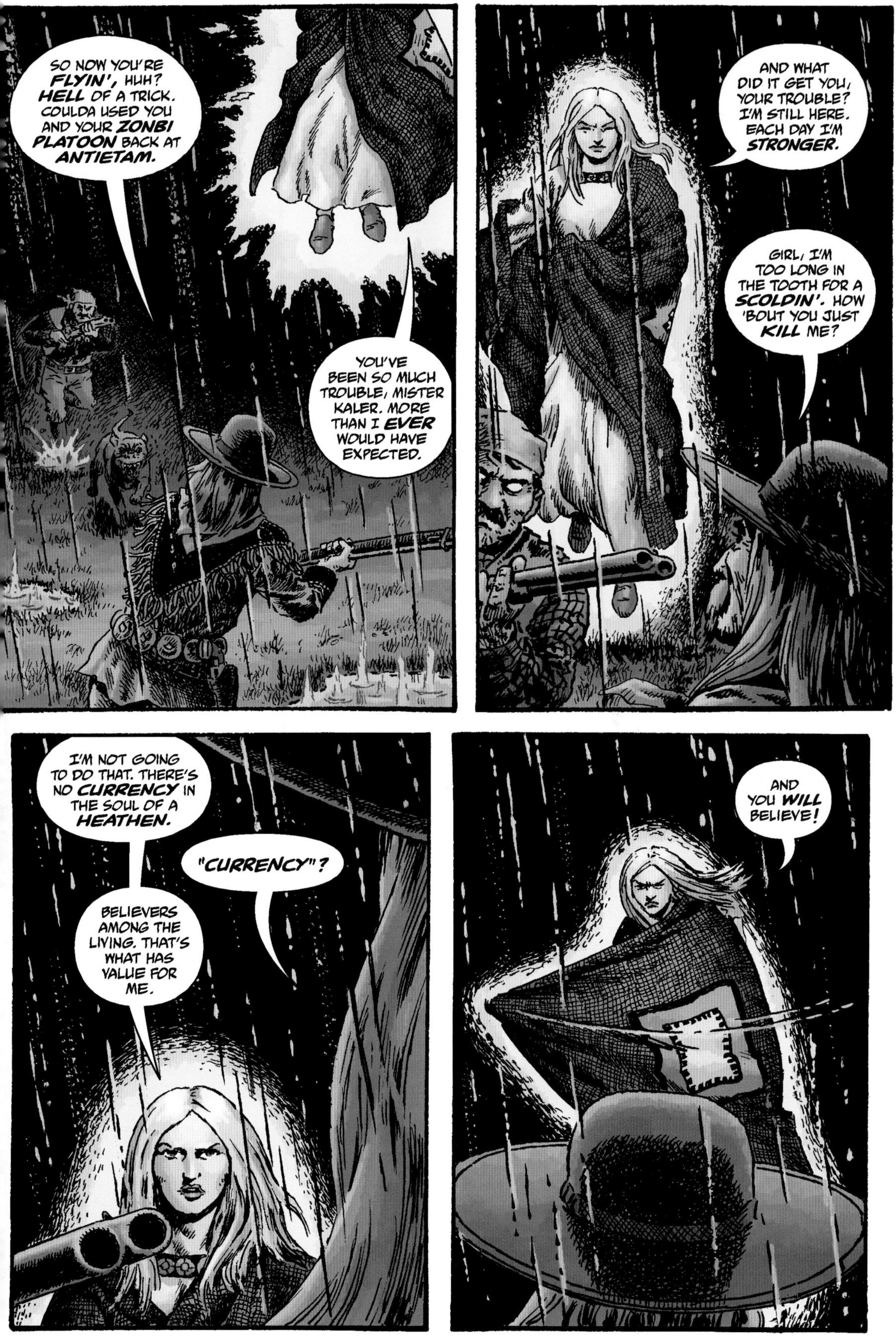
SO NOW YOU'RE FLYIN', HUH? HELL OF A TRICK. COULDA USED YOU AND YOUR ZONBI PLATOON BACK AT ANTIETAM.
YOU'VE BEEN SO MUCH TROUBLE, MISTER KALER. MORE THAN I EVER WOULD HAVE EXPECTED.
AND WHAT DID IT GET YOU, YOUR TROUBLE? I'M STILL HERE. EACH DAY I'M STRONGER.
GIRL, I'M TOO LONG IN THE TOOTH FOR A SCOLDIN'. HOW 'BOUT YOU JUST KILL ME?
I'M NOT GOING TO DO THAT. THERE'S NO CURRENCY IN THE SOUL OF A HEATHEN.
"CURRENCY"?
BELIEVERS AMONG THE LIVING. THAT'S WHAT HAS VALUE FOR ME.
AND YOU WILL BELIEVE!

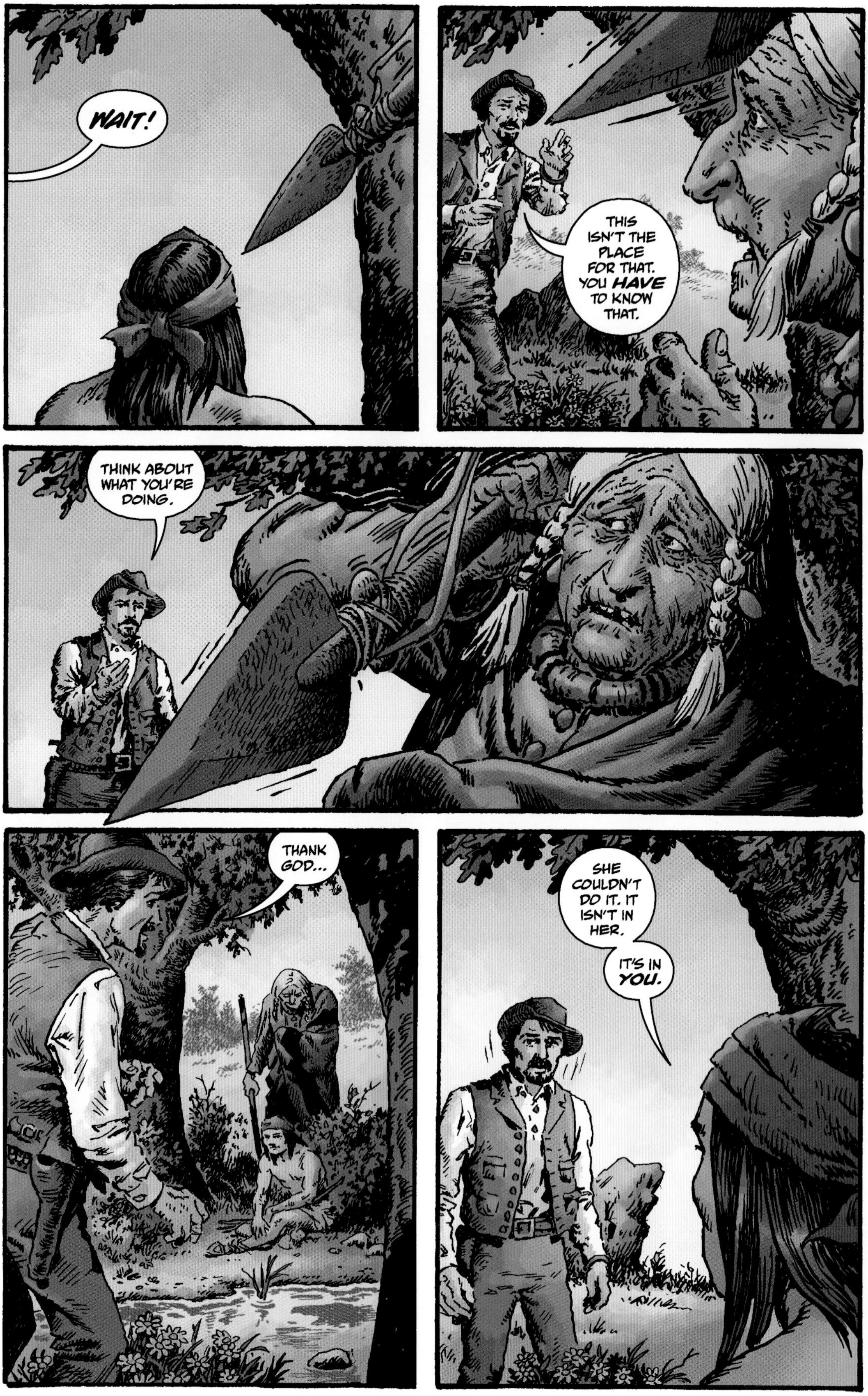
WAIT!
THIS ISN'T THE PLACE FOR THAT. YOU HAVE TO KNOW THAT.
THINK ABOUT WHAT YOU'RE DOING.
THANK GOD...
SHE COULDN'T DO IT. IT ISN'T IN HER.
IT'S IN YOU.

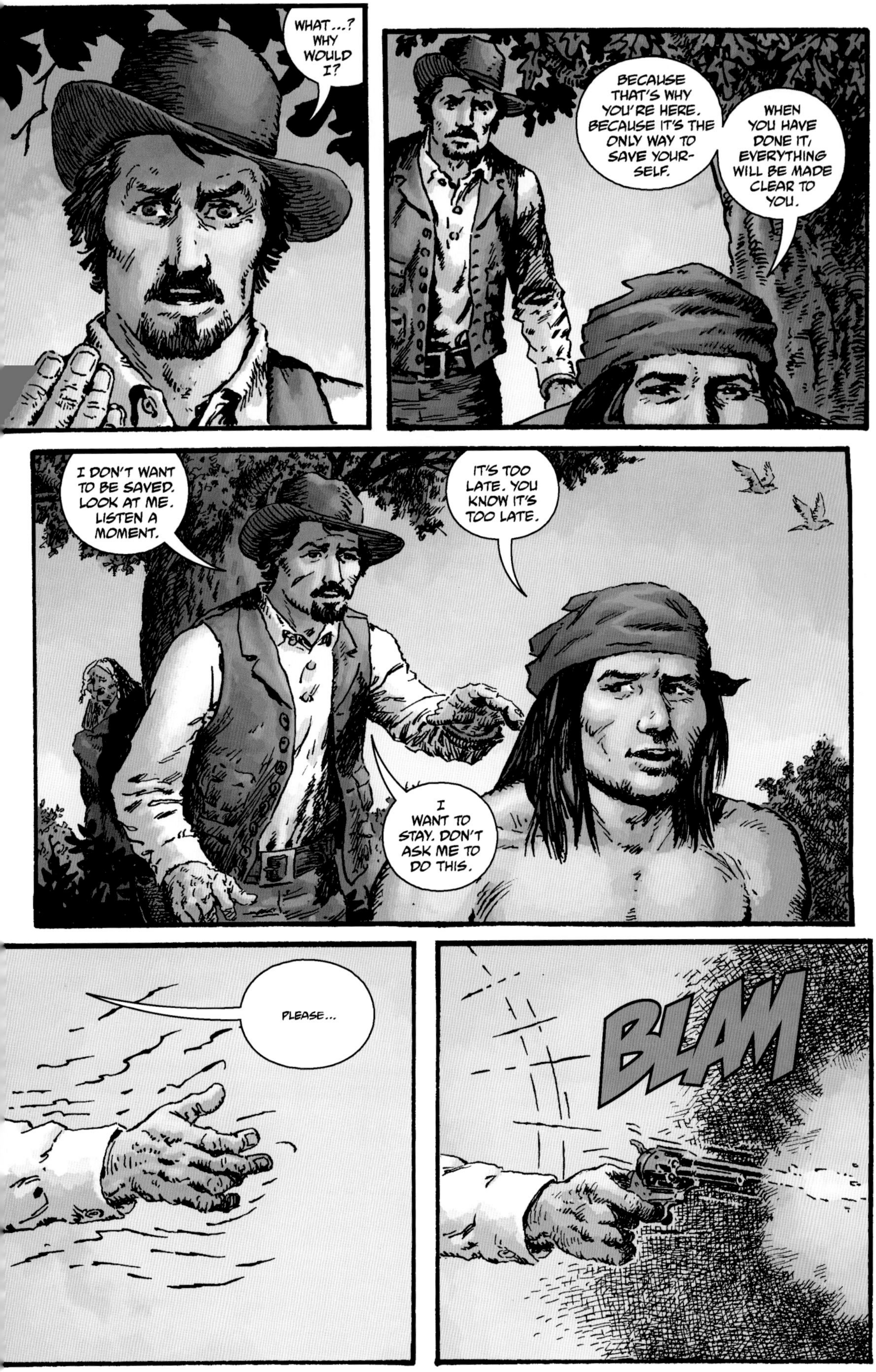
WHAT...? WHY WOULD I?
BECAUSE THAT'S WHY YOU'RE HERE. BECAUSE IT'S THE ONLY WAY TO SAVE YOURSELF.
WHEN YOU HAVE DONE IT, EVERYTHING WILL BE MADE CLEAR TO YOU.
I DON'T WANT TO BE SAVED. LOOK AT ME. LISTEN A MOMENT.
IT'S TOO LATE. YOU KNOW IT'S TOO LATE.
I WANT TO STAY. DON'T ASK ME TO DO THIS.
PLEASE...
BLAM

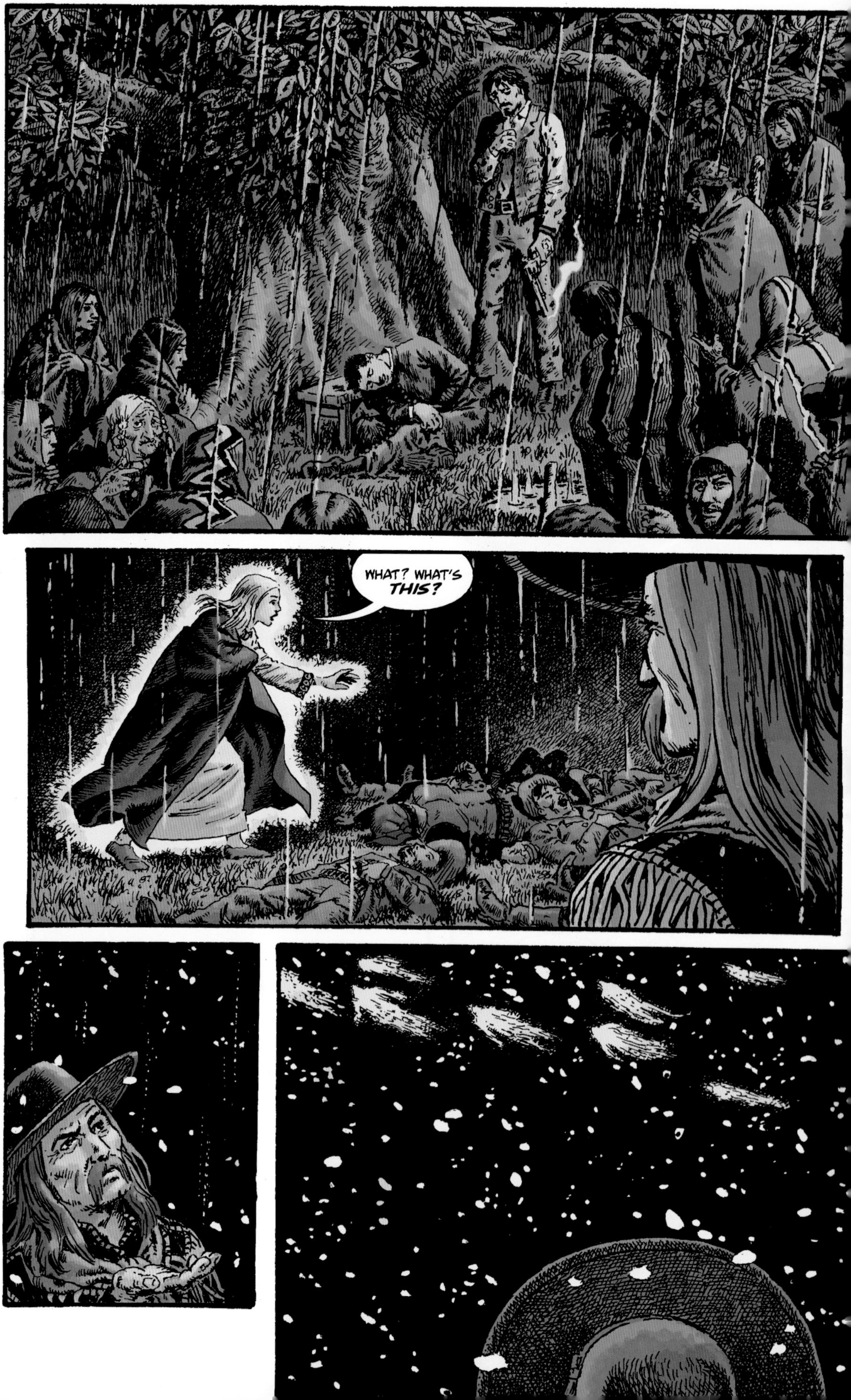
WHAT? WHAT'S THIS?

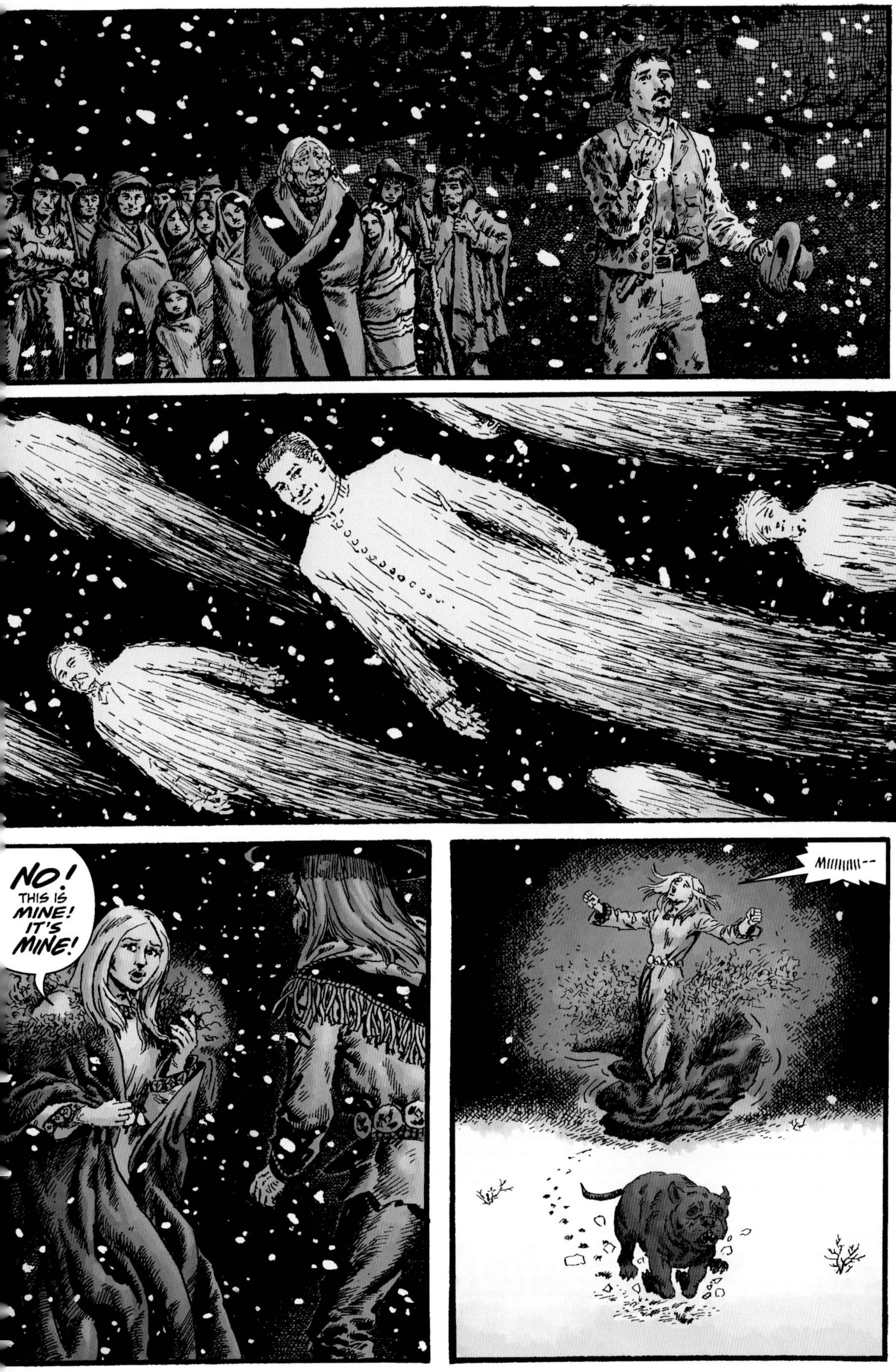
NO! THIS IS MINE! IT'S MINE!
MIIIIIIII--

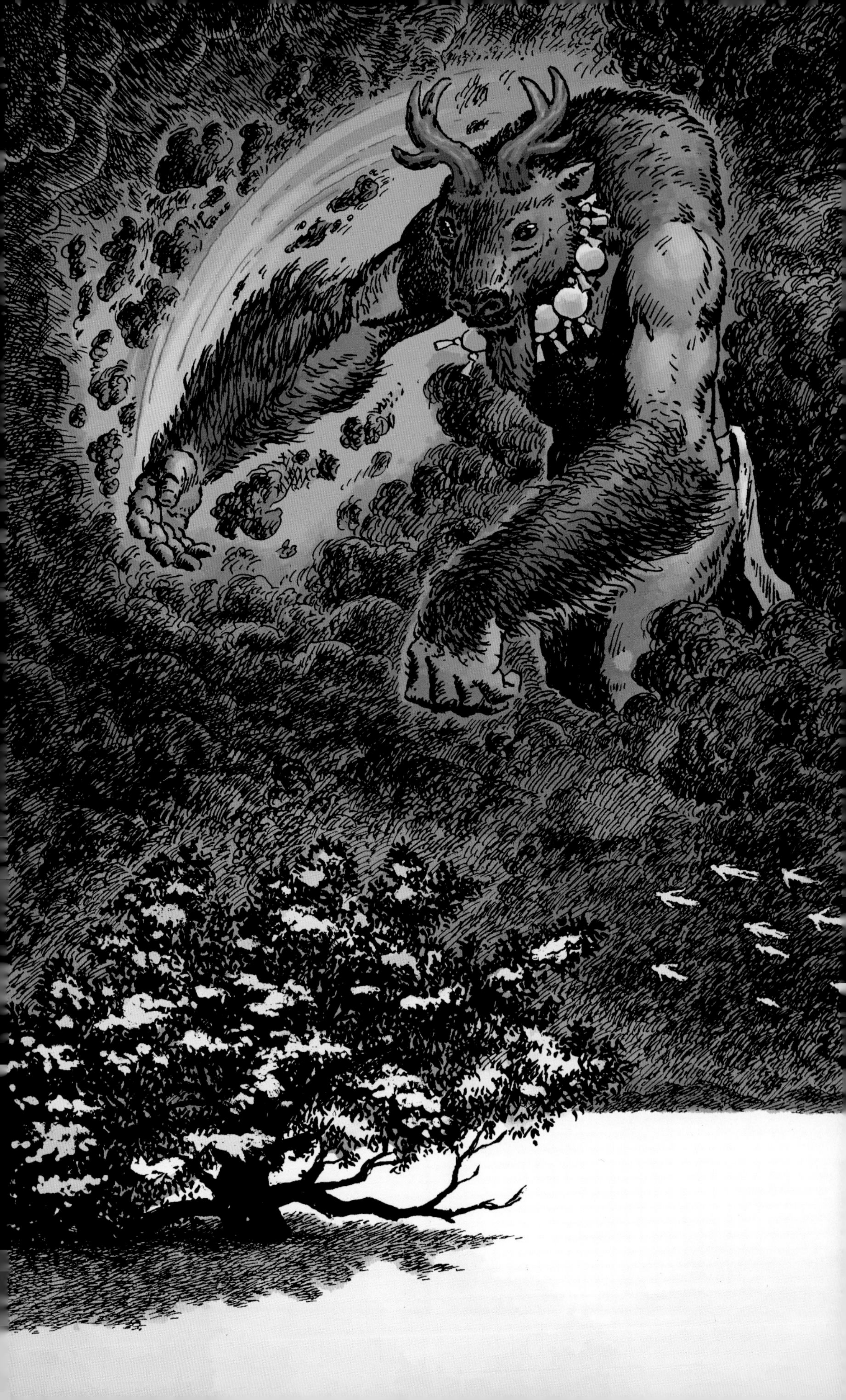

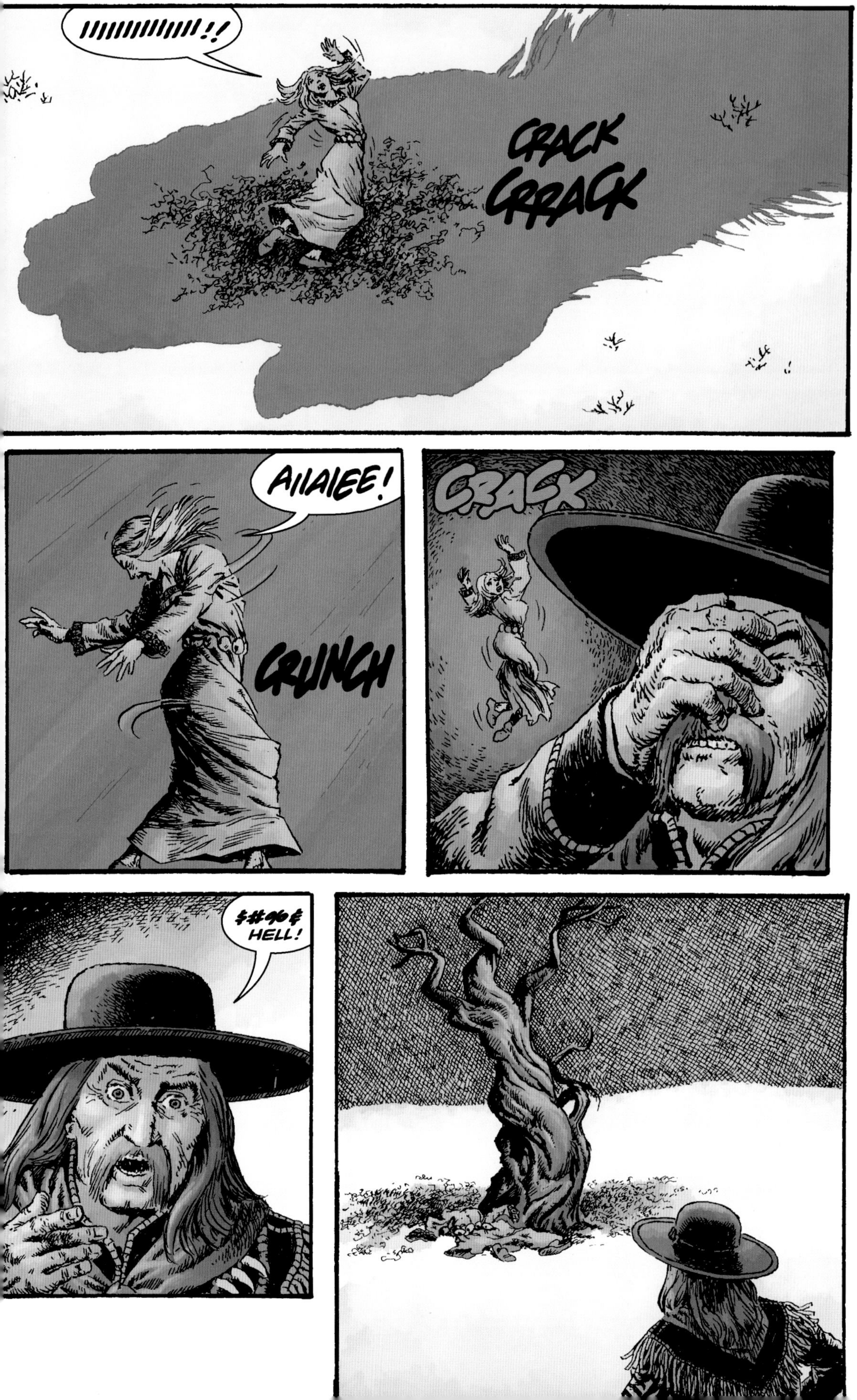
IIIIIIIIIIIII!!
CRACK
CRRACK
AIIAIEE!
CRUNCH
CRACK
$#%&
HELL!

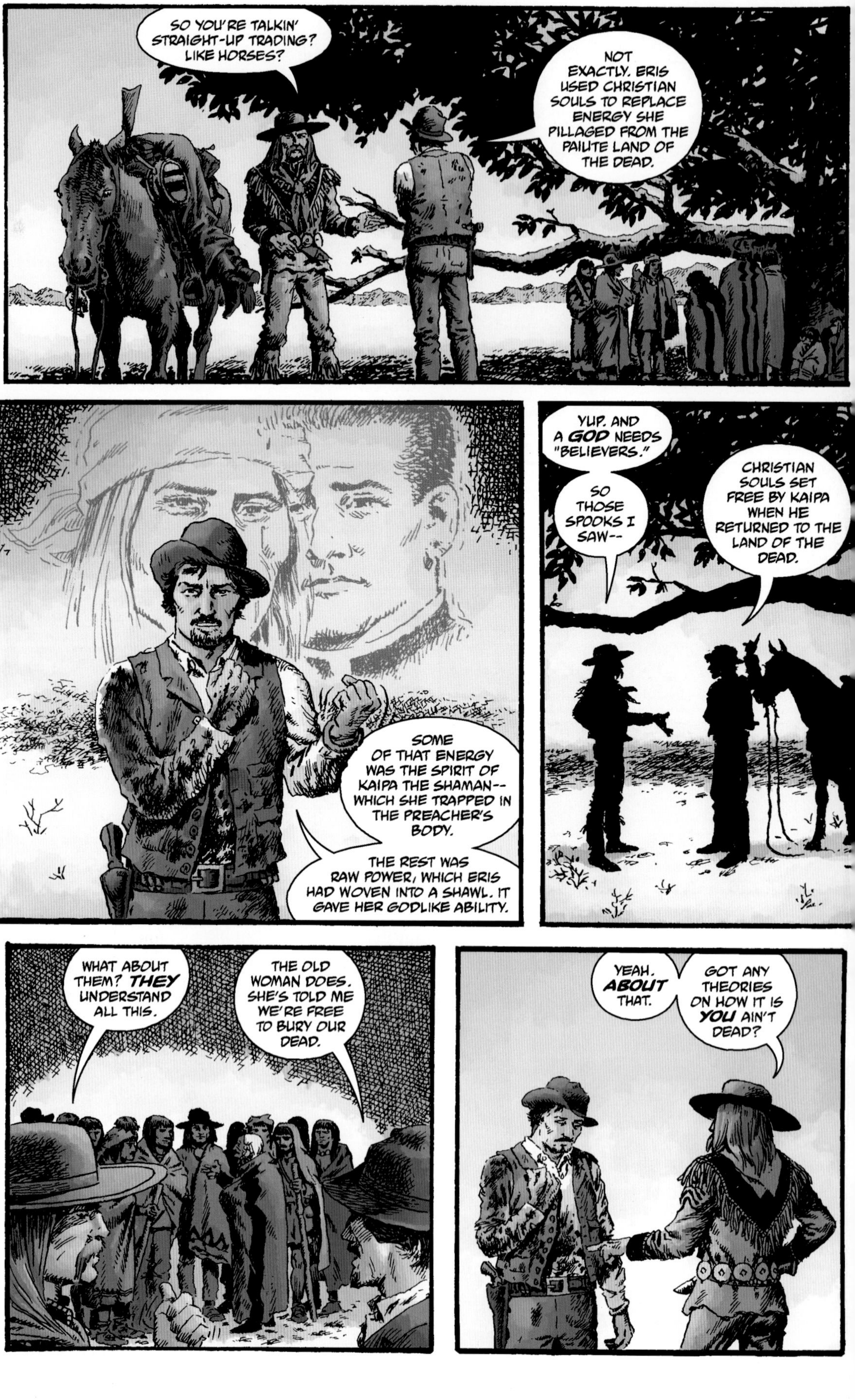
SO YOU'RE TALKIN' STRAIGHT-UP TRADING? LIKE HORSES?
NOT EXACTLY. ERIS USED CHRISTIAN SOULS TO REPLACE ENERGY SHE PILLAGED FROM THE PAIUTE LAND OF THE DEAD.
SOME OF THAT ENERGY WAS THE SPIRIT OF KAIPA THE SHAMAN--WHICH SHE TRAPPED IN THE PREACHER'S BODY.
THE REST WAS RAW POWER, WHICH ERIS HAD WOVEN INTO A SHAWL. IT GAVE HER GODLIKE ABILITY.
YUP. AND A **GOD** NEEDS "BELIEVERS."
SO THOSE SPOOKS I SAW--
CHRISTIAN SOULS SET FREE BY KAIPA WHEN HE RETURNED TO THE LAND OF THE DEAD.
WHAT ABOUT THEM? **THEY** UNDERSTAND ALL THIS.
THE OLD WOMAN DOES. SHE'S TOLD ME WE'RE FREE TO BURY OUR DEAD.
YEAH. **ABOUT** THAT.
GOT ANY THEORIES ON HOW IT IS **YOU** AIN'T DEAD?

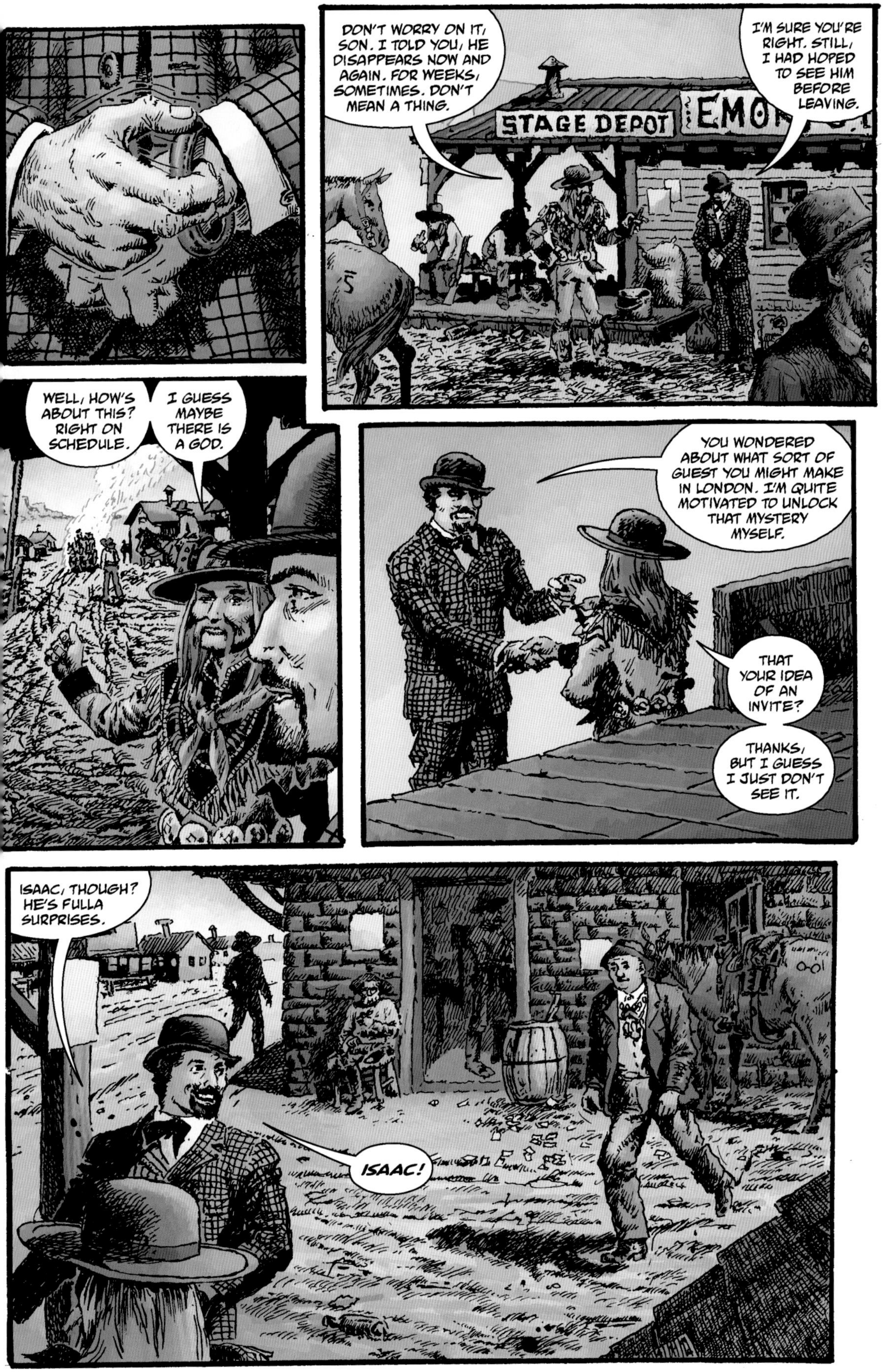
DON'T WORRY ON IT, SON. I TOLD YOU, HE DISAPPEARS NOW AND AGAIN. FOR WEEKS, SOMETIMES. DON'T MEAN A THING.
STAGE DEPOT
EMO
I'M SURE YOU'RE RIGHT. STILL, I HAD HOPED TO SEE HIM BEFORE LEAVING.
WELL, HOW'S ABOUT THIS? RIGHT ON SCHEDULE.
I GUESS MAYBE THERE IS A GOD.
YOU WONDERED ABOUT WHAT SORT OF GUEST YOU MIGHT MAKE IN LONDON. I'M QUITE MOTIVATED TO UNLOCK THAT MYSTERY MYSELF.
THAT YOUR IDEA OF AN INVITE?
THANKS, BUT I GUESS I JUST DON'T SEE IT.
ISAAC, THOUGH? HE'S FULLA SURPRISES.
ISAAC!

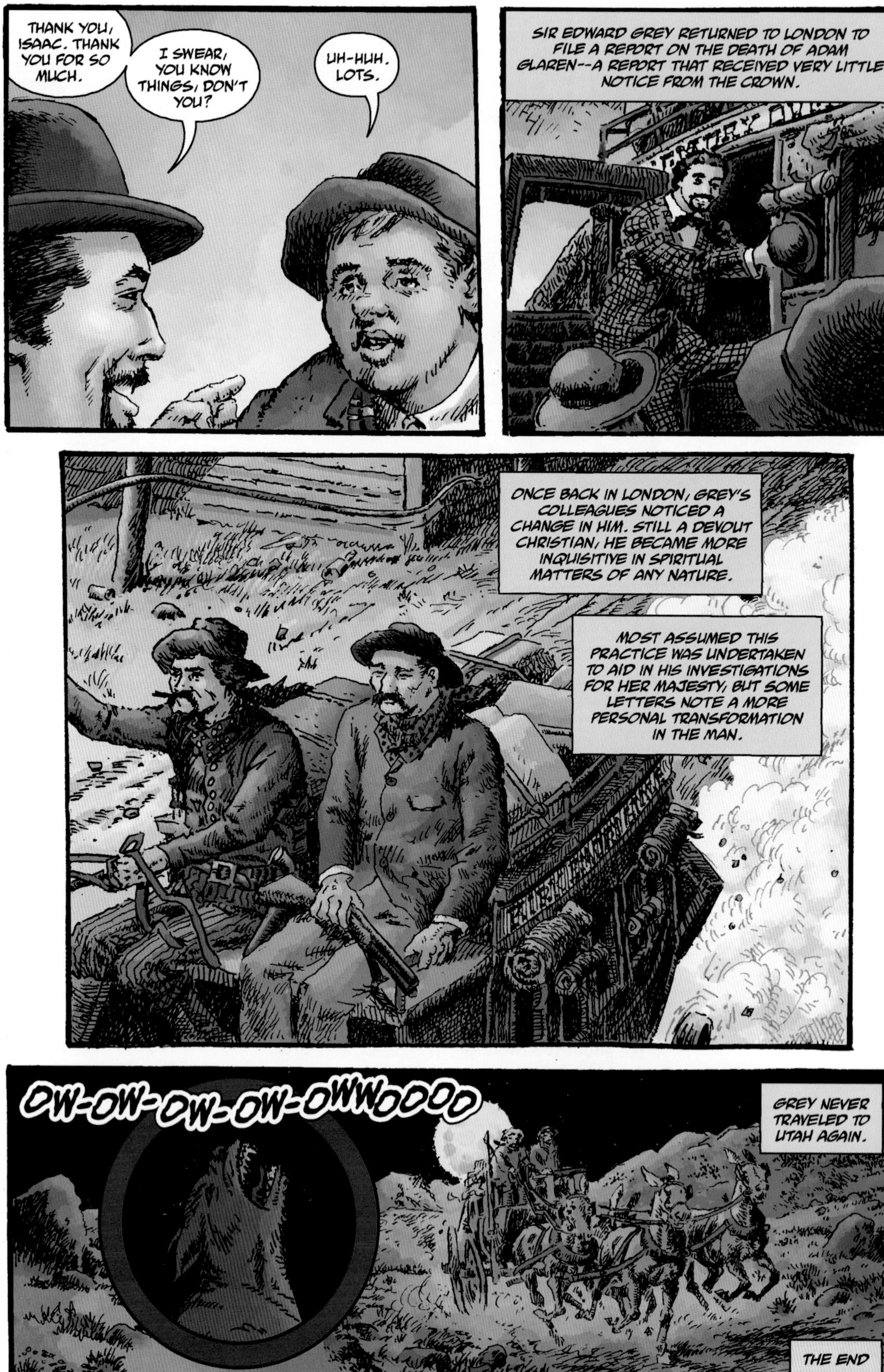
THANK YOU, ISAAC. THANK YOU FOR SO MUCH.
I SWEAR, YOU KNOW THINGS, DON'T YOU?
UH-HUH. LOTS.
SIR EDWARD GREY RETURNED TO LONDON TO FILE A REPORT ON THE DEATH OF ADAM GLAREN--A REPORT THAT RECEIVED VERY LITTLE NOTICE FROM THE CROWN.
ONCE BACK IN LONDON, GREY'S COLLEAGUES NOTICED A CHANGE IN HIM. STILL A DEVOUT CHRISTIAN, HE BECAME MORE INQUISITIVE IN SPIRITUAL MATTERS OF ANY NATURE.
MOST ASSUMED THIS PRACTICE WAS UNDERTAKEN TO AID IN HIS INVESTIGATIONS FOR HER MAJESTY, BUT SOME LETTERS NOTE A MORE PERSONAL TRANSFORMATION IN THE MAN.
OW-OW-OW-OW-OWWOOOO
GREY NEVER TRAVELED TO UTAH AGAIN.
THE END

AFTERWORD

MY BRAIN, it doesn't work the way Mike Mignola's does. Be nice if it did, but it doesn't. He wakes up in the morning and gets a glimmer of an idea and by the time he's out of the shower, he's got a whole miniseries in his head. Not me. I get a hint of an idea and then it starts running around in my brain desperately looking for other ideas (or even just other hints) to keep it company. Eventually, I get a small crowd and then I can get to work at telling an actual story, but it can take weeks—months sometimes. So you can see why it would be really easy for me to hate a guy like Mike. The only reason I don't, I guess, is because for some insane reason, Mike puts up with my glacial process. He's willing to wait, and he's come to trust that it'll be worth the wait. Truth is, it's not quite so grim as I make it sound because this modus operandi of mine is going on with several different stories simultaneously, each staking out its own corral of ideas in my brain, and each popping out and ready to write at staggered intervals so that we can still manage to get a regular B.P.R.D. book out on a timely basis. But then you have something like *Witchfinder: Lost and Gone Forever*, a book that literally took years to come together.

Long ago, over lunch, Mike and I were talking about all the (probably never-to-be-realized) possibilities of the *B.P.R.D.* universe, and I told Mike I wanted to do a series about the theft of Apache chief Mangas Coloradas's bizarrely preserved brain from the Smithsonian Institute because I love the West, and I love Native American mythology—and who doesn't like a good stolen-brain story? Realizing it wouldn't quite fit into our plan, the notion of doing such a tale sort of stuck back there in my head. Now if we could just get this notion some friends, right? Months later, Mike told me about this one character, a "villain" from a 1930s pulp-style oeuvre, who had a strange sidekick. I won't tell you more than that. They're Mike's characters, after all,

but we had a good laugh over them . . . and then the dynamic of the oddball duo ended up getting stuck back there in my brain, also lonely. Okay, now it's years later, and with *B.P.R.D.* being the success that it is, Mike asked me if there was anything else I wanted to write. "A western," was my immediate answer. Mike cocked an eyebrow and said, "What, that Indian-brain thing?" and I responded, "No. A good old nineteenth-century western." Ha ha ha. Right. A *B.P.R.D.*-universe western. Oh, well, whatever. He asked, right?

But when Mike decided he wanted to do an Edward Grey series (set in the late nineteenth century), he called me up. "Hey, still wanna do that western?" Sure, that's it. I would just use Grey. Great. But what's the story? Oh, wait, the weird duo . . . yeah, those guys . . . ummmm, well, what else? Uh-huh, that's right. Nothin' else. But I had a start, or a second start . . . or a fourth start if you're really keeping count, but a definite start, and the other pieces slowly drifted toward one another . . . slowly.

Flash-forward a few months, and Scott Allie, who had worked with the legendary John Severin on a *Conan* story (and with both of us on a *War on Frogs* one-shot) was talking to big John, trying to see if he wanted to do anything else at Dark Horse—"You know, like a western." And remarkably, this icon of western comics, this titan of the EC era, this consummate artist's artist, said, "Sure." John Severin said, "Sure," to working with me on a five-issue western series! Holy $#&! That'll speed up anybody's process—you know, unless you're a complete loser, and thankfully I'm not quite there yet. So it all came together right then because it had to. Those pieces I talked about, and others, fell into place, along with a lot of other stuff that I wish I could talk more about; however, it appears I've run outta room.

Dreadful sorry.

John Arcudi
Philadelphia

WITCHFINDER™

SKETCHBOOK

with notes from Scott Allie

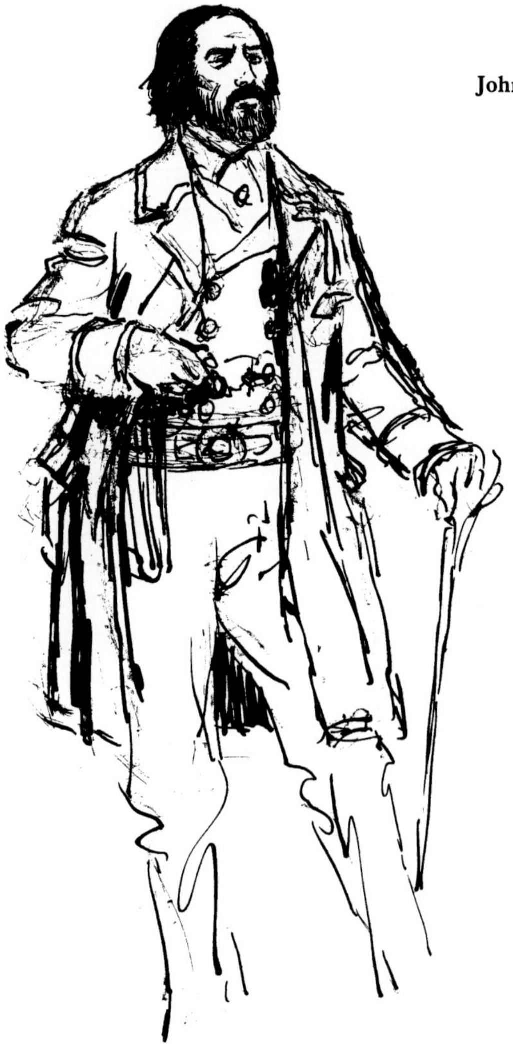

John Severin reimagines London gentleman Edward Grey for the Old West.

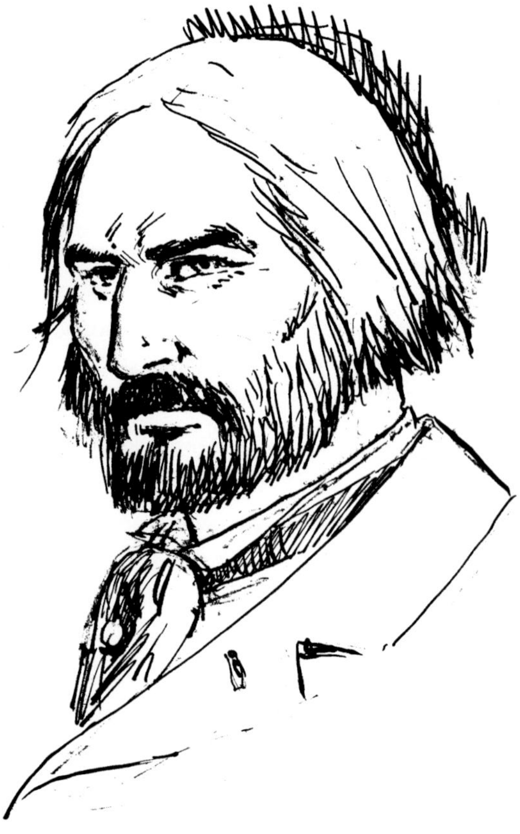

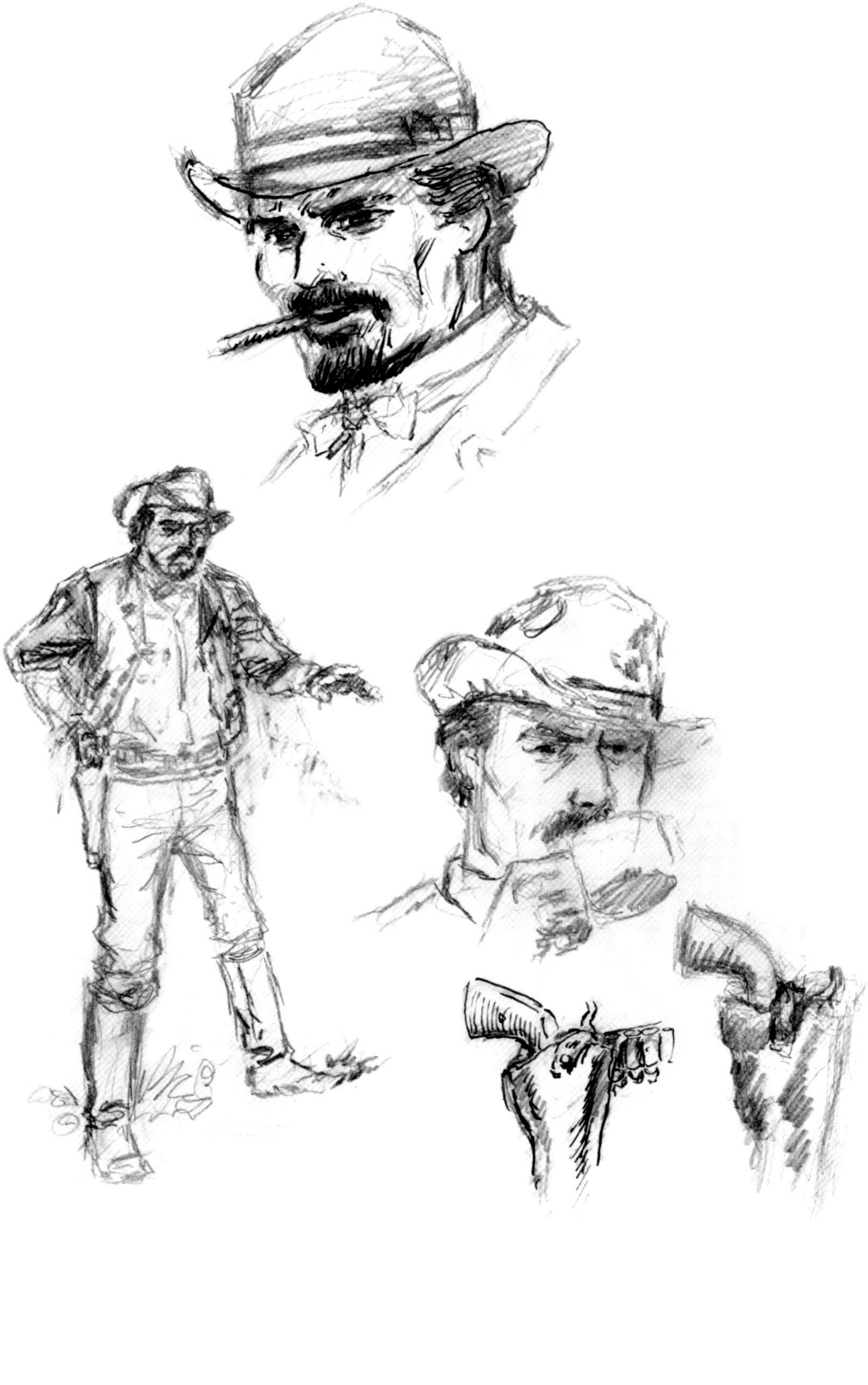

Mignola drew the initial designs for Kaler, and Severin quickly made him his own (facing page).

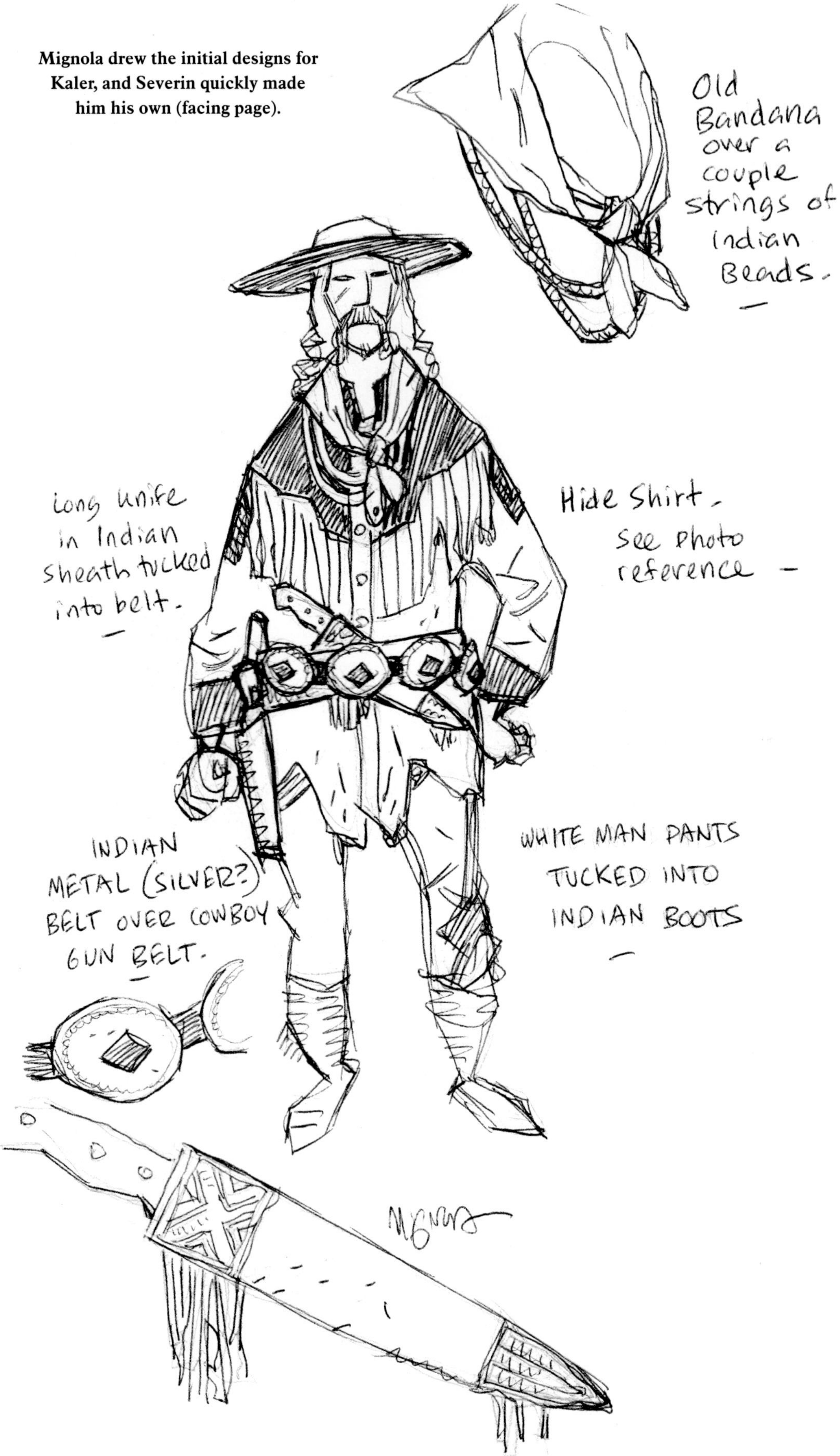
Old Bandana over a couple strings of Indian Beads.
long knife in Indian sheath tucked into belt.
Hide Shirt. see photo reference
INDIAN METAL (SILVER?) BELT OVER COWBOY GUN BELT.
WHITE MAN PANTS TUCKED INTO INDIAN BOOTS

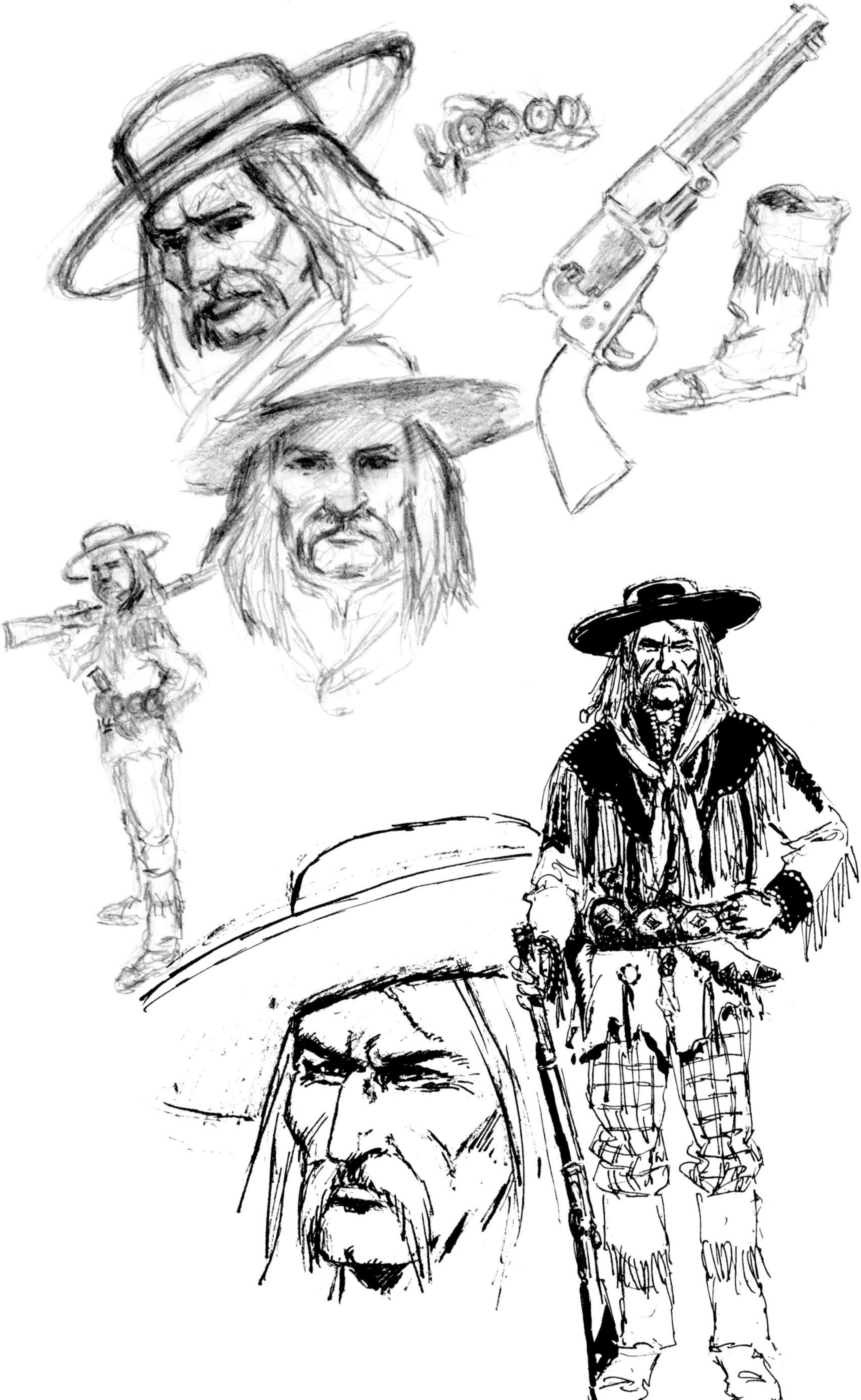

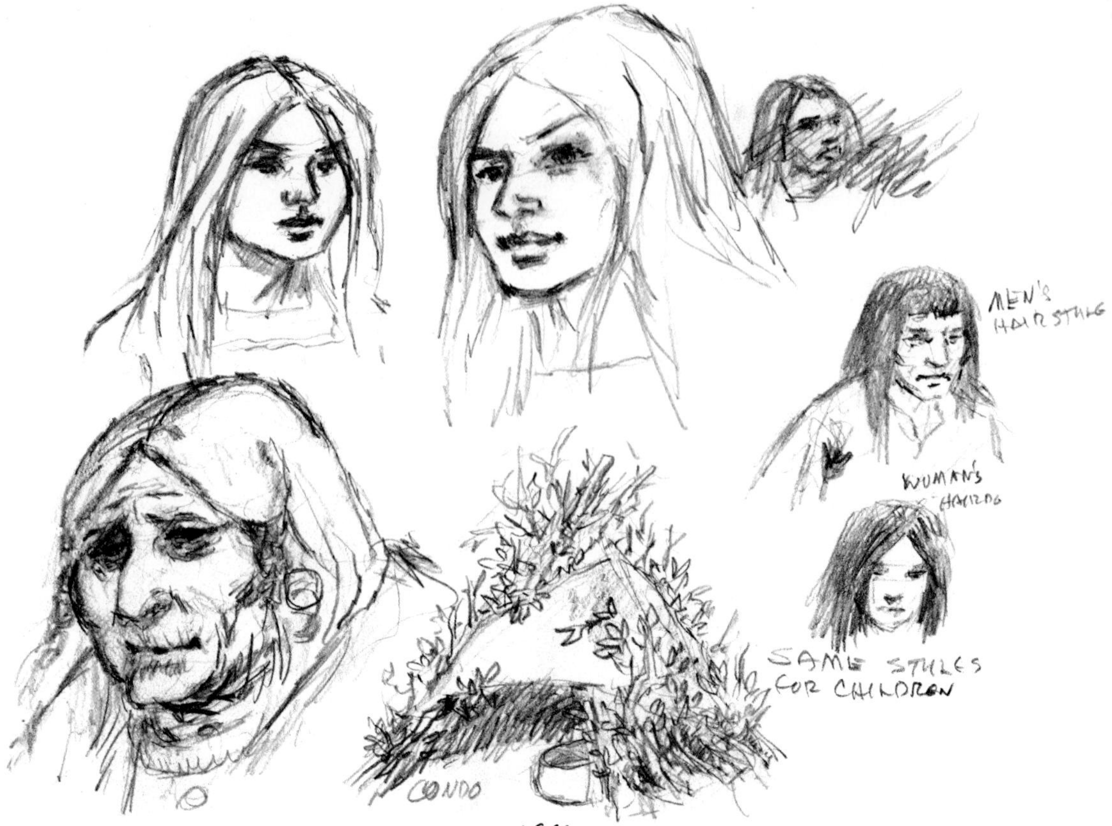
MEN'S HAIR STYLE
WOMAN'S HAIRDO
SAME STYLES FOR CHILDREN
CONDO

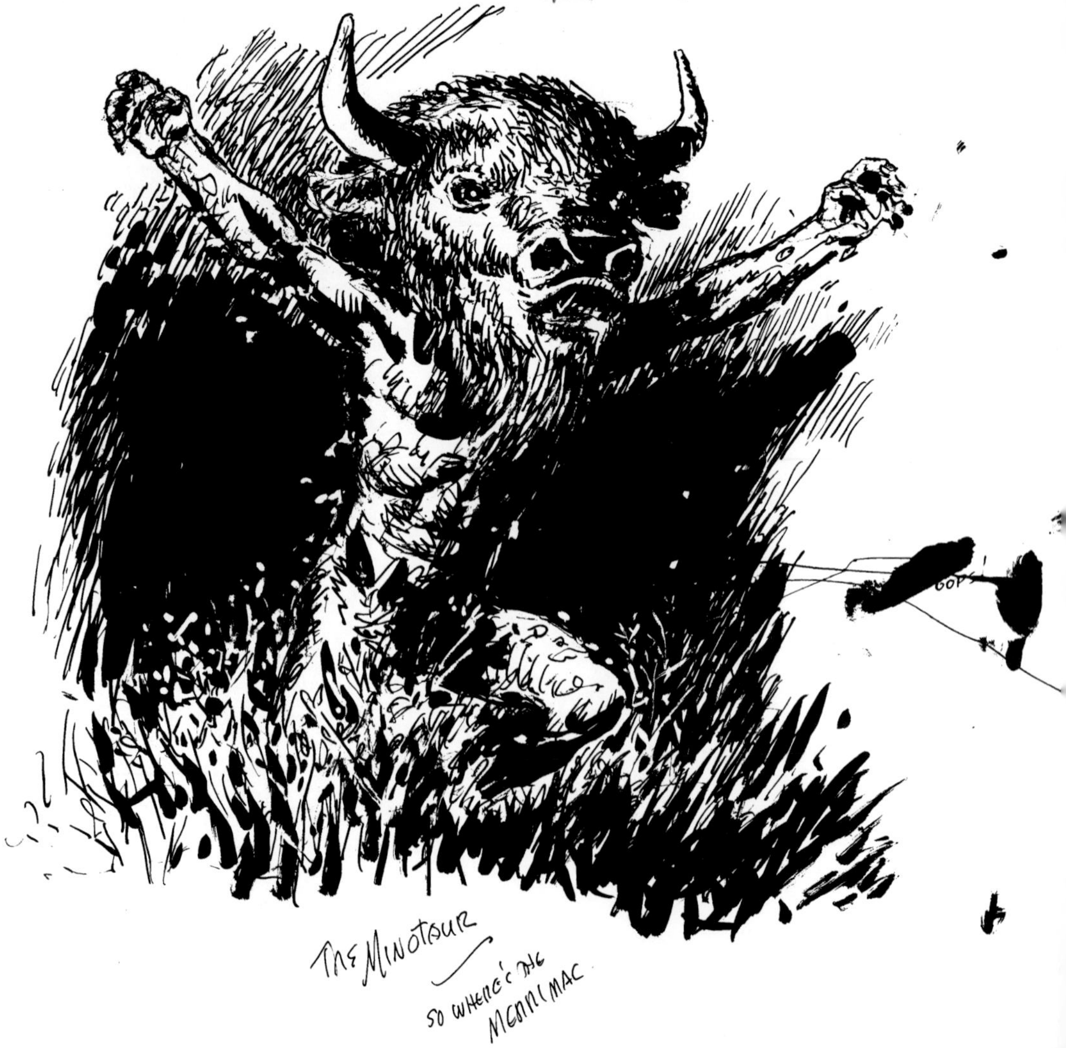
OOPS!
THE MINOTAUR
SO WHERE'S THE MERRIMAC

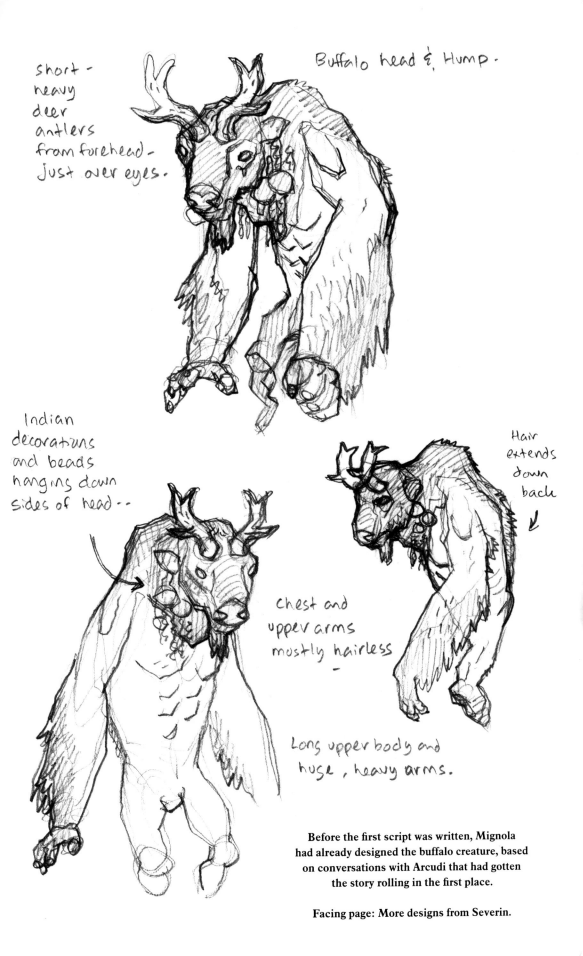

short-
heavy
deer
antlers
from forehead-
just over eyes.

Buffalo head & Hump.

Indian
decorations
and beads
hanging down
sides of head--

Hair
extends
down
back

chest and
upper arms
mostly hairless
-

Long upper body and
huge, heavy arms.

Before the first script was written, Mignola
had already designed the buffalo creature, based
on conversations with Arcudi that had gotten
the story rolling in the first place.

Facing page: More designs from Severin.

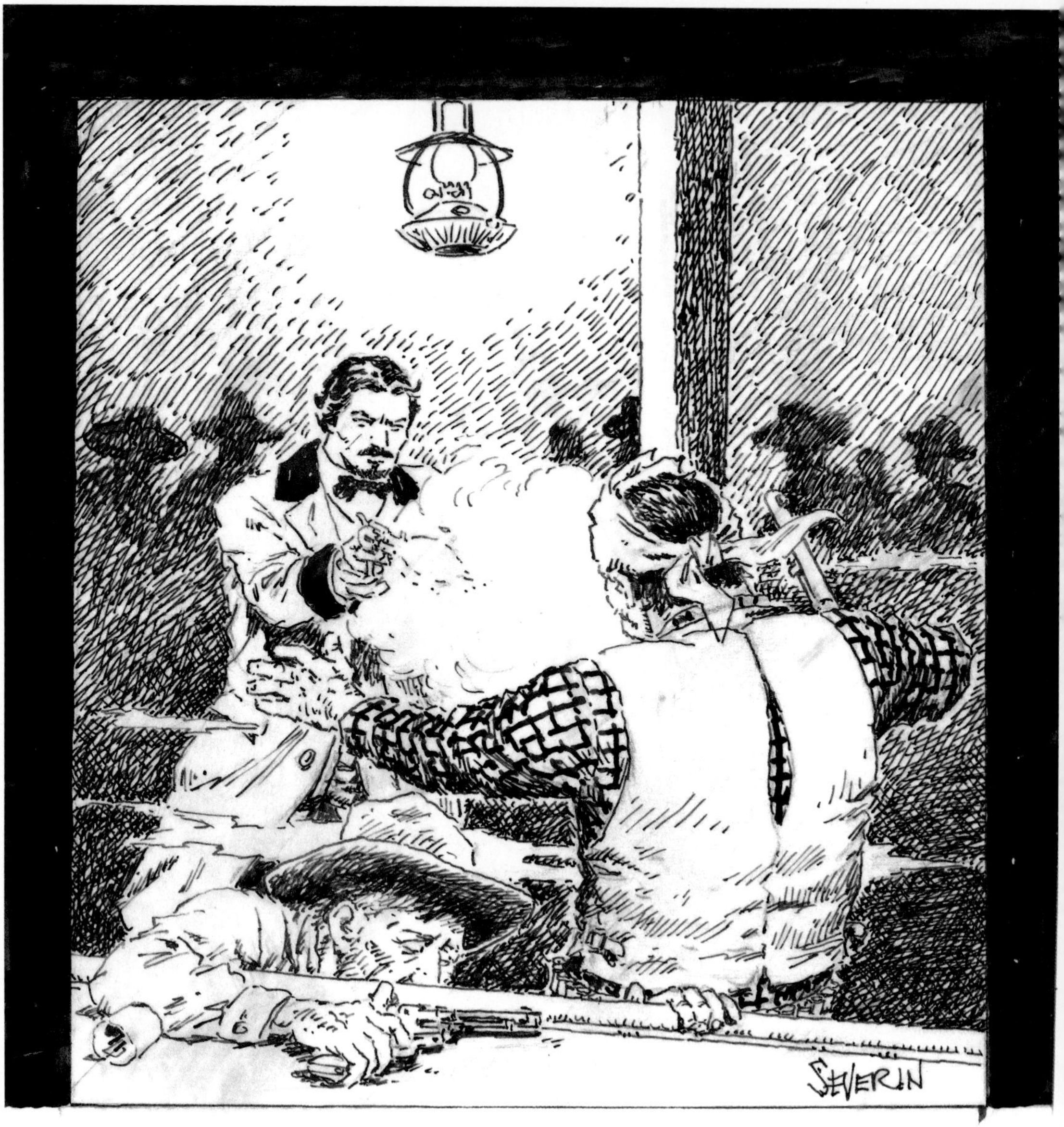
SEVERIN

Above: Severin's first cover sketch for the variant cover on issue #1. We wanted something that would address the supernatural elements of the book, so Severin provided the sketch on the facing page. The two ideas were combined into the image you see on page 2 of this volume.

Following page: Arcudi wrote pages 4 and 5 of chapter 3 to be a two-page spread, but because of the way he formatted his script, Severin misunderstood and crammed it all into a single page. We all felt very bad asking him to redraw it, but we wanted the scene to have room to breathe.

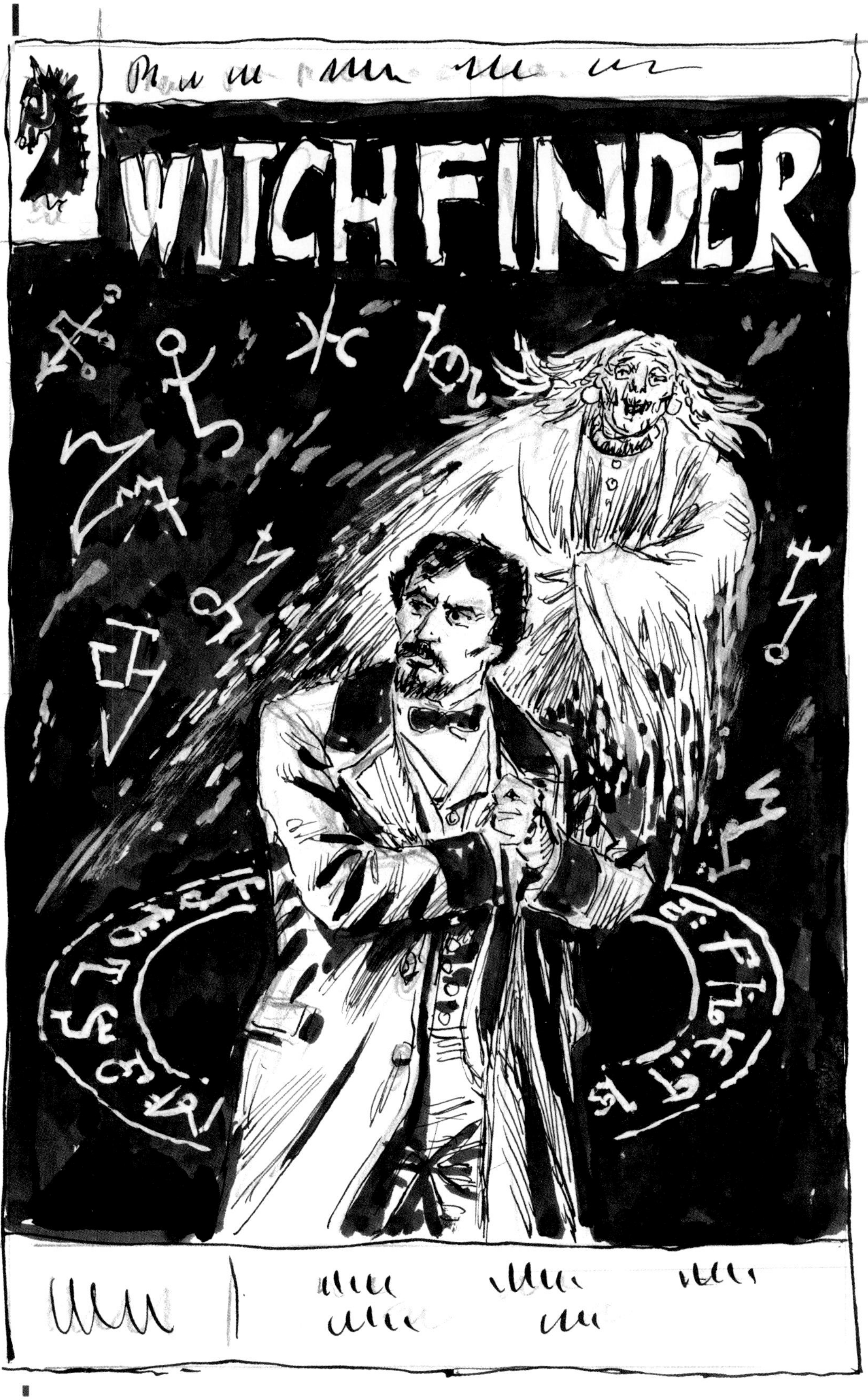
WITCHFINDER

WITCHFINDER: LOST & GONE FOREVER 3 SEVERIN 4

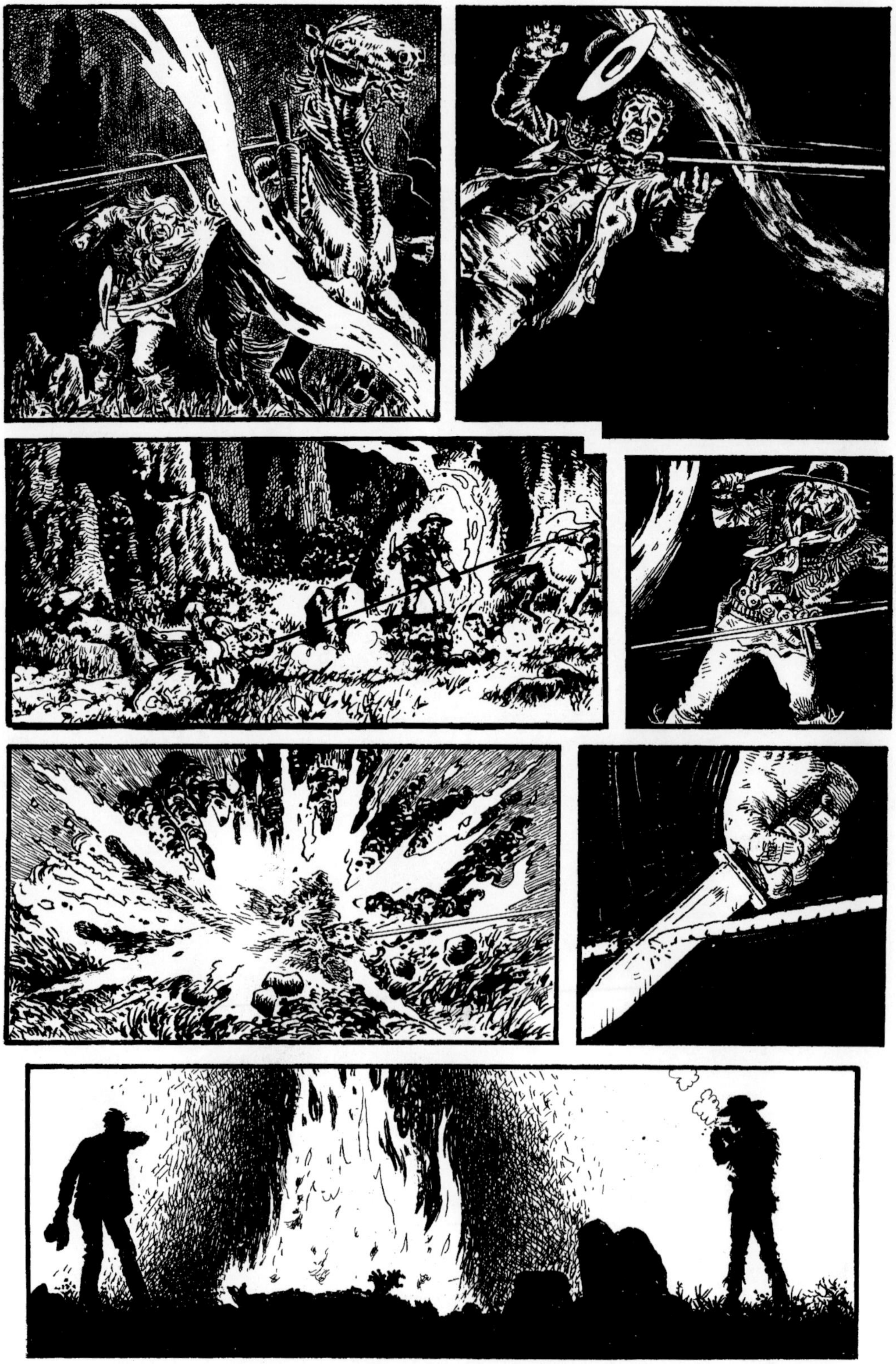

Also by MIKE MIGNOLA

B.P.R.D.: PLAGUE OF FROGS
Hardcover Collection Volume 1
By Mike Mignola, Chris Golden,
Guy Davis, and others
ISBN 978-1-59582-609-1 | $34.99

B.P.R.D.: PLAGUE OF FROGS
Hardcover Collection Volume 2
By Mignola, John Arcudi,
Davis, and others
ISBN 978-1-59582-672-5 | $34.99

B.P.R.D.: PLAGUE OF FROGS
Hardcover Collection Volume 3
By Mignola, Arcudi, and Davis
ISBN 978-1-59582-860-6 | $34.99

B.P.R.D.: THE WARNING
By Mignola, Arcudi, and Davis
ISBN 978-1-59582-304-5 | $17.99

B.P.R.D.: THE BLACK GODDESS
By Mignola, Arcudi, and Davis
ISBN 978-1-59582-411-0 | $17.99

B.P.R.D.: KING OF FEAR
By Mignola, Arcudi, and Davis
ISBN 978-1-59582-564-3 | $17.99

B.P.R.D.: 1946
By Mignola, Joshua Dysart, and Paul Azaceta
ISBN 978-1-59582-191-1 | $17.99

B.P.R.D.: 1947
By Mignola, Dysart,
Fábio Moon, and Gabriel Bá
ISBN 978-1-59582-478-3 | $17.99

**B.P.R.D. HELL ON EARTH VOLUME 1:
NEW WORLD**
By Mignola, Arcudi, and Davis
ISBN 978-1-59582-707-4 | $19.99

**B.P.R.D. HELL ON EARTH VOLUME 2:
GODS AND MONSTERS**
By Mignola, Arcudi, Davis, and Crook
ISBN 978-1-59582-822-4 | $19.99

B.P.R.D.: BEING HUMAN
By Mignola, Arcudi, Davis, and others
ISBN 978-1-59582-756-2 | $17.99

**ABE SAPIEN:
THE DROWNING**
By Mignola and Jason Shawn Alexander
ISBN 978-1-59582-185-0 | $17.99

**LOBSTER JOHNSON:
THE IRON PROMETHEUS**
By Mignola and Jason Armstrong
ISBN 978-1-59307-975-8 | $17.99

**WITCHFINDER VOLUME 1:
IN THE SERVICE OF ANGELS**
By Mignola and Ben Stenbeck
ISBN 978-1-59582-483-7 | $17.99

**WITCHFINDER VOLUME 2:
LOST AND GONE FOREVER**
By Mignola, Arcudi, and John Severin
ISBN 978-1-59582-794-4 | $17.99

**THE AMAZING SCREW-ON HEAD
AND OTHER CURIOUS OBJECTS**
Hardcover Collection
By Mignola
ISBN 978-1-59582-501-8 | $17.99

**BALTIMORE VOLUME 1:
THE PLAGUE SHIPS**
By Mignola, Golden, and Stenbeck
ISBN 978-1-59582-677-0 | $18.99

NOVELS

**LOBSTER JOHNSON:
THE SATAN FACTORY**
By Thomas E. Sniegoski
ISBN 978-1-59582-203-1 | $12.95

AVAILABLE AT YOUR LOCAL COMICS SHOP OR BOOKSTORE! • To find a comics shop in your area, call 1-888-266-4226.
For more information or to order direct visit DarkHorse.com or call 1-800-862-0052 Mon.–Fri. 9 AM to 5 PM Pacific Time.
Prices and availability subject to change without notice.

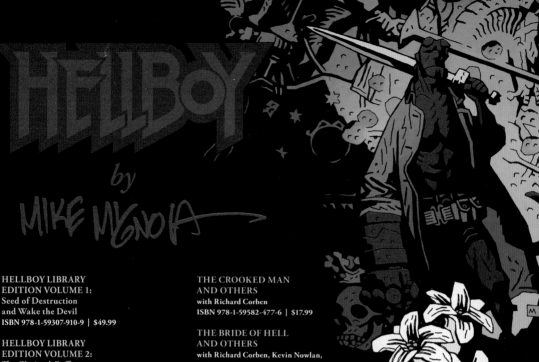

HELLBOY

by MIKE MIGNOLA

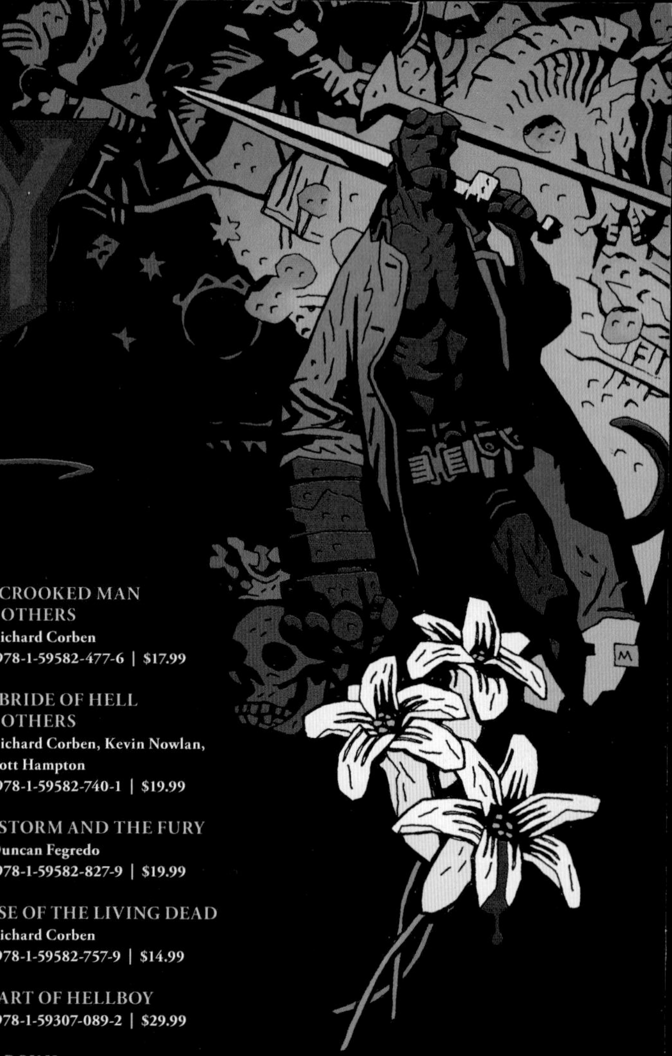

HELLBOY LIBRARY EDITION VOLUME 1:
Seed of Destruction and Wake the Devil
ISBN 978-1-59307-910-9 | $49.99

HELLBOY LIBRARY EDITION VOLUME 2:
The Chained Coffin and The Right Hand of Doom
ISBN 978-1-59307-989-5 | $49.99

HELLBOY LIBRARY EDITION VOLUME 3:
Conqueror Worm and Strange Places
ISBN 978-1-59582-352-6 | $49.99

HELLBOY LIBRARY EDITION VOLUME 4:
The Crooked Man and The Troll Witch
with Richard Corben and others
ISBN 978-1-59582-658-9 | $49.99

SEED OF DESTRUCTION
with John Byrne
ISBN 978-1-59307-094-6 | $17.99

WAKE THE DEVIL
ISBN 978-1-59307-095-3 | $17.99

THE CHAINED COFFIN AND OTHERS
ISBN 978-1-59307-091-5 | $17.99

THE RIGHT HAND OF DOOM
ISBN 978-1-59307-093-9 | $17.99

CONQUEROR WORM
ISBN 978-1-59307-092-2 | $17.99

STRANGE PLACES
ISBN 978-1-59307-475-3 | $17.99

THE TROLL WITCH AND OTHERS
ISBN 978-1-59307-860-7 | $17.99

DARKNESS CALLS
with Duncan Fegredo
ISBN 978-1-59307-896-6 | $19.99

THE WILD HUNT
with Duncan Fegredo
ISBN 978-1-59582-352-6 | $19.99

THE CROOKED MAN AND OTHERS
with Richard Corben
ISBN 978-1-59582-477-6 | $17.99

THE BRIDE OF HELL AND OTHERS
with Richard Corben, Kevin Nowlan, and Scott Hampton
ISBN 978-1-59582-740-1 | $19.99

THE STORM AND THE FURY
with Duncan Fegredo
ISBN 978-1-59582-827-9 | $19.99

HOUSE OF THE LIVING DEAD
with Richard Corben
ISBN 978-1-59582-757-9 | $14.99

THE ART OF HELLBOY
ISBN 978-1-59307-089-2 | $29.99

HELLBOY II: THE ART OF THE MOVIE
ISBN 978-1-59307-964-2 | $24.99

HELLBOY: THE COMPANION
ISBN 978-1-59307-655-9 | $14.99

HELLBOY: WEIRD TALES
VOLUME 1
ISBN 978-1-56971-622-9 | $17.99
VOLUME 2
ISBN 978-1-56971-953-4 | $17.99

HELLBOY: MASKS AND MONSTERS
with James Robinson and Scott Benefiel
ISBN 978-1-59582-567-4 | $17.99

NOVELS

HELLBOY: EMERALD HELL
By Tom Piccirilli
ISBN 978-1-59582-141-6 | $12.99

HELLBOY: THE ALL-SEEING EYE
By Mark Morris
ISBN 978-1-59582-141-6 | $12.99

HELLBOY: THE FIRE WOLVES
By Tim Lebbon
ISBN 978-1-59582-204-8 | $12.99

HELLBOY: THE ICE WOLVES
By Mark Chadbourn
ISBN 978-1-59582-205-5 | $12.99

SHORT STORIES

Illustrated by Mike Mignola

HELLBOY: ODD JOBS
By Poppy Z. Brite, Greg Rucka, and others
ISBN 978-1-56971-440-9 | $14.99

HELLBOY: ODDER JOBS
By Frank Darabont, Guillermo del Toro, and others
ISBN 978-1-59307-226-1 | $14.99

HELLBOY: ODDEST JOBS
By Joe R. Lansdale, China Miéville, and others
ISBN 978-1-59307-944-4 | $14.99

AVAILABLE AT YOUR LOCAL COMICS SHOP OR BOOKSTORE! • To find a comics shop in your area, call 1-888-266-4226.
For more information or to order direct visit DarkHorse.com or call 1-800-862-0052 Mon.–Fri. 9 AM to 5 PM Pacific Time.
Prices and availability subject to change without notice.

DARK HORSE BOOKS
DarkHorse.com